A SURVEY of BIBLE PROPHECY

Also by Arthur E. Bloomfield

All Things New
(A Study of the Revelation)

The End of the Days
(A Study of Daniel's Visions)

Signs of His Coming
(A Study of the Olivet Discourse)

The Changing Climate
and the Bible Story of Water

Ark of the Covenant

A SURVEY of BIBLE PROPHECY

Arthur E Bloomfield

Bethany Fellowship, Inc.
Minneapolis, Minnesota

FOREWORD

Mr. Bloomfield's ministry has been exciting; his messages clear and edifying. Some of the things he spoke about fifteen or twenty years ago have now entered on the world's stage.

This book, *A Survey of Bible Prophecy*, is the product of many years of intense Bible research. He has a wide knowledge of his subject. I can speak from experience, since, as a teacher, I have listened in as Mr. Bloomfield has taught our students different phases of prophecy. I know that for every Bible passage he uses he has in his mind several others to back up what he says.

This deep knowledge of the Bible has caused him some trouble with teachers who are mere echoes and not true voices of Bible prophecy. He has a rule that "if scripture has not been completely fulfilled in the past, it must yet be fulfilled in the future." He does *not* believe that the prophets used what some call "poetic license" and were experts in hyperbole. Rather, they were God's inspired spokemen whose words are valid and sure.

Mr. Bloomfield's ministry is a ministry the whole church needs. There is much confusion about the last days. His approach is to teach the principles as well as the events of prophetic scripture. *A Survey of Bible Prophecy* will prove to be a valuable book to give on God's view of this troubled world. Bible students will be glad to have a copy on their desk. Every Christian home should own one.

Arthur Bloomfield has written several other books that deal with important phases of prophecy: *All Things New* (a study in the book of Revelation), *The End of the Days* (a study of the book of Daniel), *Signs of His Coming* (commentary on the Olivet Discourse), and *The Changing Climate* (the Bible story of water).

If you haven't read these books, get at least one of them. I will venture to say that you will want to read them all. They will open your eyes to the great issues of the last days and the events that connect with the Second Coming of our Lord, Jesus Christ.

Harold J. Brokke

PREFACE

If God wanted a great oak in a certain place at a certain time, He would not have to wait until that time comes, and then get someone to dig up a big tree and transplant it. But hundreds, or even thousands, of years before, He could cause an acorn to be dropped in the right place and the tree would be growing there healthy and strong at the appointed time.

If God wanted a certain message to be given to a certain people at a certain time, He would not have to wait until that time to get someone to write the message and try to get it into circulation. Instead, He could cause the message to be written thousands of years in advance and have it in worldwide circulation, in all languages, when the time comes.

The Bible is a universal book in reference to time and place. It is for all people of all times; yet as you read any part of the Bible you get the inner feeling that the writer has in mind a goal or consummation that is to be realized at some future date. In this sense the whole Bible is prophecy.

We might cite as an illustration the teachings of Jesus. The people heard, enjoyed, and wondered, but did not comprehend the full meaning.

"When the Son of man shall come in his glory" was an event always in the mind of Christ. It was for the joy that was set before Him that He endured the cross.

All prophecy points to a certain time and involves a certain generation. Jesus spoke of it as "this generation." The prophets called it "that day."

If we read the Scriptures with this thought in mind, we find that "the end of the days" are tremendous times with unbelievable things happening. Satan and the forces of evil are very much involved. But when the enemy comes in like a flood, the Spirit of the Lord will raise up a standard against him. So God's Spirit will also be very active in those days.

Probably the most amazing feature of prophesied times is that God has staked everything on His Word. It will become the most powerful force in the entire world, and the basis of a worldwide "revival."

Either God has written the greater part of the Bible in vain or the Prophetic Word will come into its own on a grand scale.

We have an advantage over the prophets of old, because we are living nearer the time of fulfillment. After one of Daniel's visions, he said the thing was true, but the appointed time was long. That was 2500 years ago. What Daniel saw is just as true today, and the time is short, relatively short compared to the 2500 years.

The prophets did not always understand the meanings of their own words; much of what they saw will be revealed by circumstance. As we approach the end, we see more clearly. If the commentators of 100 years ago had known about the marvelous return of the Jews and their success in restoring the promised land, they would not have applied the prophecies concerning Israel to the church.

When the Jews were settled and prosperous in their own chosen lands all over the earth and Palestine was a part of the Turkish Empire, unproductive, incapable of supporting a large number of people and very hostile, no commentator would dare talk about a prosperous and powerful Jewish nation.

Today, everything has changed and there is no reason for not applying the prophecies concerning Israel literally to Israel.

The same thing may be said of many other prophecies which, because they seem so impossible, commentators had to treat figuratively; but now, a literal interpretation turns out to be the right one.

Arthur E. Bloomfield
Eustis, Florida

CONTENTS

LIST OF MAPS

LIST OF CHARTS

A SURVEY
of BIBLE
PROPHECY

Chapter 1

THE FORWARD LOOK

No Scripture stands alone. Sometimes a right understanding of one small passage will open whole sections of prophecy.

On the other hand, a small error in our thinking can hide a whole area of truth; so it becomes necessary to sweep aside unscriptural ideas that get into our minds and block our understanding. We have a definite method of doing this. It is to fix our attention on the goal (sometimes called "the end" in the Bible) and then work toward it.

If a person is lost in the woods, he will tend to go round in circles; but if he can see a tower or a landmark in the distance, he will follow a straight line. Almost all the confusion in the religious world today (and it will increase still more when prophecy begins to be fulfilled) is due to the fact that the churches have been looking at the Bible as history, and so, looking in the wrong direction, they have no view of the goal.

There is a tower. There is a landmark. There is a "time of the end" thoroughly developed in the Bible. Find out what it is; understand the meaning of the prophecies concerning it; and you have laid out for yourself a straight path through what may, at first, seem like a forest of difficulties.

That is the main purpose of a chart or map.

THE BIBLE IS PROPHECY

The viewpoint of the Bible is always forward. What you see depends largely on your viewpoint. Two people looking in opposite directions do not see the same things.

The historian looks back. He sees only the past, sometimes a little of the present. He stops writing history when he reaches his own time.

From childhood we have been taught to look back. We go to Sunday School and we are told of things that happened two or three or four thousand years ago. The world might be falling apart around us, or great prophecies may be unfolding, but our eyes are fixed on ancient times.

The Bible always looks ahead. Bible writers saw the same things that we see, but they saw them against the background of the future, rather than the background of the past.

The Bible is an ancient book. So we have assumed that a study of the Bible is a study of the past, but our assumption is false. The Bible tells its story, not with the past in mind, but with the future in clear view. Even the purely historical portions of the Bible are written as if the historian were stating the past and viewing all events in the light of the future.

> Then went king David in, and sat before the Lord, and he said, Who am I, O Lord God? and what is my house, that thou hast brought me hitherto? And this was a small thing in thy sight, O Lord God; but thou hast spoken also of thy servant's house for a great while to come. And is this the manner of man, O Lord God?—II Sam. 7:18, 19

You cannot read very far in any historical book of the Bible without encountering some statement which shows the writer realized that what he was saying was part of an overall plan that would have its culmination a long time in the future. A prophet wrote as one looking forward.

We miss the point altogether when we look at these events as a historian looking into the past. The Bible is God's book. It is a revelation of His eternal program. The Bible was conceived before any of the things it records happened.

"According as he hath chosen us in him before the foundation of the world."—Eph. 1:4. "I will open my mouth in parables; I will utter things which have been kept secret from the foundation of the world."—Matt. 13:35.

God had something in mind—a very definite goal—when He created the world. All the Bible points toward that goal. It is the development of one master plan. It always looks ahead. In that sense, the entire Bible is prophecy. A study of prophecy is a study of the Bible. A study of the Bible without the prophetic forward look is merely a study of certain aspects of history. Prophecy is history from God's viewpoint.

"Thy word is a lamp unto my feet, and a light unto my path." —Ps. 119:105. It is the path ahead that the Word is supposed to light, not the one behind. What is going to happen to a church that always looks backwards with its light pointed toward the rear? This might not be too serious if the path ahead were straight and smooth; but when the road ahead becomes uncertain and full of pitfalls, the church must either turn around and let a little light shine on the road ahead or fall by the wayside. Prophecy is light on the road ahead at a time when we all need some assurance. It is the forward look.

"We have also a more sure word of prophecy; whereunto ye do well that ye take heed, as unto a light that shineth in a dark place, until the day dawn, and the day star arise in your hearts."—II Pet. 1:19.

THE WORD OF GOD

The Bible has many writers but only one Author. This becomes increasingly evident the moment we begin to see the Bible from God's viewpoint. Genesis is the book of beginnings, but everything begun in Genesis is finished in the Bible. In many cases what is begun in Genesis is brought to its consummation in Revelation.

God always finishes what He starts; He leaves nothing hanging in midair. In most cases the consummation is future at the time of writing, so the Bible is written as one standing at the beginning and looking toward the consummation of all things. How far distant is this event?

It is not, as so many assume, untold thousands of years ahead. The time is relatively short. We can get some idea of the time by counting the years between the high points of the Bible story. Let us take a quick review: From Adam to the Flood was about 1600 years. The Flood was a major event and is used as an illustration of the coming world disaster. "As it was in the days of Noah."

Then about 100 years after that came the confusion of tongues which changed the history of the world as nothing else ever has.

Three hundred years later came the call of Abraham which began a new process, affecting the whole world for all time.

Four hundred and thirty years after the call of Abraham came the Exodus from Egypt, which was attended by a long series of miracles.

In another 500 years the temple was dedicated. Then after another 500 years the Jews were returning from exile where they had been for 70 years. After another 500 years or so Christ was born.

This dispensation has been running now for over 1900 years, so we are actually living on borrowed time. Many signs of prophetic significance are beginning to appear. For instance, a Jewish state in Palestine, a threat of world destruction, the common market, the growing necessity of a world government, wars and commotions everywhere, an uneasiness in the churches, the feeling that something is wrong with the church message and program, a movement toward one church, which could spark a whole new era of church history. A new, more spiritual church is sure to emerge to offset the world church.

That which is begun in Genesis, the book of beginnings, is finished in the Bible, usually in Revelation, the book of consummations. The chart on the next page gives the details.

THE CONSUMMATION OF ALL THINGS

Gen. 1:1	Heaven and Earth	Isa. 65:17 Isa. 66:22 Rev. 21:1
Gen. 1:3	Light	Rev. 21:23
Gen. 1:8	Heaven (Sky)	Hag. 2:6, 7 Heb. 12:26-28
Gen. 1:10	Sea (Seas)	Rev. 21:1
Gen. 1:11	Vegetation	Isa. 35:1, 2
Gen. 1:14-16	Sun, Moon and Stars (Signs)	Matt. 24:29 Rev. 6:12-17
Gen. 1:20-25	Animal Life	Isa. 11:6-9
Gen. 1:26	Man (Human Race)	Isa. 35:10 Rev. 21:3-5 Rev. 21:24
Gen. 2:9	Tree of Life	Rev. 22:2
Gen. 2:12	Gold and Precious Stones	Rev. 17:4 Rev. 21:18-21
Gen. 3:1	Satan	Rev. 20:1-3 Rev. 20:10
Gen. 3:13	Sin	Rev. 21:7, 8
Gen. 3:15	Prophecy	Rev. 22:10
Gen. 3:17, 18	Curse	Rev. 22:3
Gen. 3:19	Death	Rev. 21:4
Gen. 4:4	Redemption by Blood	Rev. 5:9
Gen. 4:17	Cities	Rev. 21:9, 10
Gen. 6:1-7	Signs of Coming Judgments	Matt. 24:37-39
Gen. 7 and 8	The Flood	Luke 17:26 Matt. 24:37-39
Gen. 9:11-16	Rainbow Covenant	Rev. 4:3 Rev. 10:1
Gen. 11:1-8	Confusion of Tongues	Zeph. 3:9 Acts 2:8
Gen. 12:1-3	Jewish Nation Foretold	Ezek. 37
Gen. 14:1	Nations	Dan. 7:14 Dan. 7:27 Rev. 21:24

THE STRUCTURE OF PROPHECY

There are three main lines of prophecy in the Bible:

The Nations
The Jews
The Church (and the kingdom)

There are three books that deal specifically with these main lines:

The Nations—Daniel
The Jews—Ezekiel
The Church—Revelation

Each main line has a destination or goal. The purpose of a chart or map is to show the goal and the way to it.

Inasmuch as the Bible is written from the standpoint of one looking ahead, you may expect to find prophecies in almost every part. But without the three mainline books it would be difficult to fit them into the sequence. It might be asked, "Why didn't God tell the whole story in one place?" The reason would be evident if you tried to do it.

Minute details concerning side issues cannot be put into the main narrative without destroying its continuity. It would be like writing a history of the United States and trying to put in every detail about every phase of life. Such subjects as sports, art, literature, and religion would have to be treated separately.

The same is true of prophecy. It covers a vast range of subjects and we need books or passages which are devoted to special parts of the program, or deal with them in a special way.

The Old Testament prophetical books may be grouped into two general classes: (1) those that deal with both their own times and the future, and (2) those that deal only with the future. The prophets themselves indicate in which group their writings fall. If a book is to treat of its own times, it is necessary to know what those times are; therefore the book will begin by stating the date and place. For instance: "The vision of Isaiah, the son of Amoz, which he saw concerning Judah and Jerusalem in the days of Uzziah, Jotham, Ahaz, and Hezekiah, kings of Judah."—Isa. 1:1.

If, however, a prophecy is concerning the future only, there is no need for a statement as to its time and place. When these are omitted, the book is concerned only with the time of the end. For instance: "The vision of Obadiah. Thus saith the Lord God concerning Edom; We have heard a rumour from the Lord, and an ambassador is sent among the heathen, Arise ye, and let us rise up against her in battle."—Obad. 1.

This groups the prophets as follows:

BOTH CURRENT AND FUTURE		ALL FUTURE
Isaiah	Amos	Joel
Jeremiah	Micah	Obadiah
Ezekiel	Zephaniah	Nahum
Daniel	Haggai	Habukkuk
Hosea	Zechariah	Malachi

(Zephaniah has only a little concerning his own time. Zechariah mentions the time but not the place: his prophecy is nearly all future.)

In That Day

"In that day" always indicates that the prophet is starting a new subject. It does not point back to the previous prophecy but ahead to the Day of the Lord. When the American army was poised in England for the invasion of Europe, the big question was "When?" The date was kept secret. It was called "D Day."

The prophets did not know the date of the Day of the Lord about which they wrote, so they called it "that day." So when the prophet begins by saying "In that day," he is beginning a new subject not necessarily connected with what has gone before. Usually he is adding details which had to be left out of the main story.

A very important illustration of this rule may be seen in Daniel 12:1:

> And at that time shall Michael stand up, the great prince which standeth for the children of thy people: and there shall be a time of trouble, such as never was since there was a nation even to that same time: and at that time thy people shall be delivered, every one that shall be found written in the book.

The commentators stumble over the phrase, "at that time." They argue, "How can it be that after Antichrist has been destroyed and the kingdom of Christ has come, there is a time of trouble such as never was since there was a nation?"

But Jesus quoted this statement in Matthew 24:21 and applied it to the same time as Daniel 11, not afterwards. The fact is that in Daniel 12:1 "at that time" does not mean at the end of the events of Daniel 11. The prophet means that he is going back to fill in a detail left out in the main sequence.

THE GOAL OF ALL PROPHECY

Your understanding of the whole Bible will be influenced by your conception of God's ultimate purpose behind His dealings with men. Is God doing something of an eternal nature? Are we in the midst of a vast process that will reach into eternity and extend into the far reaches of the heavens? Why is there to be a new heaven and a new earth?

How can we understand the process if we do not know the end? Or, if we have an entirely wrong idea of the end, and what it will be like, how can we possibly understand the process? Strange things are to happen at the end of this age; we might even call them weird or fantastic. People will be puzzled. There will be many false prophets. You will certainly be deceived if you do not know the program and realize exactly what is happening.

By the program, we mean God's purpose in creation and in redemption, and how He will bring about the results He originally planned. God is the Creator of a universe so vast that man could never discover its outer limits, if, indeed, there are any outer limits. Any program that involved the suffering and death of His Son for the purpose of winning a Bride who would be joint-heirs with Him would be something tremendous, even for heaven. Then what would it mean to the earth? We must begin to appreciate the bigness of the program we are in.

Young people in college are asking, "What is the meaning of life?" They will never find out unless they discover what God is working in this world. Some people think God is doing the best He can to make the world better. That is not it. Some people think God is going to let the world become totally evil and then burn it up. That is not it.

The Bride is the first consideration. This group is made up of tried and tested saints. That means they must live and overcome in such a world as this. They are overcomers. The word means conquerors. They have to overcome in an evil world; there is no other way.

When the Bride has been removed, then what is left will be *purged* by fire. There will still be nations here after the Millennium. The overall goal, therefore, is redemption; but each line of prophecy has its own separate goal.

It is easier to get there if you know where you are going. God may have plans that far transcend anything that man has ever conceived; but His immediate goal is revealed in the Bible. Unless we also have that goal in mind, we will have difficulty in following the prophecies which lead to that goal.

So, the rule is:

First find out where you are going. Know what is the goal.

Although the Bible has many writers, it has only one Author. Nowhere is this more evident than in prophecy. It is seen in the consistency of expression, the use of words. Determine the meaning of a symbol in one part of the Bible and you have the meaning in all parts of the Bible.

The same is true of special words and phrases, some of which are used throughout Scripture. They are used so frequently and with such emphasis that it is of prime importance to understand them.

There are two major causes of misinterpretation: (1) not knowing the goal; (2) not recognizing the expressions referring to the goal. To avoid costly errors you must

1. Know the end that God has in mind.
2. Recognize the road signs pointing to that end, such as:

> The day of the Lord
> That day
> The last days
> The end
> The time of the end
> The end of the world (age)
> At that time (and other variations)

The end is the goal, the end of the story, not a time when all things cease to be. Here are examples of clearly stated goals:

> And there was given him dominion, and glory, and a kingdom, that all people, nations, and languages, should serve him: his dominion is an everlasting dominion, which shall not pass away, and his kingdom that which shall not be destroyed.—Dan. 7:14
> And in the days of these kings shall the God of heaven set up a kingdom, which shall never be destroyed: and the kingdom shall not be left to other people, but it shall break in pieces and consume all these kingdoms, and it shall stand forever.—Dan. 2:44

"Under the whole heaven" could cover more than the earth, but it would have to include all the earth.

This earth is everlasting, "world without end."

> But Israel shall be saved in the Lord with an everlasting salvation: ye shall not be ashamed nor confounded world without end.
> For thus saith the Lord that created the heavens; God himself that formed the earth and made it; he hath established it, he created it not in vain, he formed it to be inhabited: I am the Lord; and there is none else.—Isa. 45:17, 18

"World without end" would be an everlasting world "unto the ages of the ages," or unto the ages of eternity. That it applies to the earth may be gathered from verse 18. God's purpose for the earth is, therefore, redemption, not total destruction. There is coming a day of destruction that shall burn as an oven (Mal. 4:1); but that is a purging of those things that cannot be redeemed. People will live through it (Rev. 21:24).

Here we encounter a problem inherent in all languages—the use and meaning of words. Words mean different things to different people, so we have to determine what they meant to the writers and to the hearers. Human language is not a perfect medium for the communication of ideas because words may have so many different meanings.

For instance, in the Old Testament the English word DESTROY is used to translate 40 different Hebrew words (A.V.).

Sometimes "destroy" means only to mar or disfigure. The meaning must be ascertained from the context or from the whole tenor of Scripture.

NOAH AN EXAMPLE

Noah is one of the many examples of the forward look of the Bible. Noah's forward look saved him, his family, and the whole human race. Then God, looking forward still further, made a covenant with all mankind that He never again would destroy all people as He did in the Flood but, "while the earth remaineth, seedtime and harvest, and cold and heat, and summer and winter, and day and night shall not cease."—Gen. 8:22.

> And I, behold, I establish my covenant with you, and with your seed after you; and with every living creature that is with you, of the fowl, of the cattle, and of every beast of the earth with you; from all that go out of the ark, to every beast of the earth.
> And I will establish my covenant with you; neither shall all flesh be cut off any more by the waters of a flood; neither shall there any more be a flood to destroy the earth.
> And God said, This is the token of the covenant which I make between me and you and every living creature that is with you, for perpetual generations.—Gen. 9:9-12

It would be unworthy of God to make so solemn a covenant with a mental reservation that, although He would not destroy the earth with a flood, He would destroy it with something worse—fire. The covenant is for "perpetual generations." It means that the final judgment of fire will not remove all people from the earth; but that, when it is over, there will still be nations on the earth. Armies may be destroyed without destroying all the people.

Here is a good illustration of the difference between the backward, historical look and the Bible prophetic look. Looking back, we see the rainbow covenant and say (as we have been taught) that God made a "tongue-in-cheek" promise that He would not again destroy all things as He did in the Flood knowing that next time He would destroy them by fire.

Now look at this covenant against the background of the future state as revealed by prophecy. There is coming a time of trouble such as never was since there was a nation. God will purge the earth by fire. We are told that all the green grass and one-third of the trees will be burned up, and that men will blaspheme God because of the heat.

But when the great judgment throne is set up, from which will go these judgments, it is set in the center of a rainbow.

> And he that sat was to look upon like a jasper and a sardine stone: and there was a rainbow round about the throne, in sight like unto an emerald.—Rev. 4:3

Why? It seems as though nothing could save the world. This fear is expressed by the great leaders of the nations:

> And the kings of the earth, and the great men, and the rich men, and the chief captains, and the mighty men, and every bondman, and every free man, hid themselves in the dens and in the rocks of the mountains; and said to the mountains and rocks, Fall on us, and hide us from the face of him that sitteth on the throne, and from the wrath of the Lamb: For the great day of his wrath is come; and who shall be able to stand?—Rev. 6:15-17

But the rainbow is round about the throne. The fire does not strike all the earth at once. People live through it. The nations are here when Christ comes again; otherwise, how could He rule over them with a rod of iron? (Ps. 2:9).

> And he that overcometh, and keepeth my works unto the end, to him will I give power over the nations: and he shall rule them with a rod of iron; as the vessels of a potter shall they be broken to shivers: even as I received of my Father.—Rev. 2:26, 27
> And he shall judge among many people, and rebuke strong nations afar off; and they shall beat their swords into plowshares, and their spears into pruninghooks: nation shall not lift up a sword against nation, neither shall they learn war anymore.—Micah 4:3

Again, we have been told that after Christ and the saints (working for 1000 years) have perfected the world and its inhabitants, God will burn up the whole thing and create something new to put in its place. This would be quite impossible, for Jesus said concerning the judgment prior to His return: "For in those days shall be affliction, such as was not from the beginning of the creation which God created unto this time, NEITHER SHALL BE."—Mark 13:19.

Paul said: "For he must reign, till he hath put all enemies under his feet. The last enemy that shall be destroyed is death."

If Christ reigns until He has destroyed death, then how can He burn up the earth? And why destroy that which He has died for and then has labored so hard to perfect? When Christ returns the kingdom to God it will be a perfect work, not one grand failure that has to be burned up.

God says He will make all things new, not all new things. "And I saw a new heaven and a new earth; for the first heaven and the first earth were passed away; and there was no more sea." —Rev. 21:1.

Paul said: "Old things are passed away, behold, all things are become new."—II Cor. 5:17. Paul was redeemed, not destroyed. God is going to redeem the earth and its occupants, even the animals (Isa. 11:6-9).

Redemption and destruction are opposites. That which is destroyed is not redeemed. The rainbow is the seal of God's covenant that He will redeem the earth and restore it to the condition He planned for it when He created it. This truth is expressed by Isaiah.

> But Israel shall be saved in the Lord with an everlasting salvation: ye shall not be ashamed nor confounded world without end.
> For thus saith the Lord that created the heavens; God himself that formed the earth and made it; he hath established it, he created it not in vain, he formed it to be inhabited: I am the Lord; and there is none else.—Isa. 45:17, 18

The past can only be understood if it is placed before the background of the future. Everything God does has a purpose which can be known only by looking at the consummation. This is just the reverse of what we have been taught—namely, that if we are to understand the prophets, we must know all about the times in which they lived and the conditions under which they labored.

If we are to understand the prophets, we must know the future and the goals they were talking about. The Bible must be studied with the future in mind, because that is the way the prophets were looking.

You may have seen prophetic charts which showed the world being burned up after the Millennium. If you have that picture in mind, you will be at a disadvantage because God's program calls for the redemption of everything that was lost—that God created and called good. He has established the earth and called it His footstool; He made it to be inhabited.

If the future, not the past, is the key to the whole Bible, then we must have a very clear conception of the future. As the Scriptures unfold you will see a purpose in everything God does. The purpose never changes. "The earth shall be filled with the knowledge of the glory of the Lord as the waters cover the sea." —Hab. 2:14. "Look unto me and be ye saved, all the ends of the earth."—Isa. 45:22.

Prophecy is the unfolding of God's program of redemption, the restoration of all things.

Nearly 2000 years have gone by since the last word of the Bible was written, and the signs of the approaching climax in the contest with Satan over the possession of the earth are beginning to impress themselves upon us. All the saints of the Old Testament, who lived in anticipation of God's grandest operation, had to look a long way ahead. Now, two to four thousand years may be deducted from the time appointed and we have only a short time to wait.

Not only that. We have all that the prophets recorded and all that Jesus taught, together with the marvelous book of Revelation. Yet the church today always looks back and shows no interest in what the men of old sacrificed everything to obtain. Like Lot's wife, the church has no taste for God's program of redemption. Instead of being concerned with the near future, it is all taken up with the far distant past.

Most people who call themselves Christians have nothing but contempt for what God will do; they are concerned only with what God has done. It was for the joy that was set before Him that Christ endured the cross and the shame. The time is not far away when world events will divide the church between those who will follow the greatest deceiver of all time, and those who will hold to the faith which is the substance of things hoped for, the evidence of things not seen.

All those who do not have a real love for the truth will believe the lie.

> These all died in faith, not having received the promises, but having seen them afar off, and were persuaded of them, and embraced them, and confessed that they were strangers and pilgrims on the earth.—Heb. 11:13

They saw them afar off; we see them close at hand. They did not look back longingly at the country from which they came, as so many so-called Christians today keep looking back at their experiences and the experiences of others, interested only in that which has been.

They looked for a better country, a heavenly. They didn't just think of it as a passing fancy. They believed it. It was the underlying cause of all their actions. They lived in anticipation of the promise. Think how much more we have to look forward to than they did! They did not have the prophets or the teachings of Jesus. They did not know about the Resurrection, the redemption of the earth, the rewards of the saints, the "glory that shall be revealed in us." Yet they looked ahead. We have all this information and much more, and we only look back.

"And these all, having obtained a good report through faith, received not the promise: God having provided some better thing for us, that they without us should not be made perfect."—Heb. 11:39, 40.

They saw it afar off but did not experience its fulfillment, because we are in it too. The promise includes us. We will all be glorified together. They without us will not enter into the fullness of God's program for the saints and for the world. *But we must also have the same faith.*

There are no other dispensations that we must wait for beyond the dispensation of grace. As this dispensation draws to a close we approach the time to which the Bible points. But, as usual, only those who by faith are looking ahead will understand. "The wise shall understand."—Dan. 12:10.

You do not get the full force of this truth now, because the conditions will be so much different from anything the world has ever known. When Satan's man saves the world from what seems like certain destruction and sets up a time of peace and prosperity that looks like something that will last forever; when, with his mouth speaking great things, Antichrist deceives the whole world; then the just shall live by his faith, for that will be the only evidence of things not seen. Everything that is seen will point to Antichrist.

It is true that without us they will not be made perfect, but it is also true that in that day of days we will have to have the same faith and the same forward look.

However, there is a church that Jesus said He would spue out of His mouth. Those who, like Lot's wife, are looking back will be in that church.

"Whosoever shall seek to save his life shall lose it; and whosoever shall lose his life shall preserve it."—Luke 17:33.

Under Antichrist everybody will be "living it up." The only ones found worthy to be in God's program will be those like Abraham, Isaac and Jacob and all the prophets, who look for a city that has foundations, whose builder and maker is God. It all depends on which way you are looking.

Chapter 2

THE SECOND COMING
OF CHRIST

FIVE GREEK WORDS

Five Greek words are used to express the truth of the Second Coming of Christ.

Optomai (appear)

Unto them that look for him shall he appear the second time without sin unto salvation.—Heb. 9:28

Erchomai (come)

And if I go and prepare a place for you, I will come again, and receive you unto myself; that where I am, there ye may be also.—John 14:3

Ye men of Galilee, why stand ye gazing up into heaven? this same Jesus, which is taken up from you into heaven, shall so come in like manner as ye have seen him go into heaven.—Acts 1:11

When he shall come to be glorified in his saints, and to be admired in all them that believe (because our testimony among you was believed) in that day.—II Thess. 1:10

And Enoch also, the seventh from Adam, prophesied of these, saying, Behold, the Lord cometh with ten thousand of his saints.
—Jude 14

Behold, he cometh with clouds; and every eye shall see him, and they also which pierced him: and all kindreds of the earth shall wail because of him. Even so, Amen.—Rev. 1:7

Epiphaino (appear) Epiphany

That thou keep this commandment without spot, unrebukeable, until the appearing of our Lord Jesus Christ.—I Tim. 6:14

But is now made manifest by the appearing of our Saviour Jesus Christ, who hath abolished death, and hath brought life and immortality to light through the gospel.—II Tim. 1:10

I charge thee therefore before God, and the Lord Jesus Christ, who shall judge the quick and the dead at his appearing and his kingdom.—II Tim. 4:1

Henceforth there is laid up for me a crown of righteousness, which the Lord, the righteous judge, shall give me at that day; and not to me only, but unto all them also that love his appearing.—II Tim. 4:8

Looking for that blessed hope, and the glorious appearing of the great God and our Saviour Jesus Christ.—Titus 2:13

Apokalupsis (unveiling, revelation, appearing, coming)

Wherefore gird up the loins of your mind, be sober, and hope to the end for the grace that is to be brought unto you at the revelation of Jesus Christ.—I Pet. 1:13

That the trial of your faith, being much more precious than of gold that perisheth, though it be tried with fire, might be found unto praise and honour and glory at the appearing of Jesus Christ.—I Pet. 1:7

So that ye come behind in no gift; waiting for the coming of our Lord Jesus Christ.—I Cor. 1:7

The Revelation of Jesus Christ, which God gave unto him, to shew unto his servants things which must shortly come to pass; and he sent and signified it by his angel unto his servant John.—Rev. 1:1

Parousia (presence) translated "coming"

But every man in his own order: Christ the firstfruits; afterward they that are Christ's at his coming.—I Cor. 15:23

For what is our hope, or joy, or crown of rejoicing? Are not even ye in the presence of our Lord Jesus Christ at his coming?—I Thess. 2:19

To the end he may stablish your hearts unblameable in holiness before God, even our Father, at the coming of our Lord Jesus Christ with all his saints.—I Thess. 3:13

For this we say unto you by the word of the Lord, that we which are alive and remain unto the coming of the Lord shall not prevent[precede] them which are asleep.—I Thess. 4:15

And the very God of peace sanctify you wholly; and I pray God your whole spirit and soul and body be preserved blameless unto the coming of our Lord Jesus Christ.—I Thess. 5:23

Now we beseech you, brethren, by the coming of our Lord Jesus Christ, and by our gathering together unto him.—II Thess. 2:1

And then shall that Wicked be revealed, whom the Lord shall consume with the spirit of his mouth, and shall destroy with the brightness of his coming.—II Thess. 2:8

Be patient therefore, brethren, unto the coming of the Lord. Behold, the husbandman waiteth for the precious fruit of the earth, and hath long patience for it, until he receive the early and the latter rain. Be ye also patient, stablish your hearts; for the coming of the Lord draweth nigh.—James 5:7, 8

For we have not followed cunningly devised fables, when we made known unto you the power and coming of our Lord Jesus Christ, but were eyewitnesses of his majesty.—II Pet. 1:16

And now, little children, abide in him; that, when he shall appear, we may have confidence, and not be ashamed before him at his coming.—I John 2:28

THE RAPTURE

The resurrection of the dead and the catching up of the living saints is called the Rapture. Then, for the first time in the Bible the story of redemption has two scenes of action. The saints are active in heaven and there is great activity on the earth. The time is short. It is divided into two parts, called in Revelation "the great tribulation" and the "seven last plagues."

The saints in heaven are God's agents in the redemption of the earth. Redemption requires purging, so fire is involved. Many people will live through it; so, at the end of the time of trouble, the armies of the world will be gathered together against the Lord to prevent His reign. This is called the Battle of Armageddon, although it is really fought at Jerusalem.

Christ will return in person, with His saints, at the end of this time of trouble. He will set up His kingdom and reign with His saints for 1000 years. Then there will be a change, but the kingdom will be everlasting.

So we have first, the coming of Christ FOR His saints, then the coming of Christ WITH His saints. A diagram would show it like this:

SECOND COMING

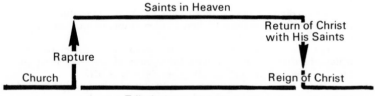

Saints in Heaven

Return of Christ
with His Saints

Rapture

Church

Reign of Christ

Tribulation and Judgment

Now let us take a closer look at the return *for* His saints. Bible students have given it the name "The Rapture" to distinguish it from the time when He comes *with* His saints.

The Second Coming of Christ is a process involving several events. The two main events come, one at the beginning and one at the end of the process. The reason is simple. There is coming a time of judgment when the earth is to be purged by fire. Jesus said it would be a time of trouble such as never was since there was a nation.

But this is not just a time of trouble; it is a punishment for sin.

> For, behold, the Lord cometh out of his place to punish the inhabitants of the earth for their iniquity: the earth also shall disclose her blood, and shall no more cover her slain.—Isa. 26:21

There will be people on the earth whose sins are forgiven. People who are under the blood of Christ cannot be punished for their sins. They have already been purged. Before the judgment comes, those people must be removed from the earth. So, the first event in the process of the Second Coming of Christ is the Resurrection or Rapture which includes the living Christians. Paul states it this way.

> For the Lord himself shall descend from heaven with a shout, with the voice of the archangel, and with the trump of God: and the dead in Christ shall rise first: then we which are alive and remain shall be caught up together with them in the clouds, to meet the Lord in the air: and so shall we ever be with the Lord.— I Thess. 4:16, 17

The Flood furnishes a good illustration of the process. It was a judgment for sin, and God saved the righteous people out of it. Noah and his family entered the ark and were carried above the Flood and then returned after the water receded. Jesus used this as an illustration of His return. There will then be more righteous people on earth than in the days of Noah. The righteous will be taken, the others left to go through the tribulation.

> But as the days of Noah were, so shall also the coming of the Son of man be. For as in the days that were before the flood they were eating and drinking, marrying and giving in marriage, until the day that Noah entered into the ark, and knew not until the flood came, and took them all away; so shall also the coming of the Son of man be. Then shall two be in the field; the one shall be taken, and the other left. Two women shall be grinding at the mill; the one shall be taken, and the other left. Watch therefore: for ye know not what hour your Lord doth come.—Matt. 24:37-42

A diagram of the Flood would be very similar to the one on the Second Coming.

NOAH

Noah in the Ark

Return after the Flood

People   Judgment   New Beginning

Corrupt   on the Earth

You will note that some of the Scriptures cited above refer to the Rapture, some to the Return in glory, others could refer to the whole process. The time between the two parts is very short.

Chapter 3

THE CHURCH AND THE KINGDOM

Each main line of prophecy has a goal. The church is no exception. The book that deals almost exclusively with the church is Revelation. The goal of the church is a new heaven and a new earth and the eternal reign of the Bride. The goal of the nations is the end of Satan's reign and the beginning of the reign of Christ and the saints over the nations of the earth. The goal of the Jews is a righteous nation and the kingdom of David.

All three goals unite in the kingdom of heaven. The church is not the kingdom, but it is a part of the kingdom. It is, in many respects, the most important part, because out of it come the rulers that will operate the kingdom. The church produces the rulers. Christ will establish the kingdom when He comes, but the process that leads up to His coming is the work of the church.

In the Old Testament the kingdom was future. "Behold, a king shall reign in righteousness, and princes shall rule in judgment." —Isa. 32:1. "Thy people shall be all righteous; they shall inherit the land for ever, the branch of my planting, the work of my hands, that I may be glorified. A little one shall become a thousand, and a small one a strong nation: I the Lord will hasten it in his time."—Isa. 60:21, 22.

The New Testament begins with the proclamation, "The kingdom of heaven is at hand." Jesus, when He established the church, began the process that will culminate in the kingdom. The kingdom was the subject which Jesus taught most systematically; and Matthew is the book that records that systematic teaching. Matthew is the book of the kingdom, yet Matthew is also the book that records the beginning of the church. "On this rock I will build my church." So, Jesus could say, "The kingdom of heaven is like unto," and then speak in parables that could apply only to the church.

The kingdom includes all the goals of prophecy and more. It is bigger than the sum of its parts. In Matthew there is a blending of the church and the kingdom, because the church is the beginning of the process by which the kingdom comes. Out of the church come the rulers of the kingdom. The goal is the everlasting kingdom—that is, the eternal reign of Christ and the saints over all things. The work of the church will not be finished until the kingdom is perfected.

The Millennium is not the length of the kingdom; it is the length of time necessary to perfect the kingdom on the earth. The kingdom is everlasting and will keep on expanding forever. "Of the increase of his kingdom and peace there shall be no end." —Isa. 9:7.

The goal of the church is not a reformed world or a better world in which to live in sin. The goal of the church is a people qualified to rule, a people qualified to be the Bride of Christ. So, the primary function of the church is to perfect the saints— that is, to prepare them for the tremendous task that lies ahead and which will reach out into eternity both in time and space.

We are dealing with God and God's program which is bigger than anything the mind of man can conceive, for it has not entered the mind of man the things that God has prepared for them that love Him.

> And he gave some, apostles; and some, prophets; and some evangelists; and some, pastors and teachers; for the perfecting of the saints, for the work of the ministry, for the edifying of the body of Christ; till we all come in the unity of the faith, and of the knowledge of the Son of God, unto a perfect man, unto the measure of the stature of the fulness of Christ.—Eph. 4:11-13

It has been said that anything man can conceive, in time, man can do. Today that reaches out into distant space; but God's program, called the Kingdom of Heaven, reaches out farther and includes more than any man can imagine.

The kingdom is big business and the saints are the operators of that business. It takes skill and understanding and experience to operate a business. It also takes a stability that could come only from an encounter with Satan. The saints are, first of all, overcomers.

BEGINNING OF THE KINGDOM OF HEAVEN

> Verily I say unto you, Among them that are born of women there hath not risen a greater than John the Baptist: notwithstanding he that is least in the kingdom of heaven is greater than he.
>
> For all the prophets and the law prophesied until John. And if ye will receive it, this is Elias, which was for to come.—Matt. 11:11, 13, 14.

Here we see the first difference between the church and the kingdom. The church began at Pentecost; the kingdom began with John the Baptist. The kingdom of heaven is like a grain of mustard seed, which was the least of all garden seeds; but, in this case, it grew to its full size as a mustard plant, and then kept on growing until it became a great tree. The kingdom began with one man, but there is no limit to its eventual size.

Jesus' first emphasis was on the greatness of the kingdom, or rather, the greatness of those in the kingdom. Jesus did not mean that John the Baptist would not be in the kingdom; but, rather, that the least person in the kingdom would be greater than the greatest man that ever lived on this earth.

John the Baptist was not Elijah. He did not fulfill Malachi 4:5, 6. "Behold, I will send you Elijah the prophet before the coming of the great and terrible day of the Lord: and he shall turn the heart of the fathers to the children, and the heart of the children to their fathers, lest I come and smite the earth with a curse."

Jesus qualified His statement by saying, "If ye will receive it"; meaning, "If you will understand what I mean." What Elijah is to the second coming of Christ, John was to the first coming of Christ.

THE GROWTH OF THE KINGDOM

Another parable put he forth unto them, saying. The kingdom of heaven is like to a grain of mustard seed, which a man took, and sowed in his field: which indeed is that least of all seeds: but when it is grown, it is the greatest among herbs, and becometh a tree, so that the birds of the air come and lodge in the branches thereof.—Matt. 13:31, 32

The usual interpretation of this parable is that the church started very small and was supposed to remain comparatively small. Actually, only a small portion of a community ever gets saved. But after the church has reached its normal size as a plant it keeps on growing until it becomes a great tree—a state church or popular church, and takes in almost everybody. The plant becomes a tree.

This is in harmony with the other parables, but there are some other considerations. The point of the parable is the small start and tremendous growth.

The kingdom started with one man. That is as small as any movement can start (the church started with a group of people). The kingdom will continue to grow until it reaches out and covers the earth. "The knowledge of the glory of the Lord will cover the earth as the waters cover the sea." That is as large as the mustard plant could get as a plant.

But the kingdom will not stop growing when it has covered the earth. "Of the increase of his kingdom and peace there shall be no end." "A little one shall become a thousand and a small one a strong nation."

This earth is too small to fulfill all the promises that God has made to His servants. This earth is a tiny speck in God's world. Even after the saints have been taken out and, in the Holy City, become a ruling class, there will still be people on the earth who can increase forever.

They will be a redeemed people. They will have survived the judgments and they will have lived through the Millennium. Revelation says that the saints will live and reign with Christ a thousand years. They will have to reign over somebody; and the reign will have to be successful, for the kingdom will be established forever on the earth. These people over whom the saints reign will be the ones who will people new worlds in space forever, an everexpanding kingdom. Then the plant will have become a great tree.

The mention of the birds of the air lodging in its branches is probably meant to indicate only the great size of the tree.

GROWTH OF THE KINGDOM

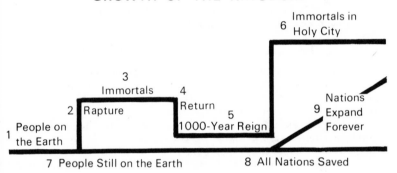

Explanation of the Chart

1. PEOPLE ON EARTH. We started with the earth before the Rapture. Now we have all kinds of people.

2. RAPTURE. The Rapture will remove the saved, leaving (a) people who lived among the saved and possibly thought they were saved; (b) the unsaved who never heard the gospel.

3. IMMORTALS. The saints, after the Rapture, will have immortal bodies like the resurrected body of Christ. Their natural place will be heaven. They are a fixed number, they will not increase.

4. THE RETURN. The saints will return with Christ.

5. THE MILLENNIUM. For 1000 years the saints will reign with Christ. The earth will be perfected and all nations will know God. During this time the nations of the earth, including Israel, will be redeemed.

6. IMMORTALS IN THE HOLY CITY. After the 1000 years there will be a change. On earth there will be a final cleansing of the nations. Then death will be destroyed. The saints will go to their final home (the Holy City) to reign over all things.

7. PEOPLE STILL ON THE EARTH. People will be on the earth all through the judgments, all through the Millennium and into eternity. The human race will be redeemed as an earthly people.

8. ALL NATIONS SAVED. "And the nations of the earth which are saved shall walk in the light of it [the Holy City]; and the kings of the earth do bring their glory and honour into it."—Rev. 21:24.

9. NATIONS EXPAND FOREVER. "Thy people shall be all righteous: they shall inherit the land for ever, the branch of my planting, the work of my hands, that I may be glorified. A little one shall become a thousand and a small one a strong nation: I the Lord will hasten it in his time." —Isa. 60:21, 22.

If each baby born is to become a nation, we will need more space than this earth provides. We are beginning to learn something of the vastness of God's creation. Now He will have a people worthy of that creation. Men want to visit other worlds. They will, in a big way. God does big things, marvelous in our eyes. The kingdom is big business. How can people get to other planets? Men are even now planning it. Are they wiser than God?

THE LAST DAYS OF THE CHURCH

There is no subject in the Bible that contains so many surprises as this one. I think it would be safe to say, "It isn't like you think." The church is an earthly organization. In heaven the saints go by other names than present-day denominations.

It is easy enough to say, "The Rapture is the next event. Therefore there are no signs of the Rapture; all prophecies of things to come before the Rapture have been fulfilled."

But that leaves whole sections of the prophetic Word that could never be fulfilled. It makes a shambles of prophecy. There is a feeling in some quarters that the church has little to do with the events of the last days of the age—that it will drift into apostasy, and then the Rapture will come. This teaching has blinded the eyes of thousands of sincere people to the most exciting truths in the Bible. This is the climax of the church age and the church will be very much involved in the close of this age. The part that the church will play in the most wonderful days since creation will unfold slowly. We will understand it better when we begin to get an understanding of God's program for the world and for the church.

The church is not just a bunch of wishy-washy, pious do-gooders. It is God's grand masterpiece with whom He will conquer and govern the world. It is the brightest star in His crown. It is the very Bride of Christ, destined to sit with Him on His throne. This age is built around the church, and the church is the very center of God's program in the last days of the church age. The entire process of redemption has been committed to the church, and there are some things that must be done while the church is still here.

The church will not be removed from the scene of action until that action is transferred to heaven. It is from heaven that the saints will judge the world. The greatest days for the church are still ahead.

We think of the church as a denomination; God does not. In fact, all denominations could defect to Antichrist; and probably most of them will, but new societies will start and the church will go right on, stronger than ever, "conquering and to conquer." There will have to be some changes, because the church has drifted into a maze of organizational activities that have little kingdom value. We need a whole new start, and we will get it.

MEANING OF THE LAST DAYS

The last days of the church could cover a period of thirty or forty years. Jesus put some limits on it when He said: "Now learn a parable of the fig tree; when his branch is yet tender, and putteth forth leaves, ye know that summer is nigh: so likewise ye, when ye shall see all these things, know that it is near, even at the doors. Verily I say unto you, This generation shall not pass, till all these things be fulfilled."—Matt. 24:32-34.

"This generation" could also be translated "THAT generation" —the generation living when these things start. The most time it can take is one generation.

Jesus told us the events that start "this generation" and the event that ends it. It starts before the Rapture when "these things begin to come to pass" (Luke 21:28); and ends with the return of Christ when "they shall see the Son of man coming in a cloud with power and great glory" (Luke 21:27).

In between these events come the tribulation and judgment of the nations. So, "this generation" covers all the time between the beginning of the signs and the return of Christ.

The beginning of these signs is not the Rapture, as so many have supposed, but conditions preceding the Rapture. Jesus referred to these beginning signs and then said: "These things must come to pass, but the end is not yet."

This leaves time for all the things that must take place before the Rapture. There are so many that they could not be put into a talk as brief as the Olivet Discourse. Jesus made a practice of not repeating what was told in other parts of the Bible. He merely added details.

The last days are not all tribulation. Many prophecies will come to complete fulfillment before the tribulation, and therefore, before the Rapture.

Many of the prophecies about these times would not make

sense if the church were not here. These will be days of great change. Institutions that cannot change will have to be discarded. The tendency among churches that cannot change will be toward the Roman Church, which does not materially change. It will be as impossible for modern denominations to change as it was for the Roman Church to change with the Reformation.

God's church of the last days will be more truly a Bible Church than we have ever had. It will be born of prophecy and will have the forward look with the exclusion of all extra scriptural doctrines.

The church of the last days will be a world-wide church on a scale that we have never known. When Communism is put down the whole world will be open to the gospel. The Holy Spirit will be in charge. Churches will not go into new fields and with their man-made doctrines compete with each other. This time it will be genuine Bible teaching with the grand climax always in view. This is a necessary prelude to the tribulation.

After the Rapture

There will be a great multitude saved after the Rapture. The gospel will be preached from heaven. It will be a warning not to receive the mark of the beast (Rev. 7:9-17; 14:6-12).

The time is short and the preaching is of an emergency nature. There will not be time for extensive teaching. The whole world will have to be made acquainted with the terms of the gospel or this tribulation preaching would have no meaning.

If an angel or messenger from heaven should fly over the United States saying, "Fear God and give him glory," everybody would know what he meant. But if the same message were preached over China as it is today, nobody would know what it meant, because, to them, there is no God. So, if there is going to be a great world-wide revival during the tribulation, there must be some extensive preparation for it before the tribulation. That is the big project of the church of the last days.

Everywhere Communism goes, false gods and heathen religions disappear. Now if Communism is suddenly wiped out, there will be an opportunity for missions that will make possible what must have been in the mind of Jesus when He said: "Go ye therefore and teach all nations, baptizing them in the name of the Father, and of the Son, and of the Holy Ghost: teaching them to observe all things whatsoever I have commanded you; and, lo, I am with you alway, even unto THE END OF THE AGE."

Chapter 4

THE KINGDOM

The subject of the kingdom is so involved in controversy that it is difficult even to attempt an orderly analysis. The difficulties are further increased by an attempt, made by some, to show a difference between the kingdom of heaven and the kingdom of God. Others try to show a difference between the gospel, and the gospel of the kingdom.

There is only one kingdom and there is only one gospel. There is only one commission to preach the gospel; that commission was given to the church. Jesus evidently used the expressions kingdom of God and kingdom of heaven interchangeably. Matthew chose kingdom of heaven; the others, kingdom of God, in reporting the same incident. Or, it may be that it is a matter of translation. Jesus spoke a form of Aramaic, while the Gospels were written in Greek. That the kingdom of heaven and the kingdom of God are the same is easily demonstrated by comparing the records. For instance:

Matthew 4:17 and Mark 1:14, 15
Matthew 5:3 and Luke 6:20
Matthew 19:14 and Mark 10:14

It is generally accepted that the church is not the kingdom, yet Jesus used the word "kingdom" freely when He was speaking about the church and salvation (Matt. 13:24; John 3:3, 5). Usually this difficulty has been met by spiritualizing the statements. This is always a dangerous practice, more apt to hide than to reveal truth.

As we study the subject throughout the Gospels, we find that the kingdom is the reign of Christ in person on this earth. It will begin with the return of Christ and last forever. Many elements will enter into the coming kingdom.

The kingdom is the climax of all prophecies concerning the Jews, the nations, and the church. It is there that all prophecy meets. No prophecy reaches beyond the kingdom, except that concerning the everlasting home of the saints, the Holy City. Both are eternal, one on earth, the other in a heavenly place. The Jews, the Gentile nations, and the church are all in the kingdom. They all have their appointed places.

THE JEWISH NATION will be there. Christ will appear as the deliverer of Jews in their hour of greatest trial. So all Israel will be saved (Rom. 11:26, 27). The kingdom of David will be revived (II Sam. 7:10, 12, 13; Luke 1:32, 33).

GENTILE NATIONS will survive the time of tribulation and plagues and will enter the kingdom age. The Lord is to rule them with a rod of iron (Ps. 2:7-9). He will judge them (Matt. 25:31). He will rebuke them for their warlike activities (Micah 4:1-3). The nations that are left after the Battle of Armageddon will be forced to worship Christ (Zech. 14:16-19).

THE CHURCH will be there. The saints will reign with Christ (Rev. 2:26, 27). The saints will be a very special group, separate from all the others. They will be the only ones in the kingdom who have passed through the resurrection or Rapture and have immortal bodies. They will be the rulers, not the subjects. They are the kingdom which comes down from heaven and is established over the nations of the earth (Dan. 7:27). In that sense the church is the kingdom, and only those redeemed by the blood of Christ may enter this kingdom.

The kingdom is now being formed in heaven. Every soul saved on earth adds one to the kingdom of heaven. The kingdom is not now growing on earth; it is growing in heaven by the preaching of the gospel on earth. The gospel we preach is the gospel of the kingdom. "Except a man be born again, he cannot see the kingdom of God." How this is to be accomplished, Jesus explained to Nicodemus. He said: "For God so loved the world, that he gave his only begotten Son, that whosoever believeth in him should not perish, but have everlasting life." This is the gospel of the kingdom. It is the gospel that Jesus preached: "Now after that John was put in prison, Jesus came into Galilee, preaching the gospel of the kingdom of God."—Mark 1:14.

It is the kingdom of David because the Son of David will reign. It is the kingdom of God because it is the workmanship of God. It is the kingdom of heaven because it comes down from heaven.

PROPHECIES APPLYING TO:

The Church: Rulers in the Kingdom

The Kingdom of Heaven
The Kingdom of God
Enter by means of conversion or the new birth . . . John 3:3, 5; Matt. 18:3
At hand (people could begin to enter) . . . Matt. 4:17; Mark 1:15; Matt. 10:7; Luke 10:9-11
Jesus preached the gospel of the kingdom . . . Mark 1:14; Luke 4:43
Belongs to the poor and persecuted . . . Matt. 5:3, 10; Luke 6:20
A difference in position in the kingdom . . . Matt. 5:19; 18:4
Righteousness required . . . Matt. 5:20; Mark 9:47; Matt. 7:21; 21:31; Luke 13:28
Seek first the kingdom . . . Matt. 6:33; Luke 12:31
Open to all people . . . Matt. 8:11; Luke 13:29
Those in the kingdom greater than John . . . Matt. 11:11; Luke 7:28

Suffereth violence . . . Matt. 11:12

The kingdom was upon them when the King was present . . . Luke 11:20; Matt. 12:28

Mysteries revealed . . . Matt. 13:11; Mark 4:11; Luke 8:10

Like seed sown . . . Matt. 13:24; Mark 4:26

Like mustard seed that becomes a tree . . . Matt. 13:31; Mark 4:30; Luke 13:18, 19

Like meal that is leavened . . . Matt. 13:33; Luke 13:20, 21

Like treasure hid in a field . . . Matt. 13:44

Like a pearl of great price . . . Matt. 13:45

Like a net containing fishes, good and bad . . . Matt. 13:47

Like a householder . . . Matt. 13:52

Peter given the keys . . . Matt. 16:19

To be seen by some before death . . . Mark 9:1; Luke 9:27

Like a king and an unmerciful servant . . . Matt. 18:23

Attitude toward the kingdom a test of discipleship . . . Luke 9:60-62

Kingdom preached since John . . . Luke 16:16

Cometh not with observation (its development is unnoticed) . . . Luke 17:20

Within you (in your midst) . . . Luke 17:21

We may make sacrifices for the kingdom's sake . . . Matt. 19:12; Luke 18:29, 30

Made up of children and those with childlike faith . . . Matt. 19:14; Mark 10:14, 15; Luke 18:16, 17

Hard for rich to enter . . . Matt. 19:23; Mark 10:23; Luke 18:24, 25

Parable of the laborers . . . Matt. 20:1

Parable of the marriage feast . . . Matt. 22:2

One of the scribes not far from the kingdom . . . Mark 12:34

Pharisees shut the kingdom against men . . . Matt. 23:13

Signs of the approaching kingdom . . . Luke 21:31

Parable of the ten virgins . . . Matt. 25:1

Passover fulfilled in the kingdom . . . Luke 22:16

Christ to drink new wine in the kingdom . . . Matt. 26:29; Mark 14:25; Luke 22:18

The Jews: The Kingdom of David

The kingdom to come from Judah . . . Gen. 49:10

The King to come from the House of David . . . II Sam. 7:12

The kingdom to be everlasting . . . II Sam. 7:13, 16; Isa. 9:7, 45:17

An Israelitish kingdom . . . Jer. 23:3-8

Jerusalem to be the capital . . . Micah 4:1-3

Jesus, the Son of David, is King . . . Luke 1:32, 33

David, a prince . . . Ezek. 34:23, 24; 37:25

The Nations: Subjects in the Kingdom

Unsaved nations will enter the kingdom . . . Zech. 14:16-19

Nations will be ruled by force at the beginning . . . Ps. 2:7-11; Rev. 2:26, 27

The saints will reign on earth over the nations for 1000 years . . . Rev. 20:4

The kingdom will be cleansed and perfected . . . Rev. 20:7-10

Kingdom prepared for those found worthy . . . Matt. 25:31-46

After the Millennium the earthly kingdom will be left to earthly people. The redeemed (with immortal bodies) will reign from the Holy City (Rev. 21:9, 10, 24).

These three elements in the kingdom—the saints, the Jews and the nations—must not be confused. There is only one kingdom. Eventually it will reach to the ends of the earth and possibly beyond, for "of the increase of his kingdom and peace there shall be no end."

But there will be two distinctly different kinds of people: (1) Those who have lived during the redemptive period, who have been born again, who have died and been raised or caught up at the Rapture. These have immortal bodies capable of inhabiting the universe. They are not earthbound. They may make their home in the Holy City and come and go "like doves to their windows" (Isa. 60:8).

(2) Then there will be Gentile nations, made up of those who are saved during the Millennium or who are born during the Millennium and after. They are of the earth. They will not go into the Holy City to live. They will inhabit the earth or the earthly kingdom forever. Everlasting life in that day will not mean that they will die and be raised; it will mean that they will never die. They will remain an earthly people. Their number will increase forever. God is not limited in His power to provide room.

The saints are a fixed number. They will not increase. They are a distinct people who live in the City of God and see His face. They are the rulers, with Christ, of all creation, heirs of all things, joint-heirs with Christ.

Redeemed Jews (those who are saved and have become immortal) are included with the saints. There is no difference because of nationality in the Holy City. Both Old and New Testament saints are there (Rev. 21:12, 14).

The earthly nation of Israel will be saved as an earthly nation and David will reign. It is the nucleus of the kingdom on earth; Christ and the saints will reign for 1000 years; after that the kingdom will assume its permanent form, with the Jews inhabiting their Promised Land and other nations living in peace with them.

The new heaven and the new earth mentioned in Revelation 20 are the result of the reign of Christ for 1000 years. "Old things have passed away, behold, all things have become new."

Chapter 5

FROM CHURCH TO KINGDOM

On the chart the red lines represent the church, or the saints. They are not called "church" after the Rapture. At the Rapture the scene of action moves to heaven and the saints are organized into groups for the work of the redemption of the earth. These groups are called Elders, Living Ones (Beasts), Horsemen and Angels.

The resurrection of the Tribulation Saints completes the number of saints in heaven (Rev. 7:9-17).

The black represents the nations and the Jews. Details will be found diagrammed on other charts.

EXPLANATION OF THE CHART

THE DISPENSATION OF GRACE began with the church and it will end with the church. The Rapture does not end the day of grace, for there will be people saved after the Rapture. The Dispensation of Grace ends with the First Resurrection.

The First Resurrection is in two parts: first, the Rapture; second, the resurrection of the Tribulation Saints, those who are killed by the beast (Antichrist). The first group is seen in heaven in Rev. 4 and 5. The second group is noted in Rev. 7:9-17. They are both seen in Rev. 20:4-6. Together they make the First Resurrection.

PHILADELPHIA AND LAODICEA are the two significant churches of the last days of the age. The Philadelphia type of church will be delivered from the time of tribulation, or trial, that is coming (Dan. 12:1-3; Rev. 3:10).

The Laodicean Church will be rejected (Rev. 3:16). The church, as an organization, will go through the tribulation, but not those individuals who were saved before the resurrection day came.

THE LITTLE HORN of Dan. 7:8 and Dan. 8:9 will rise before the Rapture. He precedes the reign of Satan.

The actual reign of Satan will start immediately after the Rapture. This is the "revelation of the man of sin" (II Thess. 2:3-9; Rev. 13:3, 4).

Rev. 13:1, 2 notes the rise of the little horn, where he is called the beast. Verses 3 and 4 show his revelation as Satan. The world will worship him as Satan, the dragon (verse 4.). The Rapture will come between the rise of the little horn and his revelation to the world as the one whom the dragon brought back to life.

From Church to Kingdom

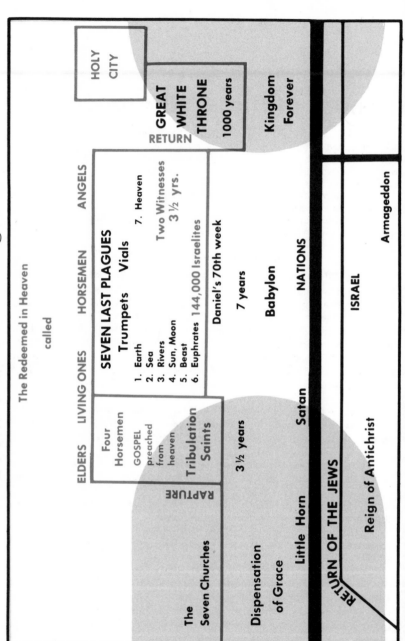

A NEW WORLD EMPIRE will be set up, at least partially, by the little horn prior to the coming of Satan. There is no record that Satan will conquer for himself an empire. He will take over, by "flattery" and treachery, one already in existence (Dan. 11:21). This will happen after the mysterious destruction or killing of the one who establishes again the "glory of the kingdom" (Dan. 11: 20). Compare this with Rev. 13:3, 4, 12, 14.

The new world empire will not cover the whole world to take in every nation. Its extent is indicated by Rev. 13:2. The lion, bear, leopard and beast are Daniel's symbols of the four empires from Babylon to Rome (Dan. 7:1-8, 17, 23, 24). This seems to indicate the territory to be included in the new empire. It may, however, include more. Ezekiel, after outlining this same general area, adds, "and many people with thee" (Ezek. 38:9).

THE RETURN OF THE JEWS coincides very closely with the Rapture. In fact, it starts before the Rapture. It is a process ending in a great mass movement. The process involves the preparation of the land. This is recorded in Ezek. 36:1-8. There will evidently be trouble in Palestine just prior to the final and complete return, while the Jews "are at hand to come." God will overrule for them. The mass return will be miraculous (Isa. 11:11-16).

Three very definite things herald the return of the Jews: (1) The prosperity of the land (Ezek. 36:8). (2) The expulsion of many Jews to Egypt (Deut. 28:68; Hosea 8:13). Great persecution will precede their deliverance (Ezek. 38:8; Ezek. 37:1, 2). (3) The appearance of the "ensign" (Isa. 11:12; Isa. 18:3).

The return of the Jews will not be by the consent of Antichrist, but in spite of him (Isa. 11:14-16).

THE RAPTURE (Luke 17:34-37; I Cor. 15:51, 52; I Thess. 4:16, 17; Dan. 12:1-3; Rev. 4:1, 2; Rev. 12:5). There is no difference between Resurrection and Rapture except that the one refers to those who are dead, and the other to those who are living. If all the dead in Christ will be raised, then all the living in Christ will be caught up. The purpose of the Resurrection and Rapture is to clothe the saved with their immortal bodies. It is the beginning of immortality. It is timed so that the living in Christ may escape the tribulation.

SAINTS IN HEAVEN. Revelation 4 to 11 records the activities of the saints in heaven after the Rapture, and the results of those administrations of judgment on the earth.

THE FOUR HORSEMEN. The elders, the living ones (A.V. beasts), the horsemen, angels with trumpets and vials—all represent saints and groups of saints who are the agents of God in the execution of the judgments written in the seven-sealed book that is being opened (Ps. 149:5-9; I Cor. 6:2; Rev. 1:6; Rev. 2:26, 27; Rev. 5:9, 10).

The four horsemen cause the gospel to be preached in the midst of judgment. The bow is the Word of God (Rev. 6:1, 2; Hab. 3:8, 9). The balance of this chapter shows God sending salvation in the midst of judgment. Rev. 14:6 shows how this preach-. ing of the gospel from heaven will appear from the earth.

THREE AND ONE-HALF YEARS is the length of time the church is persecuted before she disappears entirely at the resurrection of the Tribulation Saints. It is the length of time Antichrist will persecute the saints (Dan. 7:25; Rev. 12:6; Rev. 12:14; Rev. 13:5, 7).

"To continue" (Rev. 13:5) means to continue to make war with the saints. This is made clear in the margins of most Bibles. This is not the length of the reign of Antichrist, but the time he persecutes the saints who are saved after the Rapture. It has nothing to do with Daniel's Seventieth Week.

THE 144,000 ISRAELITES SEALED. These are Jews. They are saved after the Rapture, the same as the Tribulation Saints. But due to the fact that they are in Palestine, over which Antichrist has no power at the time, they are not subject to the persecution suffered by the Gentile converts. They are not killed; therefore, they cannot very well be raised from the dead. They will remain on the earth, the firstfruits of the kingdom of David (Rev. 7:1-8; 14:1-5).

This shows that the Jews are back in Palestine during this 3 1/2 years following the Rapture. So the return must come before the Rapture.

THE SEVEN LAST PLAGUES. The trumpets and vials are the same. The trumpets are from the standpoint of heaven and the vials from the standpoint of earth. Compare them. They are directed against the same elements. There are some variations because of the different standpoints.

		TRUMPETS	VIALS
The Earth	Rev.	8:7	16:2
The Sea		8:8, 9	16:3
The Rivers		8:10, 11	16:4-7
The Sun, Moon		8:12	16:8, 9
The Beast		9:1-12	16:10, 11
The Euphrates		9:13, 14	16:12
Heavens		11:15-19	16:17-21

THE TWO WITNESSES operate between the sixth and seventh plagues. The time of their testimony is 3 1/2 years. This is not the same period as the former 3 1/2 years out of which come the Tribulation Saints. There is no record of anyone being saved during the seven last plagues. The Dispensation of Grace has come to an end. This is wrath poured out without mixture, undiluted with grace (Rev. 9:20, 21; Rev. 16:9, 11; Rev. 14:10).

The two witnesses (Rev. 11) are sent from heaven. We are not told who they are. Their works suggest Moses and Elijah. Compare Mal. 4:5, 6. It is the function of these two witnesses to prepare the Jews for the return of Christ. They re-enact the death, resurrection and ascension of Christ. Thus the Jews will recognize Him as the one whom they have pierced (Zech. 12:10-14).

The time corresponds with the last half of Daniel's Seventieth Week. It is the great tribulation for Israel spoken of by Jesus (Matt. 24:15-22). It is followed immediately by the coming of Christ (Rev. 10:7, 11:15-19).

DANIEL'S SEVENTIETH WEEK (Dan. 9). The angel told Daniel that seventy weeks (literally, seventy sevens) had been determined upon Israel. Seventy sevens of years would be 490 years. There are 483 years to the crucifixion of Christ. That leaves 7 years yet to go. The Dispensation of Grace broke into the continuity of the 70 sevens. The Seventieth week of years will begin at the end of the Dispensation of Grace. It will last seven years, or till the Coming of Christ. The whole time between the Rapture and the Return of Christ is 10 1/2 years.

BABYLON (Rev. 17, 18) is a woman (a church), a city and a commercial institution which attains great power in the last days because of an unholy alliance with the beast. They both gain by it for a time; but, in the end, the beast will destroy the woman. The woman of the 12th chapter is the church of God; the woman in the 17th chapter is the church of Satan.

ARMAGEDDON. The Battle of Armageddon is so called because Armageddon is the place of mobilization. The scene of the battle is Jerusalem. The contestants are: on one side, Satan and the armies of the realm of Antichrist; on the other side, Christ (Ezek. 38 and 39; Joel 3:11-16; Zech. 14:1-9; Rev. 16:13-21; Rev. 19:17-21).

CHRIST WILL COME WITH HIS SAINTS (Matt. 24:30, 31; I Thess. 3:13; Jude 14; Zech. 14:5; Rev. 19:14).

THE KINGDOM (Rev. 20). A kingdom requires a king, a realm, and a reign. The King is Christ, the realm is the earth, the reign will start when the King returns. The kingdom is not of this world; it comes from heaven, but it will be established on the earth (John 18:36).

For one thousand years the kingdom will be made up of a joint rulership of the kingdom of David and the saints. After the thousand years the saints will go to their new home, the capital of the whole universe, the heavenly city. The kingdom will remain on earth, and it will be everlasting.

Unsaved nations will enter the kingdom, but they are the subjects, not the rulers. There will be a final separation and cleansing of the human race after the thousand years, but the kingdom will last forever. There will be no end to its increase. There will always be nations on the earth (Isa. 9:6, 7; Ezek. 37:21-28; Dan. 7:27; Zech. 14:16-21; Luke 1:31-33; Rev. 21:24, 26; 22:2).

THE HOLY CITY. After the thousand years there will be a change, for that is the beginning of eternity. From then on the Holy City will be the home of the saints and capital of the universe, for the throne of God is there. Only the saints (who have immortal bodies) can live in the Holy City. It will not be on the earth, but it will be near the earth. It will have life-giving power for the nations of the earth (Rev. 22:2).

The heavenly rulers will be the saints. The earthly rulers will be the house of David (II Sam. 7:8-16). The Jewish nation will never cease from the earth. The Gentile nations will also remain on the earth. After Satan is loosed to weed out the last bit of evil, the kingdom is perfected and Christ can return it to God, having put down all enemies. Then death itself can be destroyed (I Cor. 15:24-26). This is the new earth that John saw. Old things have passed away. All things have become new: the saints in the Holy City, the Jews and Gentiles made perfect on earth (Isa. 60:15-22; Rev. 21:1).

THE GREAT WHITE THRONE is the seat of the final judgment of the unsaved dead (Rev. 20:11-15). There will be two classes of people there: (1) those who have rejected Christ; (2) those who have not been saved but neither have they rejected Christ. There will be two sets of books: the book of life and the books. Those not found in the book of life are cast into the lake of fire. The others are judged according to their works as written in the books. Nothing more is told us. This is a judgment only of the dead. The living, in heaven and on earth, will have no part in this judgment (Rev. 20:11).

It is possible that the Great White Throne judgment will take place during the Millennium. It seems to start at the time of the return of Christ (Rev. 11:15-18).

Chapter 6

THE REDEMPTION
OF THE EARTH

The measure of the greatness of an executive is his ability to delegate authority. Any man who has to do everything himself will have to be satisfied with a very small business. God lost no time in giving man responsibilities. Adam gave names to the animals. God gave man dominion over all the earth.

It soon became apparent that, in the plan of redemption, God was going to use men. God did not drop an ark down from heaven to save Noah and his family. Noah had to build one for himself. Moses spoke with authority, and Peter said to the lame man, "Such as I have give I unto thee."

In the plan of redemption, the saints have a part, actually a very big part. Jesus paid the price of redemption, then delegated all authority to His followers: "Whatsoever thou shalt loose on earth shall be loosed in heaven."

God has no other plan. He has no substitutes. What we do not do will not be done. It is all up to us. The saints are God's agents in the program of redemption of the earth. They are God's only agents. No angel could save a soul or solve a problem.

This is true of the entire program, beginning with the preaching of the gospel and following through the work of the ministry, the perfecting of the saints, the running of the church, and even the interpretation of the Scriptures. But the authority does not stop there, because the program does not stop there. The saints are to be the judges of the earth, the rulers in the kingdom.

The saints are God's agents in the judgments of the last days. They are the living ones, the elders, the horsemen, and the angels with the trumpets and vials. They are the actors in Revelation, the ones who carry out the orders from the throne. They are God's agents in redemption. "Do ye not know that the saints will judge the world?"—I Cor. 6:2.

THE SCOPE OF REDEMPTION

If the process of redemption has been committed to the saints, then we should know what that program is. When we think of redemption our minds naturally go back to the cross, and then we think of people being saved. Of course, that is a part of redemption, but it is not all of it.

Redemption is restoration to the original owner of something that has been lost. If redemption is to be complete, so that Satan has no victory, then everything that was lost must be restored. So, we can get some idea of the scope of redemption by noting what was lost.

> But of the tree of the knowledge of good and evil, thou shalt not eat of it: for in the day that thou eatest thereof thou shalt surely die.—Gen. 2:17
>
> And unto Adam he said, Because thou hast hearkened unto the voice of thy wife, and hast eaten of the tree, of which I commanded thee, saying, Thou shalt not eat of it: cursed is the ground for thy sake; in sorrow shalt thou eat of it all the days of thy life:
>
> Thorns also and thistles shall it bring forth to thee; and thou shalt eat the herb of the field; in the sweat of thy face shalt thou eat bread, till thou return unto the ground; for out of it wast thou taken; for dust thou art, and unto dust shalt thou return. And Adam called his wife's name Eve; because she was the mother of all living.
>
> Unto Adam also and to his wife did the Lord God make coats of skins, and clothed them. And the Lord God said, Behold the man is become as one of us, to know good and evil: and now, lest he put forth his hand, and take also of the tree of life, and eat, and live for ever:
>
> Therefore the Lord God sent him forth from the garden of Eden, to till the ground from whence he was taken. So he drove out the man; and he placed at the east of the garden of Eden Cherubims, and a flaming sword which turned every way, to keep the way of the tree of life.—Gen. 3:17-24

This tells us what was lost and therefore what must be redeemed. We may consider it under three heads:

1. *Man lost his soul.* "In the day that thou eatest thereof thou shalt surely die."

2. *Man lost his body.* He could no longer eat of the tree of life. "For dust thou art and to dust shalt thou return."

3. *Man lost the earth.* He lost dominion over the earth and it passed into the control of Satan. It produces a living for man only by hard labor. It develops weeds and pests, disease and plagues.

If the result of sin is threefold, then redemption must be threefold. Redemption is a process that began with the cross, is continued by the gospel, and will be brought to a consummation in the day of the Lord and the reign of Christ.

The three main events in redemption follow the three points of loss:

1. *Conversion,* the saving of the soul.
2. *Resurrection,* the redemption of the body.
3. *The Second Coming of Christ,* the redemption of the earth.

The third phase of redemption concerns the earth and those who are on the earth after the Rapture. After the Rapture, the devil will be in full possession of the earth and will be reigning in the person of Antichrist.

The word redemption comes down to us from an Old Testament law. When the children of Israel possessed the Promised Land, certain provisions were made to keep the land evenly distributed among the people. It could be sold, but the bill of sale was of the nature of a lease which would expire automatically in the year of Jubilee (every fiftieth year), and the land would revert to its original owner.

If a man lost his property or sold it, thus disinheriting his children, any kinsman could buy back the land at any time by paying the value to the year of Jubilee; then the land would go back to its original owner. The man who did this was called the redeemer, and the process was known as the redemption of the purchased possession. It was a purchased possession because it had been purchased by an outsider and was subject to redemption, if a kinsman could be found who was able and willing to pay the price of redemption.

When the land was thus sold, a sort of deed was drawn up. On the inside were written the specifications and on the outside the signatures. The deed was then rolled up and sealed. A sealed deed was evidence that the land was subject to redemption. The redeemer could break the seals, which was equivalent to burning the mortgage (Lev. 25:23-28).

THE REDEMPTION OF THE EARTH

And I saw in the right hand of him that sat on the throne a book written within and on the backside, sealed with seven seals. And I saw a strong angel proclaiming with a loud voice, Who is worthy to open the book, and to loose the seals thereof?

And no man in heaven, nor in earth, neither under the earth, was able to open the book, neither to look thereon. And I wept much, because no man was found worthy to open and to read the book, neither to look thereon.—Rev. 5:1-4

Jesus is the heir of all things, and the saints with Him (Rom. 8:17). After the Rapture Satan will be in complete possession. Satan had said to Jesus, "All these [nations] will I give thee, if thou wilt fall down and worship me." If Satan had not had them to give, it would have been no temptation.

Adam sold out to Satan, and the earth became a purchased

possession. After the Rapture it will seem as if he has become the sole owner.

But God holds the deed. In His right hand there is a sealed document, legal evidence that the land is subject to redemption, if a kinsman can be found who is able and willing to pay the price of such vast proportions.

But the devil, the lawless one, knows no law. He not only refuses to vacate, but he is preparing to resist eviction. Therefore it becomes necessary for Christ to take the book, break the seals, and proceed with the authority of the open book. The breaking of the seals is the redemption of the earth.

But who is to break the seals? Who can pay the awful price of redemption? Who dares attempt the eviction of Satan? Who has a chain that can bind him? All heaven is thrown into a state of consternation. They have not forgotten the great war in heaven when Satan attempted to prevent the Resurrection; and when Michael and all his angels, the greatest force in all the universe, succeeded only in driving Satan down to the earth and strengthening his position in the world.

Michael and his angels are not equal to this emergency. "Lay thine hand upon him, remember the battle; do no more. Behold, the hope of him is in vain: shall not one be cast down, even at the sight of him? None is so fierce that dare stir him up: who then is able to stand before me?"—Job 41:8-10.

Who is able to stand before God, to take the book and break its seals? No one was found worthy. No wonder John wept at such a scene as this.

> And one of the elders saith unto me, Weep not; behold the Lion of the tribe of Judah, the Root of David, hath prevailed to open the book, and to loose the seven seals thereof.
>
> And I beheld, and, Lo, in the midst of the throne and of the four beasts, and in the midst of the elders, stood a Lamb as it had been slain, having seven horns and seven eyes, which are the seven Spirits of God sent forth into all the earth.
>
> And he came and took the book out of the right hand of him that sat upon the throne.—Rev. 5:5-7

This act, though unseen from the earth, causes great rejoicing in heaven. It is the grand climax of the whole program of redemption. All that is left now is the cleaning up: the purging out of sin, the eviction and chaining of Satan, and the restoration of the earth to the perfection which God originally created.

No event in the long history of the earth is so far reaching in its consequences as the one so simply stated: "And he came and took the book out of the right hand of him that sat upon the throne."

In order to qualify for this honor He must first suffer the

agonies of the Garden and the shame of the Cross with all the unknown suffering of bearing the sins of the world. He had to be the Lamb slain as well as the Lion of Judah.

In Jesus, our Kinsman, alone do all these things exist. He alone is both Lion and Lamb. He alone has the seven Spirits of God. He alone is able to approach the throne and take the book from the right hand of God. He alone can break its seals. He alone can redeem the purchased possession. He alone can evict Satan.

This act is the signal for the greatest outburst of rejoicing in heaven since that day in the long past when the morning stars sang together and the sons of God shouted for joy.

Christ immediately proceeds to break the seals one at a time. Each seal is a step in the redemption of the earth. As soon as a seal is broken the saints take over and carry out that part of the program. The first six seals are concerned mostly with the redemption of individuals. The seventh seal contains the seven last plagues, the trumpets and vials.

The seventh seal is concerned with the judgment of the nations and the purging out of sin and the results of sin preparatory to the reconstruction which will take place after the coming of Christ.

CHRIST TAKES POSSESSION

And I saw another mighty angel come down from heaven, clothed with a cloud: and a rainbow was upon his head, and his face was as it were the sun, and his feet as pillars of fire: and he had in his hand a little book open: and he set his right foot upon the sea, and his left foot on the earth.

And the angel which I saw stand upon the sea and upon the earth lifted up his hand to heaven. And sware by him that liveth for ever and ever, who created heaven, and the things that therein are, and the earth, and the things that therein are, and the sea, and the things which are therein, that there should be time (delay) no longer.—Rev. 10:1, 2, 5, 6

This is the same little book or scroll that first appeared in the right hand of God. The seals are now broken, the book is open. Christ is called a mighty angel. Throughout Revelation heavenly beings, whether Christ or saints or created angels, are called angels. They may be identified by their description (Rev. 1:15, 16).

The rainbow which was around the throne is now upon His head. The rainbow is the sign of God's purpose to redeem the earth and the human race rather than to destroy them. The first step is nearly over; the book is open; it is time now to take possession.

Breaking the seals is a legal process. The One who breaks

the seals has a right to take the property. This He does. "He set his right foot upon the sea, and his left foot on the earth."

This is an act of possession. This is still a legal process. It is like taking possession of land in a lawyer's office before actually moving onto the property. When the seventh trumpet sounds, Jesus and the saints will take actual possession of the earth. Then the saints will receive their inheritance.

> In whom also we have obtained an inheritance, being predestinated according to the purpose of him who worketh all things after the counsel of his own will: that we should be to the praise of his glory, who first trusted in Christ.
> In whom ye also trusted, after that ye heard the word of truth, the gospel of your salvation; in whom also after that ye believed, ye were sealed with that Holy Spirit of promise. Which is the earnest of our inheritance until the redemption of the purchased possession, unto the praise of his glory.—Eph. 1:11-14

Now we have the earnest; then we will have the inheritance. There are two kinds of possession, a purchased possession and an inherited possession. A purchased possession was insecure because it would have to be returned if a redeemer could be found. An inherited possession is forever.

The little book, or title deed, is given to John and he is told to eat it. Acting here as a type of all saints, John takes full possession by consuming the book. It becomes his forever.

Again, as a type of the saints, John was told that he must prophesy again. The gospel must be preached to all nations by the saints "flying in the midst of heaven." Out of that preaching will come a great number of all nations, and kindreds, and peoples and tongues—the Tribulation Saints.

> And the seventh angel sounded; and there were great voices in heaven, saying, The kingdoms of this world are become the kingdom of our Lord, and of his Christ; and he shall reign for ever and ever.
> And the four and twenty elders, which sat before God on their seats, fell upon their faces, and worshipped God, saying, We give thee thanks, O Lord God Almighty, which art, and wast, and art to come; because thou hast taken to thee thy great power, and hast reigned. And the nations were angry, and thy wrath is come, and the time of the dead, that they should be judged, and that thou shouldest give reward unto thy servants the prophets, and to the saints, and them that fear thy name, small and great; and shouldest destroy them which destroy the earth.
> And the temple of God was opened in heaven, and there was seen in his temple the ark of his testament: and there were lightnings, and voices, and thunderings, and an earthquake, and great hail.—Rev. 11:15-19

Before every great event there is a service of worship in

heaven, conducted by the saints, the elders and living ones taking the lead. This time they praise God because He has taken His great power and has reigned. They speak of it as an already accomplished fact, agreeing with the words of the angel who said that when the seventh trumpet sounds there will be delay no longer (Rev. 10:7).

"The nations were angry, and thy wrath has come." This is a reference to the gathering of the nations at Armageddon in anger against the Lord to prevent Christ from taking over the earth. The judgment of the dead is still future, but it is linked with the rewards of the righteous. The great white throne judgment would take time. It may start here and run all through the Millennium.

"Destroy them that destroy the earth." This is a remarkable statement. Nobody in John's day was trying or threatening to destroy the earth. Satan is the destroyer, but he never has attempted to destroy the earth. Men have destroyed cities, but to destroy the earth has been beyond human might—until now. This is the first time that Satan has had men with the capacity and willingness to destroy the earth. But it will not happen because God will act first.

The Final Earthquake

And the seventh angel poured out his vial into the air; and there came a great voice out of the temple of heaven, from the throne, saying, It is done.

And there were voices, and thunders, and lightnings; and there was a great earthquake, such as was not since men were upon the earth, so mighty an earthquake, and so great. And the great city was divided into three parts, and the cities of the nations fell: and great Babylon came in remembrance before God, to give unto her the cup of the wine of the fierceness of his wrath, and every island fled away, and the mountains were not found.

And there fell upon men a great hail out of heaven, every stone about the weight of a talent: and men blasphemed God because of the plague of the hail; for the plague thereof was exceeding great.—Rev. 16:17-21

This is the same event from the standpoint of the earth. It is the greatest earthquake since creation. The earth will reel like a drunkard so that the mountains will move into the sea. New islands, if not new continents, will appear. The whole topography of the earth will be changed.

It would seem that the whole earth is involved in this earthquake. The works of man, done in sin, must be destroyed. What is not destroyed by the earthquake will be leveled by the hail.

The reconstruction which will be accomplished by Christ and the saints in the 1000 years that are to follow will be complete.

It will be a whole new world. The old will have passed away. The whole world will be made new.

Redemption Complete

After the Millennium there will be some changes. The Holy City will come down from heaven to the proximity of the earth. This is the eternal home of the saints, the Bride of Christ.

So, there will be in the Holy City saints with glorified bodies (having passed through the Resurrection); and there will be people living on the earth in physical bodies.

These people on earth are those who have lived through the Millennium. Both places are in view in Rev. 21:24: "And the nations of them which are saved shall walk in the light of it (the Holy City): and the kings of the earth do bring their glory and honour into it."

This is after the Millennium when eternity has begun. It represents a permanent condition. There will be no more death (Rev. 21:4).

The covenants and promises of God form the great structural frame work of the Bible and are the basis of God's whole future program.

THE RAINBOW COVENANT

The rainbow covenant which God made after the Flood is especially significant because it is the one covenant which concerns the earth and every living creature. It also has the feature common to many of the covenants in that it is everlasting.

> God said, This is the token of the covenant which I make between me and you and every living creature that is with you, for perpetual generations: I do set my bow in the cloud, and it shall be for a token of a covenant between me and the earth. And it shall come to pass, when I bring a cloud over the earth, that the bow shall be seen in the cloud:
> And I will remember my covenant, which is between me and you and every living creature of all flesh; and the waters shall no more become a flood to destroy all flesh. And the bow shall be in the cloud; and I will look upon it, that I may remember the EVERLASTING covenant between God and every living creature of all flesh that is upon the earth.—Gen. 9:12-16

The covenant is for "perpetual generations." That means God will not destroy the earth or the things on the earth as He did in the Flood. The purpose and meaning of this covenant is stated in Genesis 8:21:

> And the Lord smelled a sweet savour; and the Lord said in his heart, I will not again curse the ground any more for man's

sake; for the imagination of man's heart is evil from his youth; neither will I again smite any more every thing living, as I have done.

The Earth Is Everlasting

But Israel shall be saved in the Lord with an everlasting salvation: ye shall not be ashamed nor confounded world without end. For thus saith the Lord that created the heavens; God himself that formed the earth and made it; he hath established it, he created it not in vain, he formed it to be inhabited: I am the Lord; and there is none else.—Isa. 45:17, 18

If the earth is to last forever, "world without end," it must be included in the process of redemption. The earth is subject to redemption.

And the desert shall rejoice, and blossom as the rose. It shall blossom abundantly, and rejoice even with joy and singing: the glory of Lebanon shall be given unto it, the excellency of Carmel and Sharon, they shall see the glory of the Lord, and the excellency of our God. And the parched ground shall become a pool, and the thirsty land springs of water: in the habitation of dragons, where each lay, shall be grass with reeds and rushes.—Isa. 35:1, 2, 7

The People of the Earth Will Be Redeemed

People will live on the earth forever, but they will be a people perfected during the Millennium.

And the ransomed of the Lord shall return, and come to Zion with songs and EVERLASTING joy upon their heads: they shall obtain joy and gladness, and sorrow and sighing shall flee away. —Isa. 35:10

And I heard a great voice out of heaven saying, Behold, the tabernacle of God is with men, and he will dwell with them, and they shall be his people, and God himself shall be with them, and be their God. And God shall wipe away all tears from their eyes; and there shall be no more death, neither sorrow, nor crying, neither shall there be any more pain: for the former things are passed away.—Rev. 21:3, 4.

The Animals Will Be Redeemed

The wolf also shall dwell with the lamb, and the leopard shall lie down with the kid; and the calf and the young lion and the fatling together; and a little child shall lead them. And the cow and the bear shall feed; their young ones shall lie down together: and the lion shall eat straw like the ox. And the sucking child shall play on the hole of the asp, and the weaned child shall put his hand on the cockatrice den.

They shall not hurt nor destroy in all my holy mountain: for the earth shall be full of the knowledge of the Lord, as the waters cover the sea.—Isa. 11:6-9

The wolf and the lamb shall feed together, and the lion shall eat straw like the bullock: and dust shall be the serpent's meat. They shall not hurt nor destroy in all my holy mountain, saith the Lord.—Isa. 65:25

Redemption Involves Purging

The purging comes first, the reconstruction next. Revelation chapters six through sixteen records the purging of the earth and everything on the earth.

The Millennium is the time of reconstruction. At the end of the Millennium there is a final purging of the people of the earth. Then redemption is complete and the voice from the throne of God announces the completion of the process. "Behold, I make all things new."

And he that sat upon the throne said, Behold, I make all things new. And he said unto me, Write: for these words are true and faithful.—Rev. 21:5.

Chapter 7

ISRAEL'S THREE STEPS TO THE KINGDOM

The nation of Israel did not just happen. God brought it into being by direct action and established it with a series of covenants. Israel exists today under three relationships:

Their relationship to the land
Their relationship to God—the Covenant
Their relationship to Messiah—Christ

For two thousand years they have lived without any relationship to the land, God, or Christ. God's covenant with Abraham is unconditional, but God's covenant with Israel is conditioned on their obedience. God will keep His covenant with Abraham, but to do so He will have to force the Jews to return to their covenant relationship. This is not an easy matter.

Inasmuch as the relationship is in three parts, the return will be in three steps, each one a crisis.

FIRST STEP—THE LAND

One would think that what is happening in Palestine would have the whole Christian world searching the Scriptures to see what bearing the State of Israel has on the prophecies of the last days. You would think that the beginning of the realization of so much prophecy would put the whole church in a state of expectancy. But nobody gets excited, not even those who make a special claim that they believe the whole Bible. WHY?

For one thing, things did not happen as we have been taught to expect. Many people have thought that the Rapture would come before any prophecy could be fulfilled. This has been a very serious error.

Then, too, the details of the return do not seem to correspond with the prophecy as we have understood it. There are many prophecies concerning the return of the Jews that are not in sight now. But it is better to take a second look and find out exactly what the Bible *says*, than to reject the prophecies because some things did not happen the way we thought the Bible said they would.

The return of the Jews is a very complicated process. There are so many factors involved, not the least of which is their atti-

The Middle East

Gen. 15:18 makes the
Euphrates the northern
boundary of the Promised
Land and the Nile the
southern boundary.

The land just east of the
Jordan River was
originally a part of the
Promised Land, occupied
by the Tribes of Manasseh,
Gad and Reuben.

U S S R

T U R K E Y

ARARAT

(MEDIA)

I R A N

(PERSIA)

(ELAM)

TIGRIS

EUPHRATES

(Babylon)
(SHINAR)

PERSIAN
GULF

S Y R I A

(MESOPOTAMIA)

(ASSYRIA)

J O R D A N

(CHALDEA)

KUWAIT

NEUTRAL
ZONE

(DEDAN)

CYPRUS
(KITTIM)

LEBANON
(Tyre)

MEDITERRANEAN

Armageddon

Jerusalem

Gaza

I S R A E L

DEAD SEA

(MOAB)

(EDOM)

(IDUMEA)

A R A B I A

Gulf
of
Aqaba

Suez
Canal

(GOSHEN)

E G Y P T

SINAI

Gulf
of
Suez

RED
SEA

N I L E

tude toward Christ; that is, in fact, the controlling factor. There can be no stability in Israel until Christ is King. That is the goal. The Jews will reach that goal in three steps: one is past or in progress; two are yet to come.

Between the first and second steps great changes will take place in the world. Communism will probably almost succeed in its announced intention to take over the world. Relief will come, but the benefit will be only temporary. The next world crisis of importance will be the one that produces Antichrist. The second crisis for Israel will come after that.

It seems strange that so little research has been done on this subject, seeing so much space has been given to it in the Bible. If we brought together all the prophecies concerning the return of the Jews, without an understanding of the order of events, we would have what would seem like a mass of contradictions and confused statements. It is not a simple process. It is not a matter of the Jews packing up and going to Palestine to live happily ever after.

There are three separate situations. If you take prophecies concerning one phase of the return and apply them to another, there will be difficulties. We have to get our bearings and understand the order of events. The return of the Jews from all countries at once is a much more complicated endeavor than their coming out of bondage in Egypt.

The Goal

Now the Lord had said unto Abram, Get thee out of thy country, and from thy kindred, and from thy father's house, unto a land that I will shew thee: and I will make of thee a great nation, and I will bless thee, and make thy name great; and thou shalt be a blessing: And I will bless them that bless thee, and curse him that curseth thee: and in thee shall all families of the earth be blessed. —Gen. 12:1-3

In the same day the Lord made a covenant with Abram, saying, Unto thy seed have I given this land, from the river of Egypt unto the great river, the river Euphrates.—Gen. 15:18

As for me, behold, my covenant is with thee, and thou shalt be a father of many nations. Neither shall thy name any more be called Abram, but thy name shall be Abraham; for a father of many nations have I made thee. And I will make thee exceeding fruitful, and I will make nations of thee, and kings shall come out of thee. And I will establish my covenant between me and thee and thy seed after thee in their generations for an everlasting covenant, to be a God unto thee, and to thy seed after thee. And I will give unto thee, and to thy seed after thee, the land wherein thou art a stranger, all the land of Canaan, for an everlasting possession; and I will be their God.—Gen. 17:4-8

All of God's dealing with mankind have a firm basis in the

covenants. A covenant is always a goal. It states what God intends to do. It is an outline of the plan.

The plan was outlined to Abraham progressively. Gen. 12:1-3 is a general outline. There is to be a land, the location of which is not revealed, only the promise that it will be shown to Abraham.

Abraham is to become a great nation and be a blessing to all the earth. There is one feature that is very important to the nations, and to an understanding of those portions of Isaiah, Jeremiah and Ezekiel that deal with the future of the nations around Palestine: "I will bless them that bless thee, and curse him that curseth thee."

In Gen. 15:18, the exact location of the land is given: from the river of Egypt to the River Euphrates. The Euphrates rises north of Palestine and will become the northern boundary. That would take in most of Syria and all of Lebanon. The southern boundary is to be the river of Egypt. Authorities are divided as to the meaning of the river of Egypt. The Nile is the river of Egypt, but there is a stream near what was once the border of Egypt and Israel, sometimes called the river of Egypt; actually it is only a brook. Abraham in his travels went all the way to the Nile. To Abraham the river of Egypt would be the Nile.

Gen. 17:8 adds the promise that the covenant is an everlasting covenant, and the land will be for an everlasting possession, and "I will be their God."

We may sum it up as follows:

Palestine belongs to the Jews.
They will possess it forever.
They will become a righteous nation.
God will punish nations that act against the covenant.
God will bless the nations that help the Jews in their time of trouble.

This covenant is now in process of being worked out. The land is being restored, and preparations are in progress for the second step in the fulfillment of this covenant. It took a world crisis to produce the first step; it will take a world crisis to bring about the second step—the complete possession of the land by all the Jews of the world, a complete mass return at one time. And it will take still another world crisis to consummate the final step, the establishment of the kingdom by the Messiah.

The first step in the return of the Jews required, basically, two new elements which seemed impossible.

The Need for a Crisis

1. The Jews had no great desire to remove to Palestine. They were happy and prosperous in their adopted lands. Many of them

had become rich and powerful. There was a Zionist movement, but it was opposed by many Jews. A land of sand and rocks and poverty did not seem very attractive.

Something had to happen to cause the Jews to want to settle in Palestine. A love of the land had to be revived. It had to be something drastic because only a terrific experience would give them the drive and determination necessary to face the problems and the hardships that settling there would entail.

2. The land was a part of the Ottoman Empire which extended, like a crescent, from Turkey to Egypt. Jews were not welcome, or even allowed. The prophecies about Palestine becoming a Jewish state seemed so fantastic that most commentaries spiritualized them and made them apply to the church. The land had to be freed.

Then came two world wars. The first resulted in giving the Jews a national home in Palestine—a home, not a state. Not many Jews were interested. The second world war showed the Jews that their only hope was in a state of Israel. Hitler instigated the first step in the return of the Jews; he brought on the first crisis.

Great Britain had been entrusted with a mandate to establish a Jewish home in Palestine. The execution of that mandate is one of the darkest pages in English history. They allowed only 75,000 Jews to return, and then shut off all immigration in order to appease the Arabs. Britain was engaged in some empire building in southern Arabia and needed the friendship of the Arabs.

When Hitler massacred 6,000,000 men, women and children and destroyed Jewish communities all over Europe, the only place of refuge was Palestine; but Britain refused to let the Jews enter, even when they were running for their lives. Thousands perished in an attempt to enter Palestine; others were put in concentration camps on Cyprus.

The direct result of World War II was that the British lost the mandate and the Jews forced their way into Palestine and established an independent state. This was the beginning of the fulfillment of such prophecies as:

> For thus saith the Lord God; Behold I, even I, will both search my sheep and seek them out. As the shepherd seeketh out his flock in the day that he is among his sheep that are scattered; so will I seek out my sheep and will deliver them out of all places where they have been scattered in the cloudy and dark day. And I will bring them out from the people, and gather them from the countries, and will bring them to their own land, and feed them upon the mountains of Israel by the rivers, and in all inhabited places of the country.—Ezek. 34:11-13

Before Hitler there were about twenty million Jews in the world. That number is being restored. That many Jews could not find support in Palestine in its barren state. It has lain waste for centuries, for only Jews can prosper there.

The Land Must Be Restored First

Therefore, if the land has to support so many Jews all at once, some preliminary work would have to be done. Inasmuch as Palestine would produce only for Jews, there would have to be a partial return before the whole company of Jews could be supported. The first crisis produced this preliminary return. It could not fulfill all the prophecy, but it fulfilled some of it.

We have to distinguish between prophecies concerning the Jews and prophecies concerning the land. Some prophecy concerning the land has been fulfilled by this first part of the return.

The Jews returned to their land, but they did not return to God. They returned to their language, Hebrew; they returned to their customs; they returned to their love of the land, but their attitude toward God did not change. They did it all in their own power. This is the reason there has to be a second crisis. It will take more to turn them to God than it did to turn them to the land. The next crisis will be greater than the first, not for the world, possibly, but for the Jews.

> Also, thou son of man, prophesy unto the mountains of Israel, and say, Ye mountains of Israel, hear the word of the Lord:
> Thus saith the Lord God; Because the enemy hath said against you, Aha, even the ancient high places are ours in possession.— Ezek. 36:1, 2

Notice that this prophecy is especially concerning the land, "But ye, O mountains of Israel, ye shall shoot forth your branches and yield your fruit to my people of Israel: for they are at hand to come."—Ezek. 36:8.

Almost as soon as the Jews started going back, we began getting glowing reports and pictures telling how the land was responding. Swamps were drained, trees were planted, gardens dotted the landscape, roads were built, cities sprang up; but there was one complication—the Arabs had been schooled by the British to oppose the Jews. They did not need much prodding.

The only land available to the Jews was land nobody wanted —the waste places and the rocky slopes. The Arabs said: "Aha, even the ancient high places are ours in possession."

The Jews cannot think of building their temple as long as a Moslem shrine, the Dome of the Rock, stands on the site of the Holy of Holies. This opposition of the Arabs will continue till the next crisis. The prophecy is not confirmed to the present situation. It covers all the time between the first and second crises. God himself will settle the matter with the Arabs. This will be one of the high spots of the return. Now the Jews are in Palestine by their own power.

But when all the Jews return at once under the power of God, and in complete fulfillment of the prophecies, a nation born in a day, Arab power will be destroyed. At present we see only the beginnings, but we can trace the future by studying what the Arabs will do, so first, let us look at the Arab countries and their boasted plans.

Arab Opposition

Moreover the word of the Lord came unto me, saying, Son of man, set thy face against mount Seir, and prophesy against it, And say unto it, Thus saith the Lord God; Behold, O mount Seir, I am against thee, and I will stretch out mine hand against thee, and I will make thee most desolate. I will lay thy cities waste, and thou shalt be desolate, and thou shalt know that I am the Lord.—Ezek. 35:1-4

MOUNT SEIR. The Arabs are descendants of Ishmael and Esau. Esau took a wife of the daughters of Ishmael (Gen. 28:9). In prophecy, the Arabs are always referred to by names applying to Esau (Deut. 2:4-6).

God says He will lay the land of the Arabs waste and it will be desolate. It seems that way now, but the prophecy is concerning a future punishment. God will lay their land waste because of what they do to the Jews at the time of their return. The land could not be laid waste now because it is already waste. You would not notice much difference. But the Middle East is destined to become prosperous again. Great cities will be built and the land will be filled with prosperous communities. Then this prophecy will take on real meaning.

Now we have two reasons why God will destroy the cities of the Arabs. This may seem like a severe punishment; but the provocation is going to be very great. The terms of the covenant must be carried out to the letter: "I will curse him that curseth thee."

First Reason

Because thou hast had a perpetual hatred, and hast shed the blood of the children of Israel by the force of the sword in the time of their calamity, in the time that their iniquity had an end:

Therefore, as I live, saith the Lord God, I will prepare thee unto blood, even blood shall pursue thee.

Thus, will I make mount Seir most desolate, and cut off from it him that passeth out and him that returneth. And I will fill his mountains with his slain men: in thy hills, and in thy valleys, and in all thy rivers, shall they fall that are slain with the sword.

> I will make thee perpetual desolations, and thy cities shall not
> return: and ye shall know that I am the Lord.—Ezek. 35:5-9

BECAUSE: Thou has had a perpetual hatred. "And Esau hated Jacob because of the blessing wherewith his father blessed him: and Esau said in his heart, The days of mourning for my father are at hand; then will I slay my brother Jacob."—Gen. 27:41.

Esau still has this determination. It has lasted through the years. Edom is another name for the descendants of Esau (Gen. 36:8).

They have had a perpetual hatred. This is expressed even today in their slogan: "Drive the Jews into the sea." The only reason the Arabs do not do it is because they are not strong enough. If they should try it before the time, they would probably lose more territory. Eventually, they will drive the Jews out, but that will be the second crisis.

"In the time of their calamity." The prophet is very specific about the time of this prophecy. It is the time of the iniquity of the end (R.V.), or, the time their iniquity had an end (A.V.). Either way, it is the general time of the return. The Arabs will give them trouble during the first and second crises. The third crisis is of a different nature.

Ezekiel 35 deals with what is happening now and what will happen from now till the second crisis is resolved. This is prophecy that is actually being fulfilled now. The time of their calamity is a time when they are being driven out of their home countries and have no place to go but Egypt.

This prophecy began to be fulfilled as soon as the Jews started settling in Palestine. In the beginning it was the British more than the Arabs that caused the distress. From now on it will be the Arabs, Egyptians, and Antichrist. The prophecy covers the whole time that the Jews are in process of returning. After the second crisis, the return will be complete.

Second Reason

> Because thou hast said, These two nations and these two coun-
> tries shall be mine, and we will possess it; whereas the Lord was
> there: therefore, as I live, saith the Lord God, I will even do ac-
> cording to thine anger, and according to thine envy which thou hast
> used out of thy hatred against them; and I will make myself
> known among them, when I have judged thee.
>
> And thou shalt know that I am the Lord, and that I have heard
> all thy blasphemies which thou hast spoken against the mountains
> of Israel, saying, They are laid desolate, they are given us to con-
> sume. Thus with your mouth ye have boasted against me, and have
> multiplied your words against me: I have heard them. Thus saith

the Lord God; When the whole earth rejoiceth, I will make thee
desolate.

As thou didst rejoice at the inheritance of the house of Israel,
because it was desolate, so will I do unto thee: thou shalt be desolate, O mount Seir, and all Idumea, even all of it: and they shall
know that I am the Lord.—Ezek. 35:10-15

"Because thou hast said, These two nations and these two
countries shall be mine, and we will possess it; whereas the Lord
was there." What is meant by "whereas the Lord was there"?
God's promises to Israel include prosperity in the land, earthly
goods, long life, a plentiful harvest (Deut. 28:1-14).

Therefore, if the land prospered and yielded its fruit in abundance, it was a sign that the Lord was there. For many centuries
Palestine has been waste. The Lord was not there. During those
years it made no difference who occupied the land or claimed possession of it.

But when the Jews took over some of the land, everything
changed. The covenant was about to be put back into effectiveness.
The land was being made ready for the complete return. It was
becoming miraculously productive. The Lord was there. Then, if
the Arabs made false claims they would be fighting against God.

"These two nations and these two countries." Sometimes we
think of Israel as being two countries because they were two nations for a time. There is only one nation now. Still, Palestine is
divided into two countries, held by two nations. If the Arabs
claimed just the part they now occupy, there would be no immediate crisis; but they claim the whole of Palestine—both countries.
They are determined to drive the Jews out of every inch of the
land. They say, "It is all ours and we will possess it."

Therefore prophesy and say, Thus saith the Lord God; Because
they have made you desolate, and swallowed you up on every side,
that ye might be a possession unto the residue of the heathen, and
are taken up in the lips of talkers, and are an infamy of the people:

Therefore, ye mountains of Israel, hear the word of the Lord
God; Thus saith the Lord God to the mountains, and to the hills,
to the rivers, and to the valleys, to the desolate wastes, and to the
cities that are forsaken, which became a prey and derision to the
residue of the heathen that are round about:

Therefore thus saith the Lord God; Surely in the fire of my
jealousy have I spoken against the residue of the heathen, and
against all Idumea, which have appointed my land into their possession with the joy of all their heart, with despiteful minds, to cast
it out for a prey.—Ezek. 36:3-5

The time of this prophecy can be fixed. It concerns the land.
It is addressed, not to the people, but to the mountains, the hills,
the valleys and the rivers. The time, therefore, is before the Jews

are in possession of all the land. God is talking about the land that is occupied by their enemies.

However, the Jews have to be occupying some of the land, because the Arabs are planning to cast them out and take over their possessions for a prey. It also says that this is when they are at hand to come. The mass return has not yet taken place.

The time, then, is after the preliminary return and before the great mass return when the Jews will occupy all the land. This is the time we are in now. We are actually seeing this prophecy being fulfilled. We are living between the first and second crises. Every detail is happening exactly as prophesied, even to the actual words of the Arabs.

The enemy has swallowed up the land on every side and has made it desolate. The nations round about are determined to possess the land; so, God speaks out against the nations of the Arabs because they have "appointed my land into their possession with the joy of all their heart, with despiteful minds, to cast it out for a prey." This is what they are planning to do—drive out the Jews and take their land, the land they have worked so hard to redeem. This action will bring about the second crisis.

> Therefore prophesy concerning the land of Israel, and say unto the mountains, and to the hills, to the rivers, and to the valleys, Thus saith the Lord God; Behold, I have spoken in my jealousy and in my fury, because ye have borne the shame of the heathen:
>
> Therefore thus saith the Lord God; I have lifted up mind hand, Surely the heathen that are about you, they shall bear their shame.
>
> But ye, O mountains of Israel, ye shall shoot forth your branches, and yield your fruit to my people of Israel; for they are at hand to come.
>
> For, behold, I am for you, and I will turn unto you, and ye shall be tilled and sown:
>
> And I will multiply men upon you, all the house of Israel, even all of it: and the cities shall be inhabited, and the wastes shall be builded:
>
> And I will multiply upon you man and beast; and they shall increase and bring fruit: and I will settle you after your old estates, and will do better unto you than at your beginnings: and ye shall know that I am the Lord.—Ezek. 36:6-11

Although the nations round about Israel take over the land, they will not profit by it, because the Jews are at hand to come. The full force of this prophecy will be felt when the second crisis breaks upon Israel.

From here on, Ezekiel is summarizing. It will take a little time to bring about perfection in Israel. There will yet be a third crisis.

The exciting thing about this prophecy is that it is actually being fulfilled now. We have seen it. This is the first step in a process that must continue without undue delay.

SECOND STEP—THE COVENANT

The second crisis follows somewhat the pattern of the first, only it is much more drastic. The first crisis started with one man, Hitler. The second crisis will be the work of one man, Antichrist. This gives point to the peculiar wording of the first covenant with Abraham. "I will bless them that bless thee, and curse HIM that curseth thee."

The first crisis restored a portion of the land to productivity, gave the Jews an independent state for the first time in 2500 years, and turned their faces toward Palestine. But it did not turn them to God. Therefore, they will lose the land.

Next time they will have to turn to God and repent BEFORE they get back their land. This will be the great prophesied return from all nations to possess all the land.

In the first crisis they went in on their own power. In the second crisis they will go in under the power of God, miraculously demonstrated.

The amount of Scripture involved in the second crisis is too great to deal with properly in a book of this size. From start to finish we are in the realm of the miraculous. Actually, the crisis is not the return. The crisis is over when the return starts. The whole atmosphere changes at this time. The return is the work of God just as decidedly as the Exodus from Egypt, and the miraculous acts of God will be just as sensational.

The prevailing statement is: "Then they shall know that I am the Lord." This is repeated over and over again.

It took a Hitler to turn the Jews toward Palestine. It will take a greater Hitler to turn them to God. All the persecutions for the past 2500 years have not done that. In fact, while the Jews are scattered all over the earth, no amount of persecution would make them repent and acknowledge that their troubles were due to their forsaking the Lord, although the prophets are full of warnings to that effect.

There would have to be a great gathering of Jews into one place under the most desperate conditions to bring about his result; and this is exactly what will happen.

First, we will look at the one great essential to the return: their relationship to God. This is the working out of God's covenant; and although the covenant was without conditions, there were conditions fixed as to the time that the covenant would be honored. This was told them by Moses.

> And it shall come to pass, when all these things are come upon thee, the blessing and the curse, which I have set before thee, and thou shalt call them to mind among all the nations, whither the Lord thy God hath driven thee.
> And shalt return unto the Lord thy God, and shalt obey his voice

Israel After the Six-Day War

Land east of the Jordan river occupied by the twelve tribes. This may be considered a part of the promised land.

according to all that I command thee this day, thou and thy children, with all thine heart, and with all thy soul;

That then the Lord thy God will turn thy captivity, and have compassion upon thee, and will return and gather thee from all the nations, whither the Lord thy God hath scattered thee.

If any of thine be driven out unto the outmost parts of heaven, from thence will the Lord thy God gather thee, and from thence will he fetch thee:

And the Lord thy God will bring thee into the land which thy fathers possessed, and thou shalt possess it; and he will do thee good, and multiply thee above thy fathers.

And the Lord thy God will circumcise thine heart and the heart of thy seed, to love the Lord thy God with all thine heart, and with all thy soul, that thou mayest live.

And the Lord thy God will put all these curses upon thine enemies, and on them that hate thee, which persecuted thee.

And thou shalt return and obey the voice of the Lord, and do all his commandments which I command thee this day.

And the Lord thy God will make thee plenteous in every work of thine hand, in the fruit of thy body, and in the fruit of thy cattle, and in the fruit of thy land, for good: for the Lord will again rejoice over thee for good, as he rejoiced over thy fathers:

> If thou shalt hearken unto the voice of the Lord thy God, to keep his commandments and his statutes which are written in this book of the law, and if thou turn unto the Lord thy God with all thine heart, and with all thy soul.—Deut. 30:1-10

Moses outlines the whole future of Israel. This new covenant differs from the one given Abraham in that it requires obedience on the part of the people (Deut. 29:24-28). In the state of mind of the Jews today, such obedience is entirely out of the question. The second crisis will change this.

There can be no return of the Jews until they meet God's requirements, because both parties must keep the covenant. A covenant is an agreement between two or more parties. To bring the Jews back into covenant relationship is next to impossible. The Hitler persecution came nowhere near it. Their plight will have to be so serious that complete extinction will seem certain. They will be like a valley full of dry bones. "And lo, they were very dry."—Ezek. 37:2.

The restoration of Israel will be like a resurrection from the dead; they will be so close to death as a nation.

> And it shall come to pass, that as the Lord rejoiced over you to do you good, and to multiply you; so the Lord will rejoice over you to destroy you, and to bring you to nought; and ye shall be plucked from off the land whither thou goest to possess it.
>
> And the Lord shall scatter thee among all people, from the one end of the earth even unto the other; and there thou shalt serve other gods, which neither thou nor thy fathers have known, even wood and stone.
>
> And among these nations shalt thou find no ease, neither shall the sole of thy foot have rest: but the Lord shall give thee there a trembling heart, and failing of eyes, and sorrow of mind:
>
> And thy life shall hang in doubt before thee; and thou shalt fear day and night, and shalt have none assurance of thy life:
>
> In the morning thou shalt say, Would God it were even! and at even thou shalt say, Would God it were morning! for the fear of thine heart wherewith thou shalt fear, and for the sight of thine eyes which thou shalt see.
>
> And the Lord shall bring thee into Egypt again with ships, by the way whereof I spake unto thee, Thou shalt see it no more again: and there ye shall be sold unto your enemies for bondmen and bondwomen, and no man shall buy you.—Deut. 28:63-68

"Into Egypt again with ships." Normally, you do not go from Palestine to Egypt in ships. These Jews will be coming from other parts of the world. It apparently will be Antichrist's policy not to kill them as Hitler did, but to dump them on desert sands to die.

This is the final stage of the dispersion. All the Jews will be involved this time, not just those in Germany. Conditions in the world will be much different from what they are today. We cannot judge them by present-day standards. Only under Antichrist could there be such a world-wide turning against the Jews.

> And Moses said unto the people. Fear ye not, stand still, and see the salvation of the Lord which he will show you today: for the Egyptians whom ye have seen today, ye shall see them again no more forever.—Ex. 14:13

This would be along the Red Sea, so the ships could come both from the Mediterranean Sea and the South Seas. They could come from all over the world. It is quite possible that this will be a spite action on the part of Antichrist. He will always have trouble with Egypt, for Egypt is to become a very powerful nation.

The second crisis is the attempt of Antichrist to annihilate all the Jews in the world. Some Jews will be in Egypt quite a while. Apparently Palestine and Ethiopia will be the last countries affected. When the persecution gets around to Israel they are getting close to the time of the return. This will be the time of their calamity, and the Arabs will stand in waiting to put them to the sword and take over their possessions for a prey. The Jews will have no place to go. Egypt will be overrun with them. Many of them will be consigned to the desert.

> As I live, saith the Lord God, surely with a mighty hand, and with a stretched out arm, and with fury poured out, will I rule over you:
> And I will bring you out from the people, and will gather you out of the countries wherein ye are scattered, with a mighty hand, and with a stretched out arm, and with fury poured out.
> And I will bring you into the wilderness of the people, and there will I plead with you face to face.
> Like as I pleaded with your fathers in the wilderness of the land of Egypt, so will I plead with you, saith the Lord God.
> And I will cause you to pass under the rod, and I will bring you into the bond of the covenant:
> And I will purge out from among you the rebels, and them that transgress against me: I will bring forth out of the country where they sojourn, and they shall not enter into the land of Israel: and ye shall know that I am the Lord.—Ezek. 20:33-38

The return of the Jews will be an act of God. Only God himself could save them this time. It will be by an outstretched arm and with fury poured out. They will not come straggling back to Palestine and try to buy land from the Arabs. They will follow a route which allows them to congregate in a place called the wilderness of the people, or the wilderness of Egypt. It will probably be close to the ancient land of Goshen, because they will have to cross the Red Sea again. There God will plead with them face to face.

"And I will cause you to pass under the rod, and bring you

into the bond of the covenant." The covenant with Abraham was unconditional, but the people had to be brought under the bond of the covenant before it could be put into effect. There was also a covenant with Moses and that one had some conditions.

> These are the words of the covenant which the Lord commanded Moses to make with the children of Israel in the Land of Moab, beside the covenant which he made with them in Horeb.—Deut. 29:1
>
> That thou shouldest enter into covenant with the Lord thy God, and into his oath which the Lord thy God maketh with thee this day: that he may establish thee today for a people unto himself, and that he may be unto thee a God, as he hath said unto thee, and as he hath sworn unto thy fathers, to Abraham, to Isaac, and to Jacob.—Deut. 29:12, 13

This covenant is very specific about one thing: They must remain true to God; they must keep the terms of the covenant or they cannot keep their land. Therefore, before they can return under the power of God, they must be brought again under the terms or bond of the covenant.

"And I will cause them to pass under the rod." This rod is the same as in Psalm 23: "Thy rod and thy staff they comfort me." The shepherd counted the sheep with his rod as they passed into the fold. If one was missing, a search was made. They will be brought into the bond of the covenant individually. The Jews will not at this time accept Christ. They will return to the God of their fathers. It will require a third crisis to bring them to Christ.

The Time of Their Calamity

God says He will bring them out of the countries where they have been scattered, "with a mighty hand, and with a stretched out arm, and with fury poured out." These are strong words and they tell of no ordinary circumstance. Satan, through Antichrist, will go forth in fury to do away with all the Jews in the world and thus make impossible the fulfillment of all prophecy.

It is the covenant that stands in the way of Satan. Daniel says: "His heart shall be against the holy covenant."—Dan. 11: 28.

What the Arabs did, or tried to do, during and after the first crisis, they will do on a still greater scale in the second crisis. The entire book of Obadiah concerns the time of the second crisis.

> For thy violence against thy brother Jacob shame shall cover thee, and thou shalt be cut off for ever.
>
> In the day that thou stoodest on the other side, in the day that the strangers carried away captive his forces, and foreigners entered into his gates, and cast lots upon Jerusalem, even thou wast as one of them.

But thou shouldest not have looked on the day of thy brother in the day that he became a stranger; neither shouldest thou have rejoiced over the children of Judah in the day of their destruction; neither shouldest thou have spoken proudly in the day of distress.

Thou shouldest not have entered into the gate of my people in the day of their calamity; yea, thou shouldest not have looked on their affliction in the day of their calamity, nor have laid hands on their substance in the day of their calamity;

Neither shouldest thou have stood in the crossway, to cut off those of his that did escape; neither shouldest thou have delivered up those of his that did remain in the day of distress.—Obad. 10-14

This prophecy is concerning a specific time. What is that time?

For the day of the Lord is near upon all the heathen: as thou hast done, it shall be done unto thee: thy reward shall return upon thine own head.—Obad. 15

Note also the goal of the prophecy:

But upon mount Zion shall be deliverance, and there shall be holiness; and the house of Jacob shall possess their possessions.

And the house of Jacob shall be a fire, and the house of Joseph a flame, and the house of Esau for stubble, and they shall kindle in them, and devour them; and there shall not be any remaining of the house of Esau; for the Lord hath spoken it.

And they of the south shall possess the mount of Esau; and they of the plain the Philistines: and they shall possess the fields of Ephraim, and the fields of Samaria: and Benjamin shall possess Gilead.

And the captivity of this host of the children of Israel shall possess that of the Canaanites, even unto Zarephath; and the captivity of Jerusalem, which is in Sepharad, shall possess the cities of the south.

And saviours shall come up on mount Zion to judge the mount of Esau; and the kingdom shall be the Lord's.—Obad. 17-21

Now we are in a position to understand the prophecy which will be fulfilled before the day of the Lord (while the day of the Lord is near). The fact that it is written in the past tense makes no difference to the time. The Hebrew verb had no future tense, so all prophecy in the Old Testament was originally written in either the present or past tense.

It is strangers, other than the Arabs, that will enter Palestine and drive the Jews out. The Arabs will help. This will be a time of great calamity for Israel because their land, which they have worked so hard to improve and which is their only hope in the world, is passing into the hands of their worst enemies. They have no place to go but Egypt, and Egypt hates them.

The Jew will become a stranger. He will have no land and

no home—a man without a country, a stranger wherever he goes. This condition will be much more difficult to bear after they have enjoyed a land of their own, a place of safety where they were not strangers. It is no wonder they say: "Our bones are dried, our hope is lost: and we are cut off for our parts." (an idiom meaning: It is all over with us.)—Ezek. 37:11.

If God can save them from this, it will be like opening their graves and bringing them out (Ezek. 37:12).

But first, God must put His Spirit in them (Ezek. 37:14). God cannot do that until they are willing. They will be willing only when they are ready to die. God explained this to Ezekiel at the start. He said:

"The house of Israel will not hearken unto thee; for they will not harken unto me: for all the house of Israel are impudent and hardhearted."—Ezek. 3:7.

"Neither shouldest thou have spoken proudly in the day of distress."—Obad. 12. This gives us a very vivid picture of the haughtiness of the Arabs when they see their dreams come true and see themselves taking over all the rich possessions of the Jews—"which have appointed my land into their possession with the joy of all their heart, with despiteful minds, to cast it out for a prey."—Ezek. 36:5.

> Neither shouldest thou have stood in the crossway, to cut off those of his that did escape; neither shouldest thou have delivered up those of his that did remain in the day of distress.—Obad. 14

This speaks volumes. You can just see the Jews trying to escape from the invaders, with the Arabs standing at the cross-roads to cut off their escape. Other Jews are in hiding, trying to remain in Jerusalem until the trouble blows over. They are betrayed by the Arabs and delivered up to their enemies. This is the day of their destruction.

It will not be for long because the Lord is about to act. As Ezekiel said: "But ye, O mountains of Israel, ye shall shoot forth your branches and yield your fruit to my people of Israel; for they are at hand to come. For, behold, I am for you, and I will turn unto you, and ye shall be tilled and sown."—Ezek. 36:8, 9.

At this point, Isaiah seems to give us the most information in the smallest space.

> And it shall come to pass in that day, that the Lord shall set his hand again the second time to recover the remnant of his people, which shall be left, from Assyria, and from Egypt, and from Pathros, and from Cush, and from Elam, and from Shinar, and from Hamath, and from the islands of the sea.
>
> And he shall set up an ensign for the nations, and shall assemble the outcasts of Israel, and gather together the dispersed of Judah from the four corners of the earth.

The envy also of Ephraim shall depart, and the adversaries of Judah shall be cut off: and Judah shall not vex Ephraim.

But they shall fly upon the shoulders of the Philistines toward the west; they shall spoil them of the east together: they shall lay their hand upon Edom and Moab; and the children of Ammon shall obey them.

And the Lord shall utterly destroy the tongue of the Egyptian sea; and with his mighty wind shall he shake his hand over the river, and shall smite it in the seven streams, and make men go over dry-shod.

And there shall be an highway for the remnant of his people, which shall be left, from Assyria; like as it was to Israel in the day that he came up out of the land of Egypt.—Isa. 11:11-16

"And it shall come to pass in that day (the day of fulfilled prophecy) that the Lord shall set his hand again the second time to recover the remnant of his people, which shall be left . . . "

This is the second time that the Jews have all gone back to their land by the hand of the Lord. This is going to be a miraculous proceeding from beginning to end. The Jews will be in a helpless state, even trying to sell themselves as slaves. Only a remnant will be left after the terrible persecution. They are left from:

ASSYRIA. There are no Assyrians now. Antichrist is called the Assyrian by Isaiah. So Antichrist's empire may be called Assyria in prophecy.

EGYPT. There are few, if any, Jews in Egypt now, but a great company will be there for some time before the return. The return will be by way of Egypt.

PATHROS, CUSH. Cush is Ethiopia. Pathros is north of Ethiopia, a part of Egypt or the Sudan. There are Jews in Ethiopia, the only known descendants of the priesthood. Emperor Haile Selassie is a Jew, a descendant of King Solomon. He claims to have the original Ark of the Covenant, and there is a great deal of evidence that it is there, in the keeping of the priests.

ELAM AND SHINAR. Shinar is the site of Ancient Babylon. Elam is east of Shinar. It is not an independent country now, but it will be—not only independent, but great. There are some amazing prophecies concerning it. It is in Shinar and Elam that the wealth of the world will center in those days, and naturally it would attract many Jews. Prophecy shows how great changes will take place in that part of the world.

HAMATH. This points to territory north of Palestine which will be well developed during that time of world prosperity and which, therefore, will contain many Jews.

ISLANDS OF THE SEA. This is an idiomatic expression often used to indicate far distant lands. The Jews will come from the four corners of the earth (verse 12).

"He shall set up an ensign for the nations." This will be God's doings. The ensign stands for His power (as did the ark). It is not only a rallying point for the Jews, but it is a signal to the nations that God is doing something for Israel. The ensign is not a flag or banner; although it is sometimes translated banner. It is an obejct having all the characteristics of the ark of the covenant. It first appears in Ethiopia where it causes the destruction of Israel's enemies. From there it is taken to Mt. Zion (Isa. 18).

"And shall assemble the outcasts of Israel." They will be outcasts in all countries, but God will assemble them into one place in Egypt so that they can go back in a body, as they came out of Egypt the first time. They will have no army and no power except God's power exemplified by the ensign.

"They shall fly upon the shoulders of the Philistines toward the west." There are no Philistines left in the world. The same rule applies: the prophet used the name of an ancient people to tell of a future people that had some of the same characteristics. "Philistines" means "strangers in the land." Possibly it should be left untranslated and read: "strangers from the west." This would then apply to Antichrist's armies which come in from the west. Only by the power of God, as was demonstrated by the ark, could a company of helpless slaves drive out armed forces as powerful as those of Antichrist.

"They shall spoil them of the east together." This confirms our previous statement. There are people from the east and from the west that have taken over Palestine. Those from the east would be Arabs, in contrast with those strangers that came in from the west. The whole process is very clear. The Arabs could not, of themselves, take Palestine away from the Jews; but strangers from the west come in with great power and drive the Jews before them. Then the Arabs, standing by, complete the slaughter.

When the Jews come back, led by the ensign, they will first fly upon the strangers from the west, and then spoil their enemies from the east. They will take back all of Palestine, including Jerusalem and the temple site, which is now occupied by a Moslem shrine called the Dome of the Rock. Then the Jews will build their own temple. This could only be done by the power of God, such as was exercised when they took Jericho.

> And the Lord shall utterly destroy the tongue of the Egyptian sea; and with his mighty wind shall he shake his hand over the river, and shall smite it in the seven streams, and make men go over dryshod.—Isa. 11:15

The tongue of the Egyptian Sea is that part which the Children of Israel crossed when Moses led them out of Egypt the first time. This will be the second time (verse 11). They will again cross the Red Sea on dry ground. "And with his mighty wind shall he shake his hand over the river . . . and make men go over dry-shod."

> And I will sow them among the people: and they shall remember me in far countries; and they shall live with their children, and turn again.
>
> I will bring them into the land of Gilead and Lebanon; and place shall not be found for them.
>
> And he shall pass through the sea with affliction, and shall smite the waves in the sea, and all the deeps of the river shall dry up: and the pride of Assyria shall be brought down, and the sceptre of Egypt shall depart away.
>
> And I will strengthen them in the Lord; and they shall walk up and down in his name, saith the Lord.—Zech. 10:9-12

GILEAD. The far eastern part of Palestine beyond the River Jordan. A nation called Jordan now occupies this land. A part of Palestine is on the Jordan side of the river.

LEBANON. The far northern part of Palestine, now occupied by Lebanon and Syria. When the Jews go back under the power of God, they will not stop till they have occupied all the land that God promised Abraham in the covenant. The drying up of the water is literal, as it was the first time; but it is also symbolic of what God is going to do to Egypt and Assyria (nations in Antichrist's empire). Many chapters in prophecy are given over to the destruction of the countries that oppose the Jews in the time of their calamity.

THE SEVEN STREAMS (Isa. 11:15) would refer to the Nile delta. Evidently there will be Jews on the western side of the river who will pass over both the river and the Red Sea dryshod.

> And there shall be an highway for the remnant of his people, which shall be left, from Assyria; like as it was to Israel in the day that he came up out of the land of Egypt.—Isa. 11:16

THE HIGHWAY. There was no road leading through the Red Sea. It was not that kind of a highway. There were no signposts, but there was a pillar of cloud by day and a pillar of fire by night. There were no drive-ins, but there was manna every morning and water out of the rock. There were no repair shops, but their shoes did not wear out. The whole trip was miraculous. It will be the same when God again, the second time, recovers His people which are left (after the persecution) from Egypt and from all the places where they have been scattered.

> The word that came to Jeremiah from the Lord, saying, Thus speaketh the Lord God of Israel, saying, Write thee all the words that I have spoken unto thee in a book. For, lo, the days come, saith the Lord, that I will bring again the captivity of my people Israel and Judah, saith the Lord: and I will cause them to return to the land that I gave to their fathers, and they shall possess it.

And these are the words that the Lord spake concerning Israel and concerning Judah. For thus saith the Lord; We have heard a voice of trembling, of fear, and not of peace.

Ask ye now, and see whether a man doth travail with child? Wherefore do I see every man with his hands on his loins, as a woman in travail, and all faces are turned into paleness?

Alas! for that day is great, so that none is like it: it is even the time of Jacob's trouble; but he shall be saved out of it. For it shall come to pass in that day, saith the Lord of hosts, that I will break his yoke from off thy neck, and will burst thy bonds, and strangers shall no more serve themselves of him:

But they shall serve the Lord their God, and David their king, whom I will raise up unto them. Therefore fear thou not, O my servant Jacob, saith the Lord; neither be dismayed, O Israel: for, lo, I will save thee from afar, and thy seed from the land of their captivity; and Jacob shall return, and shall be in rest, and be quiet, and none shall make him afraid.

For I am with thee, saith the Lord, to save thee: though I make a full end of all nations whither I have scattered thee, yet will I not make a full end of thee: but I will correct thee in measure, and will not leave thee altogether unpunished.—Jer. 30:1-11

There is a tremendous amount of prophecy concerning the return of the Jews. We refer to this passage only as an example. Note the following points:

1. *The statement of the goal* (vs. 3). The Jews will return to their land and possess it. They will not share it with others. They will not live in a land that others possess, but "they will possess their possessions."—Obad. 17.

2. *It is a time of trembling, fear, and not of peace* (vs. 5) Does this mean after the return, during the return, or before the return? We must remember that there are three crises, each one worse than the one before it. Some of the details are so much alike that one prophecy might serve for both. Sometimes the prophet saw the entire process in one view and did not distinguish the three parts. When you are looking at a time two or three thousand years in the future, events that are only a few years apart would seem as one process.

We are now living in the very midst of these things; some are past, some are present, and some are future, so we are very conscious of the timing and the sequence.

3. *It is the time of Jacob's trouble* (vss. 6, 7). He will be saved out of it. This could apply to both the second and third crises. They are here thought of as one process, which they are, but there will be a time of peace in between.

4. *God will break the power of Antichrist* (vs. 8). Antichrist does not appear in the first crisis, but he is the prime mover in the second and third. The Jews will get complete victory over him when they return under the power of God. But some of them will

make a deal with Antichrist and that will bring on the third crisis.

5. *They will serve the Lord their God and David their king.*
This brings us very definitely to the third crisis. They cannot have
a king until they accept Christ, not only as King, but as the one
they crucified. This will take a third crisis. That is called Armageddon.

THE THIRD STEP

Why must there be a third crisis for Israel? They have returned to God; they have been brought back under the covenant;
they are in full possession of the land; they have a temple; they
are at peace; they have God's promised protection.

Israel has been in this situation before. When they were about
to enter the Promised Land, the Lord told them:

> . . . Behold, I make a covenant: Before all thy people I will do
> marvels, such as have not been done in all the earth, nor in any
> nation: and all the people among which thou art shall see the work
> of the Lord: for it is a terrible thing that I will do with thee.—
> Ex. 34:10

God did all those things when He led them across the Jordan
on dry ground, and the walls of Jericho fell down at the blowing
of trumpets. Their enemies were defeated before them, and the
land was divided among the tribes, but their faithfulness did not
last, so we read:

> And the children of Israel did evil in the sight of the Lord, and
> served Baalim:
> And they forsook the Lord God of their fathers, which brought
> them out of the land of Egypt, and followed other gods, of the gods
> of the people that were round about them, and bowed themselves
> unto them, and provoked the Lord, and served Baal and Ashtaroth.
> And the anger of the Lord was hot against Israel, and he sold
> them into the hands of their enemies round about, so that they could
> not any longer stand before their enemies.
> Whithersoever they went out, the hand of the Lord was against
> them for evil, as the Lord had said, and as the Lord had sworn unto
> them: and they were greatly distressed.—Judges 2:11-15

They will do the same thing again. The return of the Jews
from all countries will be accompanied by the same marvelous
miracles. They will drive out their enemies by the power of God.
They will possess their land and they will experience an unheard-
of prosperity.

Prophecy indicates that the Jews will go deeper into sin before
the third crisis than ever before in their history. Even idolatry
will be rampant. A great deal of Old Testament prophecy is given
over to it. The entire book of Malachi is on this subject.

For the day of the Lord of hosts shall be upon every one that is proud and lofty, and upon everyone that is lifted up; and he shall be brought low:

And upon all the cedars of Lebanon, that are high and lifted up, and upon all the oaks of Bashan,

And upon all the high mountains, and upon all the hills that are lifted up,

And upon every high tower, and upon every fenced wall,

And upon all the ships of Tarshish, and upon all pleasant pictures.

And the loftiness of man shall be bowed down, and the haughtiness of men shall be made low: and the Lord alone shall be exalted in that day.

And the idols he shall utterly abolish.

And they shall go into the holes of the rocks, and into the caves of the earth, for fear of the Lord, and for the glory of his majesty, when he ariseth to shake terribly the earth.

In that day a man shall cast his idols of silver, and his idols of gold, which they made each one for himself to worship, to the moles and to the bats;

To go into the clefts of the rocks, and into the tops of the ragged rocks, for fear of the Lord, and for the glory of his majesty, when he ariseth to shake terribly the earth.—Isa. 2:12-21

Men are doing great things today, even by modern standards. But this is only the beginning; unheard-of things are ahead that stagger the imagination. The most astonishing things in this picture is the return to idolatry. This will, of course, be promoted by Satan's Church, Babylon the great. To what extent this practice is carried on in Israel is not certain. Isaiah writes about the whole world. But when the world becomes "as it was in the days of Noah," the Jews will be the greatest offenders.

The power behind all this is the presence of Satan in the person of Antichrist. He will get into Israel, not at first by war, but by craft. Daniel says: "After they join themselves unto him [Antichrist], he worketh deceit, and hath increased, and hath been strong by a few of the nation."—Dan. 11:23 (Young's Literal Translation).

If Antichrist has so much power that he can easily put down the most formidable opposition, and if he can almost control the world by his supernatural power (Rev. 13), how can he be stopped by so little a nation as Israel? Antichrist will not soon forget the miracles of the return. The ensign, probably the ark of the covenant (Jer. 3:16), will be on Mt. Zion. There will be signs even more startling than those produced by Antichrist and there will be evidence of God's protection for which even Antichrist will have respect. Antichrist must first break down God's protection. He must overcome the covenant. His historic way of doing this is to bring Israel into sin.

Daniel says he (Antichrist) will confirm the covenant with many for one week (of years). The many may be leaders in the nation although few in number as compared to the entire population. He will become strong with a few. When the Jews turn to Antichrist for protection they turn away from God. The ark always lost its power when the Israelites left the Lord. They will "forsake the holy covenant" (Dan. 11:30).

The result is: Satan will bring the armies of the world against the Jews. This is known as the Battle of Armageddon. The word Armaggedon appears only once in the Bible (Rev. 16:16): "And he gathered them together into a place called in the Hebrew tongue Armageddon."

Armageddon comes from a Hebrew word meaning "hill of Megiddo." It is a low plateau in the northwestern part of present-day Palestine, the battleground of ancient times. But there is no mention of any battle being fought there in the last days. Armageddon is the gathering place. The battle is fought at Jerusalem (Zech. 14).

Joel 2 also describes the battle, as does Rev. 19:11-21.

ARMAGEDDON

There is an interesting difference of opinion about the prophetic future of Russia. Prophecy, to many people, means Ezekiel 38. It has been the most talked about and written about of all prophetic chapters. If the usual interpretation of that chapter should fail, because of the defeat of Russia or a change in world politics, as, for instance, the rise of China as a world power, or the appearance of Antichrist, many people would almost lose their faith.

There are two ways of approaching a passage of Scripture. One way is to make it prove something that you have already decided; the other way is to find out exactly what it says regardless of your own belief. Nobody would ever read Russia into Ezekiel 38 if he did not have Russia in mind and was trying to make it fit into the prophecy.

Ezekiel 33:21 begins a new section, the Return of the Jews. This may be outlined as follows:

The Goal: 33:21—34:31

I will bring them out from the people, and gather them from the countries, and will bring them to their own land, and feed them upon the mountains of Israel by the rivers, and in all the inhabited places of the country.

And I the Lord will be their God, and my servant David a prince among them; I the Lord have spoken it.

Opposition of the Arabs: 35:1—36:8

This covers the time between the first and second crises. The occupation and restoration of the land will be opposed.

The Regathering and Cleansing: 36:9-38

The time covered is from the second crisis to the kingdom age. Arab opposition has been overcome. All the Jews occupy all the land. But we still have Antichrist to deal with.

Vision of Dry Bones: 37

The condition of Israel just before the return (37:1-3).
Israel is a nation again, but without the Holy Spirit (37:4-8).
God will give them His Spirit (37:9-14).
Israel and Judah will become one nation (37:15-22).
They will be cleansed, and God will dwell with them (37:23-28).

Ezekiel 38 and 39 concentrate on the final phase of the return—the destruction of the armies that come against Jerusalem. This is a detailed study of the third crisis. First, let us look at the goal.

And I will set my glory among the heathen, and all the heathen shall see my judgment that I have executed, and my hand that I have laid upon them.

So the house of Israel shall know that I am the Lord their God from that day and forward.

And the heathen shall know that the house of Israel went into captivity for their iniquity: because they trespassed against me, therefore hid I my face from them, and gave them into the hand of their enemies: so fell they all by the sword.

According to their uncleanness and according to their transgressions have I done unto them, and hid my face from them. Therefore thus saith the Lord God: Now will I bring again the captivity of Jacob, and have mercy upon the whole house of Israel, and will be jealous for my holy name; after that they have borne their shame, and all their trespasses whereby they have trespassed against me, when they dwelt safely in their land, and none made them afraid.

When I have brought them again from the people, and gathered them out of their enemies' lands, and am sanctified in them in the sight of many nations;

Then shall they know that I am the Lord their God, which caused them to be led into captivity among the heathen: but I have gathered them unto their own land, and have left none of them any more there.

Neither will I hide my face any more from them: for I have poured out my spirit upon the house of Israel, saith the Lord God.
—Ezek. 39:21-29

This is exactly the same goal as expressed in many other places. It is the "end." "So the house of Israel shall know that I am the Lord their God from that day and forward."—Ezek. 39:22.

All the prophecies concerning Israel end in the same place— the total restoration of Israel to its promised place in the kingdom. But the details at this point are so many that they have to be treated each in its own way. The theme of this chapter is the final battle.

Gog and the Land of Magog

And the word of the Lord came unto me, saying,
Son of Man, set thy face against Gog, the land of Magog, the chief prince of Meshech and Tubal, and prophesy against him,
And say, Thus saith the Lord God; Behold, I am against thee, O Gog, the chief prince of Meshech and Tubal.—Ezek. 38:1-3

The Revised Version (1901) changes the wording in one respect. It reads "Prince of Rosh" instead of "chief prince." The R.S.V. reads "chief prince," which is correct. Rosh is the Hebrew word for first or chief. It is not the name of any place or country (or people). Nathan J. Stone, in *Moody Monthly* (about 1948), wrote:

"Whatever justification there may be for referring the names mentioned in Ezekiel 38 to Russia and cities in that land, such interpretation of the Hebrew words is purely arbitrary. It is not based on the root meaning of these words. This is particularly true of the word Rosh interpreted as Russia. . . . This is based on Hebrew vowels invented a thousand years after the Old Testament was written. The word rosh never means anything but first or chief."

The Pulpit Commentary gives both translations and says either one is possible, but rosh occurs 456 times in the Old Testament and nowhere is it translated as a proper noun.

Here is illustrated the right and wrong way to interpret Scripture. The wrong way is to find some country that has a name remotely like the Hebrew word (when pronounced in English). This, of course, would be only guesswork. Russia comes from a Finnish word meaning rowers (of a boat) while rosh is a Hebrew word meaning chief. There is no connection in history, prophecy, ethnology or etymology.

The right way is to determine the Bible use of a word, especially the way the writer of the book uses the word. In Ezekiel, rosh occurs in only one other place—Ezekiel 27:22: "The merchants of Sheba and Raamah, they were thy merchants: they occupied in thy fairs with chief of all spices, and with all precious stones and gold."

Here rosh is translated "chief" even by the Revised Version. In fact, it would be quite difficult to make the Jews put Russia in place of rosh when one of their most sacred holidays was Rosh Hashana, the first day of the new year. The Jewish Bible reads "chief prince" in this portion.

THE STORY

Ezekiel, chapters 35-37, tells of the conditions in Palestine at the time of the return of the Jews: the enraged opposition of the surrounding nations, the fruitfulness of the land under Jewish control, and the mighty return.

In chapter 38, the Jews are all safely residing in the Promised Land. They have turned to God under pressure but there has been no real change of heart. They will turn to God in dire extremity, only to forget Him when the crisis is past. When this story opens, the world is in turmoil. Six plagues have left the nations in a state of desperation. This is the meaning of 39:2: "I will turn thee back and leave but a sixth part of thee." Literally, "I will six thee." That is, "I will afflict thee with six plagues" (margin). Only Palestine is prosperous.

Antichrist cannot allow such conditions to continue. The Jews' prosperity is, in fact, the direct result of Antichrist's attempt to destroy them. God answered by returning them to Palestine with a great show of strength. After the plagues, all nations will sorely need what the Jews have in abundance; so, when Antichrist tries to seize it, a world war will threaten. All nations will start toward Palestine (Zech. 14:2).

Only by a swift movement, with overwhelming force, could such a movement be a success. There will be no weapons for such an army after the plagues of the trumpets and vials (Revelation). This sudden move by Antichrist necessitates the use of wooden weapons hastily made from tools at hand.

"Prepare war, wake up the mighty men, let all men of war draw near; let them come up: beat your plowshares into swords, and your pruninghooks into spears: let the weak say: I am strong." —Joel 3:9, 10.

These crude weapons will be sufficient because the Jews will be unprepared and unarmed, "dwelling without walls or gates." Speed seems to be the first consideration. Antichrist tries to accomplish his purpose of annihilating the Jews before he can be stopped. Satan knows he has but a short time. This is far more than a war of Antichrist against the Jews; it is the final attempt of Satan to retain possession of the earth. This makes it the subject of much prophecy.

GOG AND MAGOG. This term applies to a super-enemy of God. It is used in the same way in Rev. 20:8. The time difference is a thousand years, but the circumstances are similar. Satan is again at large, and he gathers a great host against the Lord. When Satan operates in person on the earth, he is known as Gog and Magog.

The invasion of Palestine by the nations will turn out to be a battle against the Lord, for "then shall the Lord go forth and fight against those nations, as when he fought in the day of battle. And his feet shall stand in that day upon the mount of Olives which is before Jerusalem on the east."—Zech. 14:3, 4.

It is easy to identify Gog. God says of him: "Art thou he of whom I have spoken in old time by my servants the prophets of Israel, which prophesied in those days, many years, that I would bring thee against them?"—Ezek. 38:17.

There is only one such man mentioned by the prophets as coming against Israel in the last days. He goes by different names, but it is always the same man, the man we call Antichrist. Gog is not the name of any man in the Bible. It is the name of Satan when he becomes a man in Antichrist. After the Rapture, Antichrist is Satan in the flesh; then he is Gog. In Revelation we have the dragon and the beast. The dragon is Gog in Ezekiel and the beast is Magog. We have the same situation, only the names are different. We will not know the exact names until they arrive on the scene.

> And I will turn thee back, and put hooks into thy jaws, and I will bring thee forth, and all thine army, horses and horsemen, all of them clothed with all sorts of armour, even a great company with bucklers and shields, all of them handling swords:
>
> Persia, Ethiopia, and Libya with them; all of them with shield and helmet:
>
> Gomer, and all his bands; the house of Togarmah of the north quarters, and all his bands: and many people with thee.—Ezek. 38:4-6

The land of Magog, Antichrist's empire, is divided into three parts:

1. Meshech and Tubal
2. Persia, Ethiopia, Libya
3. Gomer, Togarmah and their bands

Put yourself in Ezekiel's place. He was looking 2500 years into the future, to a time when world conditions would be so different that no words could be found to express them. His problem was to name the countries that would come into existence at some future time and constitute the empire of a man known to Ezekiel only as Gog.

This had to be so perfectly done that people living on the other side of the world and under very different circumstances would be able to read and understand it.

Three of those countries were in existence in Ezekiel's day

and would remain to the end. These Ezekiel could call by name—
Persia, Ethiopia, Libya.

The others, whose names are not known, would have to be
identified in some other way. Ezekiel uses the only means available
to him: he called the countries by the names of their founders.
After the Flood, the grandsons of Noah went out in several directions and peopled certain lands. Ezekiel identifies these lands by
the names of the grandsons of Noah.

> Now these are the generations of the sons of Noah, Shem, Ham,
> and Japheth: and unto them were sons born after the flood.
> The sons of Japheth; Gomer, and Magog, and Madia and Javan,
> and Tubal, and Meshech, and Tiras.
> And the sons of Gomer; Ashkenaz, and Riphath, and Togarmah.
> —Gen. 10:1-3

All the names are there. Maps showing the posterity of Noah
differ slightly, as there are some uncertainties; but they are accurate enough for our purpose. You will note that Ezekiel considers
Palestine the center of the earth. In fact, that is the meaning of
"in the midst of the land" (verse 12). Ezekiel starts at the north
and makes a complete circle around Palestine.

MESHECH AND TUBAL. These men settled somewhere in
the neighborhood of the Caucasus Mountains between the Black
and Caspian Seas. This now belongs to Russia, but in the past
it was independent and probably will be again under Antichrist.
Antichrist's empire will be made up of independent countries volun-
tarily supporting him (Rev. 17:17).

PERSIA, ETHIOPIA, LIBYA. Persia is now called Iran. Ethiopia is the oldest continuing country. Its importance lies in the
fact that it is the home of many Jews who trace their ancestry
back to the priests of Solomon's day. They are called Falashas,
and are supposed to be the custodians of the Ark of the Covenant.
It will be the scene of Antichrist's first major defeat (Isa. 18).
After the Jews leave to return to Palestine, Ethiopia will join with
Antichrist (Dan. 11:43). Libya is North Africa. Both Ethiopia and
Libya will be confederate with Egypt in the end (Jer. 46:8-10;
Ezek. 30:4-6).

GOMER. Gomer settled in Turkey. His descendants peopled
most of Europe, especially the northern parts. This included Germany, but the word Germany does not come from Gomer. The
Galatians of Asia Minor were called Gomerites by Josephus.
Gomer, therefore, became the forefather of many nations which
would be in the world empire of the last days. So Ezekiel says,
"And all his bands."

TOGARMAH. Togarmah was the son of Gomer and would
therefore have the same line of descent. Concerning Togarmah,
Whedon's Commentary says: "The Armenians, according to their

historians, had Thorgon for their founder and called themselves the house of Thorgon. They originally dwelt in Armenia and Asia Minor, but poured across the Hellespont into Europe before the dawn of history and, according to Sallust, spread over the Mediterranean peninsulas, even to Spain."

Again, we have the mention of many bands coming out of Togarmah. This completes the circle and covers the same territory that is in the four world empires of Daniel and, according to Revelation, make up Antichrist's empire.

Revelation also puts these nations into three groups. "And I saw three unclean spirits like frogs come out of the mouth of the dragon, and out of the mouth of the beast, and out of the mouth of the false prophet. For they are the spirits of devils, working miracles, which go forth unto the kings of the earth and of the whole world, to gather them to the battle of that great day of God Almighty."—Rev. 16:13, 14.

AND MANY PEOPLE WITH THEE. This completes the number and could include people from all parts of the world, nations that are confederate with Antichrist. Two important countries are omitted from this list that would naturally be named. They are Babylon and Egypt.

How could Ezekiel list the nations surrounding Palestine and leave out the two most important ones? The reason may be discovered. Babylon will be wiped out as a nation by what is called the drying up of the Euphrates. The destruction of Babylon comes before the coming of Christ and therefore before Armageddon (Rev. 18).

Egypt also will be completely destroyed just prior to Armageddon (Ezek. 29:6-13).

> Be thou prepared, and prepare for thyself, thou, and all thy company that are assembled unto thee, and be thou a guard unto them. After many days thou shalt be visited: in the latter years thou shalt come into the land that is brought back from the sword, and is gathered out of many people against the mountains of Israel, which have been always waste: but it is brought forth out of the nations, and they shall dwell safely all of them.
>
> Thou shalt ascend and come like a storm, thou shalt be like a cloud to cover the land, thou, and all thy bands, and many people with thee. Thus saith the Lord God; It shall also come to pass, that at the same time shall things come into thy mind, and thou shalt think an evil thought:
>
> And thou shalt say, I will go up to the land of unwalled villages; I will go to them that are at rest, that dwell safely, all of them dwelling without walls, and having neither bars nor gates, To take a spoil, and to take a prey; to turn thine hand upon desolate places that are now inhabited, and upon the people that are gathered out of the nations, which have gotten cattle and goods, that dwell in the midst of the land.—Ezek. 38:7-12

"That are assembled unto thee" (Ezek.) "And he gathered them together" (Rev.).

"Be thou a guard unto them." The word "guard" has the meaning of dictator. Gog is not a king. Daniel says they will not give him the honor of a king. He is a dictator or guard.

"In the latter years." The prophets invariably indicated the time of fulfillment in some way. This is the most direct. It has the same significance as "the time of the end."

"Thou shalt be visited." Literally, "Thou shalt come into prominence," or "Thou shalt become notorious." To invade Israel after what God has done for the Jews and what God has said about them dwelling safely, is an act of great daring. The world will be amazed. This is sheer desperation on the part of Antichrist.

"The land that is brought back from the sword" (vs. 8). The people have been put to the sword. This is a reference to the second crisis when a great massacre takes place in Israel so that only a remnant is left.

"Which have been always waste." The three crises for Israel cannot be a long time apart, for then the land would not always have been waste. If Palestine should come back to productivity, as it is doing, it could not then be said to have always been waste, unless the third crisis follows so soon that the reference is to the time before the great return. This whole process is one process that comes in the latter days. If it starts, it will have to finish on time. Here is a valuable and somewhat exciting indication of time. Palestine is returning to productivity. We are actually in the process.

"They shall dwell safely, all of them." Palestine will not be a very safe place during this raid, but God has decreed that they shall dwell safely; therefore, any invasion of Palestine will bring swift action. Christ will appear and fight for them and return them to their homes. This decree that they shall dwell safely does not stop the invasion, but it does bring swift action from God both to punish the invaders and to restore that which is lost.

"Thou shalt ascend" (vs. 9). Today we would say, "Thou shalt take off." They will come by air, like a storm cloud. Speed is important. If they are to take a spoil they must get there before the other nations do.

"An evil thought" (vs. 10). This evil thought is amplified in verses 11 and 12.

The places that were desolate are now inhabited. They have gotten cattle and goods. A book could be written today about the desolate places that are now inhabited. That one sentence summarizes the whole story of the return of the Jews. In time the Jews will inhabit all the former desolate places. In spite of their enemies, the Jews have prospered so that they are the envy of all the nations round about them. When the world is suffering the famines and the pestilences that are coming in the tribulation, then all nations will envy Israel.

> Sheba, and Dedan, and the merchants of Tarshish, with all the young lions thereof, shall say unto thee, Art thou come to take a spoil? hast thou gathered thy company to take a prey? to carry away silver and gold, to take a great spoil?—Ezek. 38:13.

"Sheba, Dedan and the Merchants of Tarshish, with all the young lions thereof." This is a fourth group. There is also a fourth group in Revelation called the kings of the east (Rev. 16:12), not because they are eastern countries such as China or Japan, but because they will come into Palestine from the east. They could come from any part of the world.

The exact location of Sheba and Dedan will not be known until they appear on the scene. They would seem to be located in Arabia and Africa. They will be parts of an empire or group that remains independent of Antichrist.

Tarshish is Gibraltar. It was the farthest known port in the world. Jonah tried to flee to Tarshish because he wanted to get as far away as he could. It would, therefore, represent a distant but unknown land which in the last days would have a world-wide influence. The young lions would be offshoots of that country or commonwealth.

Sheba and Dedan are mentioned first. They will assume great importance and possibly dominate the commonwealth. If we were to apply this prophecy to our day, we would have to think of Great Britain and the United States. The young lions would be the other countries that have come out of England. They will remain an independent group, never completely subjected to Antichrist.

They will send a note of protest when Antichrist makes plans to invade Palestine. That sounds natural. They will evidently get little satisfaction so the only way they can protect their own interests is to go into Palestine by a different route. The eastern approach will be the only one that Antichrist does not control. The Lord will have "dried up" that part of Antichrist's empire.

"To take a great spoil." This would suggest that the Jews will be comparatively prosperous when the rest of the world is in trouble.

> Therefore, son of man, prophesy and say unto Gog, Thus saith the Lord God; In that day when my people of Israel dwelleth safely, shalt thou not know it?
>
> And thou shalt come from thy place out of the north parts, thou, and many people with thee, all of them riding upon horses, a great company, and a mighty army:
>
> And thou shalt come up against my people of Israel, *as a cloud* to cover the land; it shall be in the latter days, and I will bring

> thee against my land, that the heathen may know me, when I shall be sanctified in thee, O Gog, before their eyes.
>
> Thus saith the Lord God; Art thou he of whom I have spoken in old time by my servants the prophets of Israel, which prophesied in those days many years that I would bring thee against them?—Ezek. 38:14-17

"In the latter days." Again the time is specified. It is a time when God is going to make himself known to all nations by the miraculous destruction of His enemies.

> And it shall come to pass at the same time when Gog shall come against the land of Israel, saith the Lord God, that my fury shall come up in my face.
>
> For in my jealousy and in the fire of my wrath have I spoken, surely in that day there shall be a great shaking in the land of Israel;
>
> So that the fishes of the sea, and the fowls of the heaven, and the beasts of the field, and all creeping things that creep upon the earth, and all the men that are upon the face of the earth, shall shake at my presence, and the mountains shall be thrown down, and the steep places shall fall, and every wall shall fall to the ground.
>
> And I will call for a sword against him throughout all my mountains, saith the Lord God: every man's sword shall be against his brother.
>
> And I will plead against him with pestilence and with blood; and I will rain upon him, and upon his bands, and upon the many people that are with him, an overflowing rain, and great hailstones, fire, and brimstone.
>
> Thus will I magnify myself, and sanctify myself; and I will be known in the eyes of many nations, and they shall know that I am the Lord.—Ezek. 38:18-23
>
> My fury shall come up in my face. He that sitteth in the heavens shall laugh; the Lord shall have them in derision. Then shall he speak unto them in his wrath, and vex them in his sore displeasure.—Ps. 2:4, 5

THE EARTHQUAKE. Earthquakes are frequent all during the last days. "And earthquakes in diverse places."—Matt. 24:7. But the final one is the greatest. It is not an ordinary earthquake which shakes only a small portion of the earth. The final earthquake makes the entire earth reel like a drunkard so that the mountains are moved into the sea. Compare Isa. 24:18-23 and Rev. 16:17-20.

THE HAIL. "And there fell upon men a great hail out of heaven, every stone about the weight of a talent [about 60 lbs.]: and men blasphemed God because of the plague of the hail; for the plague thereof was exceeding great."—Rev. 16:21.

"Every man's sword shall be against his brother." This is a peculiar characteristic of Armageddon. "And I will overthrow the throne of kingdoms, and I will destroy the strength of the heathen [the nations]; and I will overthrow the chariots, and those that ride in them; and the horses and their riders shall come down, every one by the sword of his brother."—Haggai 2:22.

Also Zech. 14:13. Zechariah gives the most details about how the armies will be destroyed (Zech. 14:9-15).

Therefore, thou son of man, prophesy against Gog, and say, Thus saith the Lord God; behold, I am against thee, O Gog, the chief prince of Meshech and Tubal: and I will turn thee back, and leave but the sixth part of thee, and will cause thee to come up from the north parts, and will bring thee upon the mountain of Israel: and I will smite thy bow out of thy left hand, and will cause thine arrows to fall out of thy right hand.

Thous shalt fall upon the mountains of Israel, thou, and all thy bands, and the people that is with thee: I will give thee unto the ravenous birds of every sort, and to the beasts of the field to be devoured. Thou shalt fall upon the open field: for I have spoken it, saith the Lord God. And I will send a fire on Magog, and among them that dwell carelessly in the isles; and they shall know that I am the Lord.

So will I make my holy name known in the midest of my people Israel; and I will not let them pollute my holy name any more: and the heathen shall know that I am the Lord, the Holy One in Israel. Behold, it is come, and it is done, saith the Lord God; this is the day whereof I have spoken.—Ezek. 39:1-8

This is a restatement with added details. "This is the day whereof I have spoken." Again the prophet tells us when this will happen. There is only one such day about which God has spoken. Nearly all the prophets have something to say about it. The earth could not survive two such experiences.

And they that dwell in the cities of Israel shall go forth, and shall set on fire and burn the weapons, both the shields and the bucklers, the bows and the arrows, and the handstaves, and the spears, and they shall burn them with fire seven years:

So that they shall take no wood out of the field, neither cut down any out of the forests; for they shall burn the weapons with fire: and they shall spoil those that spoiled them, and rob those that robbed them, saith the Lord God.

And it shall come to pass in that day, that I will give unto Gog a place there of graves in Israel, the valley of the passengers on the east of the sea: and it shall stop the noses of the passengers: and there shall they bury Gog and all his multitude: and they shall call it The valley of Hamongog.

And seven months shall the house of Israel be burying of them, that they may cleanse the land.

Yea, all the people of the land shall bury them; and it shall be to them a renown the day that I shall be glorified, saith the Lord God.

> And they shall sever out men of continual employment, passing through the land to bury with the passengers those that remain upon the face of the earth, to cleanse it: after the end of seven months shall they search.
>
> And the passengers that pass through the land, when any seeth a man's bone, then shall he set up a sign by it, till the buriers have buried it in the valley of Hamongog.—Ezek. 39:9-15

Mention has been made of horses and chariots; now we find wooden weapons. This does not sound like modern warfare. Why wooden weapons that burn? The seven last plagues, six of which precede the gathering of the armies, are sent to cleanse the earth of the results of sin in preparation for the establishing of the kingdom. They are administered from heaven against predetermined objectives. No armament factories would be left in operation. So, when the whole world is armed at once, they will have to beat their plowshares into swords, and their prunning-hooks into spears. The weak will have to say, "I am strong" (Joel 3:10).

> And, thou son of man, thus saith the Lord God; Speak unto every feathered fowl, and to every beast of the field, Assemble yourselves, and come; gather yourselves on every side to my sacrifice that I do sacrifice for you, even a great sacrifice upon the mountains of Israel, that ye may eat flesh, and drink blood.
>
> Ye shall eat the flesh of the mighty, and drink the blood of the princes of the earth, of rams, of lambs, and of goats, of bullocks, all of them fatlings of Bashan.
>
> And ye shall eat fat till ye be full, and drink blood till ye be drunken, of my sacrifice which I have sacrificed for you.
>
> Thus ye shall be filled at my table with horses and chariots, with mighty men, and with all men of war, saith the Lord God.
>
> And I will set my glory among the heaven, and all the heathen shall see my judgment that I have executed, and my hand that I have laid upon them.—Ezek. 39:17-21

This is exactly parallel to Rev. 19:17-21. There could not be two such experiences, for Jesus said, "For then shall be great tribulation, such as was not since the beginning of the world to this time, no, nor ever shall be."—Matt. 24:21.

This also identifies Gog and Magog. Satan is cast into the bottomless pit and the beast (along with the false prophet) is cast into the lake of fire. They are the leaders of the armies that come against the Lord.

Chapter 8

THE NATIONS

THE GOAL

> And in the days of these kings shall the God of heaven set up a kingdom, which shall never be destroyed: and the kingdom shall not be left to other people, but it shall break in pieces and consume all these kingdoms, and it shall stand for ever.—Dan. 2:44

"And it shall stand forever." This is the goal because it is the final state which does not change. The most often repeated feature of the kingdom that Christ will establish is that it will last forever.

> Of the increase of his government and peace there shall be no end, upon the throne of David, and upon his kingdom, to order it, and to establish it with judgment and with justice from henceforth even for ever. The zeal of the Lord of hosts will perform this—Isa. 9:7. Compare Luke 1:32, 33.

It may be argued that the word "forever" is not used in the original because there was no such word. A literal translation might be, "unto the ages of the ages," and therefore it could have an end. This is taken care of by some such statement as "and of his kingdom there shall be no end" (Luke 1:33).

The kingdom will be established by a process which will take some time. The *process* will come to an end, but the kingdom is everlasting.

> Then cometh the end, when he shall have delivered up the kingdom to God, even the Father; when he shall have put down all rule and all authority and power. For he must reign, till he hath put all enemies under his feet. The last enemy that shall be destroyed is death.—I Cor. 15:24-26

The end, here, is not the end of all creation but the end of the process that establishes the kingdom of God. Christ must reign till He has put down all His enemies. The last enemy to be destroyed is death. The process is not complete till death is destroyed. When death is destroyed there can be no more death; then the kingdom over the whole earth will be everlasting.

> And in the days of these kings shall the God of heaven set up a kingdom, which shall never be destroyed: and the king-

97

dom shall not be left to other people, but it shall break in pieces and consume all these kingdoms, and it shall stand for ever.— Dan. 2:44

"In the days of these kings." When will the kingdom of God be set up? This is not something in the far distant future. It will come while certain nations are still in existence.

Daniel uses Nebuchadnezzar's dream of a great image to predict the course of history. He mentions four great world empires. They turned out to be: the Babylonian, the Persian (Medes and Persians), the Grecian, and the Roman. The Roman was the only one that would not have a successor. Instead, it would be divided into many parts, indicated by the toes of the image.

Daniel made two statements concerning these nations. They would exist right down to the end. They could not be united to form another great European Empire. In a later vision we find that Antichrist will bring them together briefly by their own consent, but Antichrist will never be given the honor of a king. The nations will remain independent.

So, Daniel said: (1) They could not be conquered. (2) They could not be united.

Therefore, these nations that came out of the Roman Empire will remain until the coming of Christ. They represent the end-time nations.

So, the end of the nations as they now are would be the time of the end of the prophecy. World War I did not make any material change. Neither did World War II. Neither will the Common Market. But Armageddon and the coming of Christ will make a change.

This new kingdom that Daniel sees will not be perfected instantly. The stone destroys the image, and then begins to grow. Eventually it covers the earth, but that will take time. The kingdom cannot be perfected instantly. People cannot be changed that fast. In fact, it will take a thousand years to bring total accomplishment. It is one thing to put a King in Jerusalem and proclaim Him to be the King of kings and Lord of lords. It will be another thing to bring the whole world into harmony with His reign.

The kingdom at first is not the reign of Christ over a perfect world; it is the perfect reign of Christ over the world—the world as He finds it.

No sooner will He set up His rule than some nations will make preparations to start another war. They will yield only to superior force. Two references will give you the "feel" of the situation that will exist at the beginning of the kingdom age.

But in the last days it shall come to pass, that the mountain of the house of the Lord shall be established in the top of the mountains, and it shall be exalted above the hills; and people shall flow unto it.

And many nations shall come, and say, Come, and let us go up to the mountain of the Lord, and to the house of the God of Jacob; and he will teach us of his ways, and we will walk in his paths: for the law shall go forth of Zion, and the word of the Lord from Jerusalem.

And he shall judge among many people, and rebuke strong nations afar off; and they shall beat their swords into plowshares, and their spears into pruninghooks: nation shall not lift up a sword against nation, neither shall they learn war any more.

But they shall sit every man under his vine and under his fig tree; and none shall make them afraid: for the mouth of the Lord of hosts hath spoken it. For all people will walk every one in the name of his god, and we will walk in the name of the Lord our God for ever and ever.—Micah 4:1-5

Mountain is a symbol for nation (Dan. 2:35, 44). Other mountains would be other kingdoms or nations. (King or kingdom may be used for a nation without any reference to its form of government.) Hills could be lesser nations.

"All people will walk every one in the name of his god." It will take time to make the worship of God universal over all the earth. Isaiah states the end but not the means to the end: "For the earth shall be full of the knowledge of the Lord, as the waters cover the sea."—Isa. 11:9.

Zechariah also sees the end: "And the Lord shall be king over all the earth: in that day there shall be one Lord, and his name one."—Zech. 14:9.

And it shall come to pass, that every one that is left of all the nations which came against Jerusalem shall even go up from year to year to worship the King, the Lord of hosts, and to keep the feast of tabernacles.

And it shall be, that whoso will not come up of all the families of the earth unto Jerusalem to worship the King, the Lord of hosts, even upon them shall be no rain. And if the family of Egypt go not up, and come not, that have no rain; there shall be the plague, wherewith the Lord will smite the heathen [the nations] that come not up to keep the feast of tabernacles.

In that day shall there be upon the bells of the horses, HOLINESS UNTO THE LORD: and the pots in the Lord's house shall be like the bowls before the altar. Yea, every pot in Jerusalem and in Judah shall be holiness unto the Lord of hosts; and all they that sacrifice shall come and take of them, and seethe therein; and in that day there shall be no more the Canaanite in the house of the Lord of hosts.—Zech. 14:16-21

There were three great yearly feasts: Passover, Pentecost, and Tabernacles. After the kingdom is established, Passover and Pentecost would represent something that had been fulfilled. Any keeping of these feasts would be in the nature of a memorial. But the feast of Tabernacles represented a continuing condition— possession of the land, and, by extension, a perfect world order under Christ. Of course, not all the people of the earth could come to Jerusalem at once, but all nations would have to be officially represented.

A canaanite would be an ungodly person.

All the nations will send armies against Jerusalem to try to prevent the reign of Christ. That is known as the Battle of Armageddon. The battle is fought at Jerusalem, not Armageddon. Armageddon is the place where the armies gather. All those armies will be destroyed. The nations that sent them will have to acknowledge the authority of Christ by officially attending the feast of Tabernacles.

Now we have two lines of thought which may seem to be in conflict.

1. The dominion under the whole heaven shall be given to the people of the saints of the Most High.

2. There will always be nations having rulers and kings.

After the thousand year reign of Christ and the saints, and death is destroyed, we read, "Behold the tabernacle of God is with men, and he shall dwell with them, and they shall be his people, and God himself shall be with them, and be their God. And God shall wipe away all tears from their eyes; and there shall be no more death, neither sorrow, nor crying, neither shall there be any more pain; for the former things are passed away." Even after the Holy City has become the eternal home of the saints. We read: "And the nations of them which are saved shall walk in the light of it; and the kings of the earth do bring their glory and honour into it."—Rev. 21:24.

So, there will always be nations and rulers on the earth. This problem of the relationship of the saints, when solved, will open up new vistas of truth.

Jesus is, at His second coming, King of kings and Lord of lords. There must then be other kings and other lords. Jesus is not called King of saints (except once in Rev. 15:3, which is an inaccurate translation. It should read "King of the ages"). There will be earthly kings even though there is a heavenly dominion.

The Word of God will go forth from Jerusalem, but it will go first to the kings and rulers of the nations. Neither Christ nor the saints will have time for the petty duties of earthly rulers. The dominion of the saints is greater than the earth and continually expanding.

Notice that Dan. 7:27, which tells of the dominion of the saints, also mentions the dominions of the earth which will serve Him.

So, there will always be earthly dominions even after the saints possess the kingdom. The saints will sit with Christ on His throne, but they will not again possess mortal bodies and sit on earthly thrones. That would be somewhat beneath those who have resurrected bodies and whose sphere of operation is the entire created universe, who sit with Christ on His throne and are joint-heirs with Him.

Now that we know what is the end of the matter, we are in a stronger position to discover the means to that end. We know what the nations are like now. We know what they will be like when the plan is complete. The next question is, therefore, how do we get from here to there? How will the nations be brought under control? And what will be the world events that will accomplish the prophesied program?

> And in the days of these kings shall the God of heaven set up a kingdom, which shall never be destroyed: and the kingdom shall not be left to other people, but it shall break in pieces and consume all these kingdoms, and it shall stand for ever.
>
> Forasmuch as thou sawest that the stone was cut out of the mountain without hands, and that it brake in pieces the iron, the brass, the clay, the silver, and the gold; the great God hath made known to the king what shall come to pass hereafter: and the dream is certain, and the interpretation thereof sure.—Dan. 2: 44, 45

God writes history not after it happens but before it happens. This requires a new technique.

It will pay you to stop and think about this. Think of the conditions in the world today, not only here, but in Africa, Russia, China, India, Palestine. Then contrast this with the perfect conditions as seen by the prophets.

What could bring about such a drastic change? If the change is tremendous, then the conditions or events that produce it must be tremendous. Prophecy is the story of how God is going to accomplish the impossible. Extreme changes require extreme measures.

DANIEL 2

In Daniel 2, we have the simplest use of symbols. That makes it a good starting place. A great image, the subject of the king's dream, is used like a cartoonist uses his imagination to express truth by a picture.

1. *The Head of Gold.* The Babylonian Empire. This was in existence at the time. (For maps see Daniel's Second Vision.)

Head of Gold

The Babylonian Empire

2. *The Arms of Silver.* Persia and Media (Cyrus, the Persian, conquered the Medes and out of two nations made one empire). The Empire of the Medes and Persians followed the Babylonian.

3. *The Trunk of Brass.* Greece or the Grecian Empire. That was the empire of Alexander the Great who conquered the Persian Empire.

4. *Legs and Feet of Iron.* The Roman Empire—one leg Asia and the other Europe. The Roman Empire was always so divided. In point of time, the Roman Empire did not follow immediately after the fall of the Grecian. There were some intervening wars, but it was the next world empire. In a treatment as short as this, many unimportant details have to be left out. They may not have seemed unimportant at the time, but they are not essential to the development of the program. This is an important point and should be carefully noted, because it illustrates one feature of the prophetic method. Only world movements are considered—that is, movements that change the course of history.

For instance, World Wars I and II were not really world wars. Only now would it be possible to have a truly world war. After those wars were over, the nations settled down substantially

Arms of Silver

The Persian Empire

as they were before. These wars were not prophetic material.

They did have some results that connect with prophecy. Those results were mostly in Palestine. But "in the days of these kings" something will happen that will change the world drastically. Prophecy will be concerned with that. We are preparing now for the time of those prophecies. They will be so terrific that even the churches will be changed materially.

Note what happens to the toes of the image. Follow the same method of interpretation. Just as the arms and legs represented parts of the empire, so the toes represent parts of the empire after it is divided. The toes are the final state. They represent "kings," Daniel's word for nations. It is in the days of these nations that God will set up His kingdom. The Roman Empire was the last of the world empires before the kingdom comes. It had no successor, as did the others.

That is the point of this prophecy. Babylon had a successor —Persia. Persia had a successor—Greece. Greece had a successor—Rome. But Rome had no successor. It was not conquered. Instead, it was divided. The toes represent the nations into which the Roman Empire was divided. These nations are still with

Trunk of Brass

The Grecian Empire

us and it will be in the days of these nations, while they still exist, that the kingdom of God will be established in the world.

Ten, in prophecy, is a round number, indicating an approximate, or unknown, or changing number. In the end there may be exactly ten nations in Antichrist's federation. Many of the present-day boundaries are artificial.

There are two elements in the toes: iron and clay. Both are explained. Iron represents strength, empire strength. It is the element of which the empire was made. These separate nations will have in them the strength of the iron. They cannot be conquered. They will remain to the end as independent nations. If any other nation tries to absorb them, that nation will eventually go down to defeat, but the Roman Empire nations will remain.

There is also clay in the toes, the only sign of weakness in the entire image.

> And the fourth kingdom shall be strong as iron; forasmuch as iron breaketh in pieces and subdueth all things: and as iron that breaketh all these, shall it break in pieces and bruise. And whereas thou sawest the feet and toes, part of potters' clay and part of iron, the kingdom shall be divided; but there shall be in it of the strength of the iron, forasmuch, as thou sawest the iron mixed with miry clay.

And as the toes of the feet were part of iron, and part of clay, so the kingdom shall be partly strong, and partly broken. And whereas thou sawest iron mixed with miry clay, they shall mingle themselves with the seed of men: but they shall not cleave one to another, even as iron is not mixed with clay.

And in the days of these kings shall the God of heaven set up a kingdom, which shall never be destroyed: and the kingdom shall not be left to other people, but it shall break in pieces and consume all these kingdoms, and it shall stand for ever.—Dan. 2: 40-44

The clay separates the nations so they cannot get together to form a United States of Europe. Even intermarrying will not bring them together. Under Antichrist there is a brief semblance of union. Daniel does not recognize this as an empire. It is never quite stable. Trouble soon breaks out among them. Daniel says Antichrist will not be given the honor of a king (Dan. 11:21).

The World-Wide Aspect of Prophecy

And wheresoever the children of men dwell, the beasts of the field and the fowls of the heaven hath he given into thine hand, and hath made thee ruler over them all. Thou art this head of gold.

And after thee shall arise another kingdom inferior to thee, and another third kingdom of brass, which shall bear rule over all the earth.—Dan. 2:38, 39

Daniel answered and said, Blessed be the name of God for ever and ever: for wisdom and might are his: And he changeth the times and the seasons: he removeth kings and setteth up kings: he giveth wisdom unto the wise, and knowledge to them that know understanding: He revealeth the deep and secret things; he knoweth what is in the darkness, and the light dwelleth with him.—Dan. 2:20-22

"Which shall bear rule over all the earth." This prophecy has a world-wide aspect. It is, first, a prophetic history of Bible lands, and second, a history of the world in type. Here we have an example of the use of both symbols and types. As symbols, they tell the story of four limited world empires, which never covered much of the earth.

As types, these four empires represent all nations, "wheresoever the children of men dwell." All history revolves around the people that came from those countries, especially the Roman Empire. In the end, Babylon will be again the center of religion, commerce, and power which will involve the whole world.

This prophecy is basic. The other visions of Daniel are extensions of certain features of this one. Without this image as our guide, the other visions would be difficult indeed. The visions

Legs and Feet of "Iron"

of Daniel are progressive. Each one adds details not found in the others. The details that are added are mostly concerning the end time. At that time the whole world will be involved. It is that feature that we must now consider.

> Thou sawest till that a stone was cut out without hands, which smote the image upon his feet that were of iron and clay, and brake them to pieces.
>
> Then was the iron, the clay, the brass, the silver, and the gold, broken to pieces together, and became like the chaff of the summer threshingfloors; and the wind carried them away, that no place was found for them: and the stone that smote the image became a great mountain and filled the whole earth.
>
> Forasmuch as thou sawest that the stone was cut out of the mountain without hands, and that it brake in pieces the iron, the brass, the clay, the silver, and the gold; the great God hath made known to the king what shall come to pass hereafter: and the dream is certain, and the interpretation thereof sure.—Dan. 2: 34, 35, 45

When the stone, which represents the kingdom of God, strikes the toes, the entire image crumbles. This seems strange, because when the stone strikes, all there is left of the image are the toes. The gold, silver and brass are gone. They represent empires that have long since disappeared. Yet the image seems to be standing intact when the stone strikes.

So we take it that this image represents, not only the four empires of the past, but also a great world power of the future. The image will stand again; that is, these countries will be revived. The Middle East will again become the center of world power and influence. Antichrist's political power will extend to the limits of these former empires.

This gives us our first glimpse of the extent of Antichrist's dominion.

The Dream Is Certain

Nearly 2500 years have gone by since these words were written. Everything happened just as Daniel said. Daniel himself lived to see the fall of Babylon and the beginning of the Persian Empire. Daniel stood at the beginning of these events and looked ahead. Now we stand near the end and look back and see how certain the dream was.

That is another value of this vision. Because of the fact that it is mostly in the past, we can test our method of interpretation. Now we only have to apply what we have learned about how God writes history to the other visions. That is what makes this a basic prophecy.

Chapter 9

DANIEL'S SECOND VISION

DANIEL 7

On four different occasions Daniel was given revelations concerning the political future of the world. None of these visions are complete in themselves; each omits important details found in the others. The details increase as we approach the end.

Symbols have their limitations. One symbol cannot express all the facts in a series of events. Ten toes might symbolize the nations that grew out of the Roman Empire, but to show what happens to those nations would take different symbols.

The first three empires are treated briefly, merely by way of introduction. The rest of chapter 7 deals with Antichrist, from his rise to his fall.

In chapter 2 Nebuchadnezzar saw the vision, and Daniel told the interpretation. In chapter 7, Daniel saw the vision and the angel told the meaning (Dan. 7:17).

"King" in Daniel means nation or the ruler of a nation. The exact reference can be ascertained from the context. We will follow Daniel's example and pass hurriedly over the events of the past and spend our time, as Daniel does, on the future.

A chart will be the quickest way to get our bearings.

A HARMONY OF CHAPTERS 2 AND 7

Chapter 2		Chapter 7
Head of Gold	BABYLON	Lion—king of beasts
Arms of Silver	PERSIA	Bear—2 sides, 2 ribs
Trunk of Brass	GREECE	Leopard—4 heads
Legs of Iron	ROME	Beast—iron teeth
Ten Toes	NATIONS	Ten Horns
	ANTICHRIST	Little Horn
Stone	KINGDOM OF GOD	Saints Reign

108

THE BABYLONIAN EMPIRE

And four great beasts came up from the sea, diverse one from another. The first was like a lion, and had eagle's wings: I beheld till the wings thereof were plucked, and it was lifted up from the earth, and made stand upon the feet as a man, and a man's heart was given to it.—Dan. 7:3, 4

For a fuller explanation of the lion symbol, read Dan. 4:30-33. The animals have an advantage over the image in that they can express action. Still there is always enough correspondence between them so that we can get our bearings. The chief of metals becomes the king of beasts.

The purpose of the second vision is not to duplicate the first, but to add details, especially toward the time of the end. Jesus used the same method in the 13th chapter of Matthew. There we find seven parables, all about the kingdom. Jesus changed symbols to show new things.

THE PERSIAN EMPIRE

And behold another beast, a second, like to a bear, and it raised up itself on one side, and it had three ribs in the mouth of it between the teeth of it: and they said thus unto it, Arise, devour much flesh.—Dan. 7:5

The bear has two sides. He gets up first on one side, then on the other. The image had two arms which we labeled Media and Persia. They were united in the breast to form one empire. Media was the older. It came up first; then when Persia came the bear was on all fours.

THREE RIBS. The Persian empire extended itself over more territory than the Babylonian. It captured more countries. These are the ribs.

THE GRECIAN EMPIRE

After this I beheld, and lo another, like a leopard, which had upon the back of it four wings of a fowl; the beast had also four heads; and dominion was given to it.—Dan. 7:6

FOUR WINGS. The Grecian Empire extended itself in all directions, taking in still more territory. It had only one emperor, Alexander the Great. When he died, his empire was divided into four parts—toward the four winds of heaven (Dan. 8:8).

THE ROMAN EMPIRE

After this I saw in the night visions, and behold a fourth beast, dreadful and terrible, and strong exceedingly; and it had great iron teeth: it devoured and brake in pieces, and stamped the

Empire

Dan.

Daniel uses four symbols to indicate the four world empires. Revelation uses the same symbols to indicate the territory that will be involved in the kingdom of the Beast (Rev. 13:1-2). Daniel says, "As concerning the rest of the beasts, they had their dominion taken away: yet their lives were prolonged for a season and time." This would indi-

ntichrist

13:1-3

cate that the four world empires would pass out of existence but not forever. Of course, they could not exist again to the same extent that they did formerly, because their territories overlapped. This map represents prophetic lands where the great final action will take place.

residue with the feet of it: and it was diverse from all the beasts
that were before it; and it had ten horns.—Dan. 7:7

The fourth beast is not named but is called simply a beast.
It corresponds to the legs of iron and represents the fourth world
empire, the Roman. Iron is again mentioned as characteristic of
this empire. It was the Roman Empire that scattered the Jews
after the fall of Jerusalem in A.D. 70 and persecuted the Christians for hundreds of years.

THE NATIONS

I considered the horns, and, behold, there came up among them
another little horn, before whom there were three of the first horns
plucked up by the roots: and, behold, in this horn were eyes like
the eyes of man, and a mouth speaking great things.—Dan. 7:8

The ten toes and the ten horns represent the nations of
the Roman world that will be in power when Antichrist rises.
That is where most of the action takes place. Those nations hold
the key to the future. That is where to look for any action that
starts the fulfillment of prophecy. Daniel says, "I considered
the horns." Daniel watched the horns. He knew that it was among
the horns that the action would start. Unless they become involved with prophetic lands, Russia, China, and Africa are relatively unimportant. Like Daniel, we must watch the horns.

ANTICHRIST

Antichrist is not mentioned in chapter 2. Here is where we
get the new information. Now the action starts, made possible
by the new symbols. From now on details multiply. Daniel asks
questions. He knows what questions to ask—the very ones you
would ask if you had a chance. From here on we are dealing
not with symbols but with the explanation of the symbols.

THE KINGDOM OF GOD

And he shall speak great words against the most High, and shall
wear out the saints of the most High, and think to change times
and laws: and they shall be given into his hand until a time and
times and the dividing of time. But the judgment shall sit, and
they shall take away his dominion, to consume and to destroy it
unto the end.
    And the kingdom and dominion, and the greatness of the kingdom under the whole heaven, shall be given to the people of the
saints of the most High, whose kingdom is an everlasting kingdom,
and all dominions shall serve and obey him.—Dan. 7:25-27

This is the final phase of both visions. The kingdom here

is not the kingdom of David. That is everlasting also, but it is limited to a strip from the River of Egypt on the south to the Euphrates on the north. The kingdom of David is one of the dominions of the earth. The saints will reign with Christ over all dominions. The kingdom of God is unlimited as to time and extent. "Of the increase of his kingdom and peace there shall be no end."

There is only limited value in trying to draw a picture of a hideous beast with horns coming out of its head. We have something better than a picture of the symbol. We have a picture of the fulfillment. Daniel considered the horns. We follow his example when we study a map of what the horns stood for. Daniel was not interested in any movement among the horns that left them intact, as all wars to date have done. A few border lines may have changed, but the nations are still there.

ANTICHRIST'S ORIGIN

"There came up among them another little horn." The symbol can represent both the nation and the man (dictator). It starts with a nation and ends with a man. The man becomes more important than the nation because he takes over many nations. The man must have a country. He is, after all, a dictator. Primarily, the horns are nations. Another horn would be another nation.

This horn is called little. It is little at the start, but Daniel later says, "Whose look was more stout than his fellows."

Note that it does not say that one of the ten horns became more stout than its fellows. The little horn is not one of the original ten (as Italy, for instance), but *another one;* still it is among them, or, as in the margin, between them. This puts some limitations on the place that Antichrist can come from. The little horn represents a comparatively new country, one that comes up near the time of the end. It is not an old country like Syria.

Eyes, Mouth

In this horn were eyes like the eyes of man, and a mouth speaking great things (Dan. 7:20). From this point on we are dealing with a man. The country is no longer important, for he takes over many countries. It is not uncommon for a symbol to be used as the name of a man. (For instance, a lamb was a symbol of Christ, but the symbol became the name when He was called the Lamb of God.)

Now the little horn becomes the name of a man. "I beheld then because of the voice of the great words which the horn spake." Revelation also mentions this feature. "And there was given unto him a mouth speaking great things."—Rev. 13:5.

If we think of the eyes in the same way, then they too are a characteristic of the man, an identifying mark. Eyes speak of unusual intelligence or knowledge. In this case there is something supernatural about them. Satan's cunning shines through them. In the next vision this is explained further.

> And in the latter time of their kingdom, when the transgressors are come to the full, a king of fierce countenance, and understanding dark sentences, shall stand up."—Dan. 8:23

It is probably this feature that captivates the world. It will be almost impossible to resist those eyes. When the world is in a state of hopelessness and terror with no way out, here is a man who seems to know exactly what to do and how to do it. Of course it will be wrong, but it will seem right at the time. Even church leaders will get enthusiastic over him. Everybody will be deceived—except those who recognize him for what he is. The only ones who can do that are the ones who know the prophecy. That is what prophecy is for.

He will speak great things and he will do great things. Is the world paralyzed with terror? He will destroy the cause of the terror. Is Communism threatening the safety of the world? He will put an end to Communism. Never again will Russia be a great power.

Are the nations in a state of depression? He will form a world-wide common market and revive commerce and trade on a scale never dreamed of before, enriching all peoples (Rev. 18). In the temptation, Christ forced Satan to reveal his overall strategy (Matt. 4:1-11).

1. *An appeal to the physical*

"Command these stones to be made bread." Satan will promise the world prosperity, even luxury. All politicians know the value of that appeal. That is how they win elections. The man that dares promise the most usually gets the most votes. The world will fall hard for Antichrist's promise of prosperity.

2. *An appeal to man's religious nature*

"Then the devil taketh him up into the holy city, and setteth him on a pinnacle of the temple." Antichrist will have a religion and a great world church. Revelation uses a whole chapter to reveal it. Even now we can see a tendency for all religions to get together. Satan may be able to unite them. Antichrist will be a very "religious" man, but his religion will center in himself. This fact may not be too apparent at the start. We are dealing with the greatest deceiver of all time.

3. *The desire for power*

"Again, the devil taketh him up into an exceeding high mountain, and showeth him all the kingdoms of the world and the glory of them." Power corrupts men. Satan's princes will have more power than most independent rulers.

Prosperity, piety, power. This sums up Antichrist's strategy. Of these the most effective is prosperity. That may be why so much space is given to it in the Bible.

"Before whom were three of the first horns plucked up by the roots." This is explained in verse 24. "He shall subdue three kings." He will conquer three countries.

If Antichrist appears as the savior of the world, it would not be necessary for him to conquer free countries; they would naturally cooperate, especially if their prosperity depended upon it. Any government that turned down what Antichrist has to offer would fall immediately.

Military campaigns outside the Roman Empire would not be in view here, so we do not know what may happen in Russia, China or the United States. But within the boundaries of the Roman Empire there are now three countries which do not have the power of self-determination. They belong to a foreign power. They are Hungary, Rumania and Bulgaria. Many changes may come before that time, but as of now these three countries would have to be pulled up by the roots. This would probably involve defeating Russia.

Communism is no good to Antichrist. He will not be controlled by a party. He is not an atheist. He will believe in a god. At the start he will be supported by many churches and church leaders. Only gradually will he replace God. If Antichrist will show himself as god, the people must believe in a god (II Thess. 2:4).

> I beheld till thrones were cast down, and the Ancient of days did sit, whose garment was white as snow, and the hair of his head like pure wool: his throne was like the fiery flame, and his wheels as burning fire.
>
> A fiery stream issued and came "forth before him: thousand thousands ministered unto him, and ten thousand times ten thousand stood before him: the judgment was set and the books were opened.—Dan. 7:9, 10

Here we have a principle of interpretation. A break is made in the narrative to show something happening in heaven at the same time. If you leave out verses 9 and 10, there is no break in the continuity. The scene in heaven corresponds with Rev. 4, which happens immediately after the Rapture.

The scene shifts back to heaven again in verses 13, 14. This time Revelation 5 is in view. Something is happening in heaven at the same time that these things are happening on the earth. Such action in heaven can come only after the saints get there, because they are the actors. So, verse 9 indicates the time of the Rapture.

After the Rapture, Satan will never go unchallenged. The horn will speak great words, but God will have an answer. This is the day of the Lord. God will answer with judgment and fire.

> As concerning the rest of the beasts, they had their dominion taken away: yet their lives were prolonged for a season and time.—Dan. 7:12

The rest of the beasts would be the lion, bear and leopard—that is, the former world empires. As empires, they have already gone out of existence, but they have remained as separate peoples. In time, these three old empires will be restored, somewhat smaller in extent, because their territory overlapped. Revelation mentions all four in connection with the rise of Antichrist. Their dominion was taken away, but they still exist and will again be the center of world power. They will be a part of Antichrist's kingdom.

As a man, Antichrist will never conquer the whole world; but as Satan his influence will be universal.

Chapter 10

ANTICHRIST

The reason for Antichrist is simple: Whoever holds dominion must occupy. When the atom bomb was made the basis of our military might, the question arose: Why do we need an army? The answer is: You may conquer a country with atomic power, but to hold it you must occupy it.

The same is true of the earth. Spiritual power is not enough; you have to have manpower. Satan is a spirit and as such has great power; he seems to be always victorious. But there is a threat to his world program. This threat is contained in a promise and prophecy concerning God's Son: "Ask of me, and I will give thee the nations for thine inheritance, and the uttermost parts of the earth for thy possession."

There is only one way Satan can meet this threat of physical occupancy and that is to match it with a man of his own. Satan needs a man, a man to whom he can give the nations. Of this man, Revelation says,

"The dragon gave him his power and his throne and great authority." Satan must have a man who can muster the nations of all the world against the Lord.

Antichrist is Satan's answer to Christ. While Christ remains in heaven—at the right hand of God—Satan is comparatively secure in his position as the prince of this world. As long as people are being born faster than they are being saved, it may be said that Satan is doing very well in his battle for the complete possession of the earth.

But signs of the coming of Christ to set up His own worldwide reign would certainly cause a great stir among Satan's principalities and powers. The earth has seen many a crisis, but nothing to be compared with an all-out war between two great spirit forces for the dominion of the earth.

Here we have the reason for such astonishing statements as:

> And there was war in heaven: Michael and his angels fought against the dragon; and the dragon fought and his angels, and prevailed not: neither was their place found any more in heaven. And the great dragon was cast out, that old serpent, called the Devil, and Satan, which deceiveth the whole world: he was cast out into the earth, and his angels were cast out with him.
> —Rev. 12:7-9

> And I stood upon the sand of the sea, and saw a beast rise up out of the sea, having seven heads and ten horns and upon his horns ten crowns, and upon his heads the name of blasphemy. And the beast which I saw was like unto a leopard, and his feet were as the feet of a bear, and his mouth as the mouth of a lion: and the dragon gave him his power, and his seat [throne] and great authority.—Rev. 13:1, 2

There is a plain reference here to Daniel's vision of four world empires. There seems to be some confusion in our thinking about this man. Nearly all the difficulties are bound up in one fact: Antichrist is a man and also Satan. It might be more accurate to say that the man becomes Satan. This happens when Satan, by means of a death and resurrection, takes on this man's body. Yet they remain two separate individuals—this is the mystery.

Daniel sees only the man, but in Revelation, Antichrist is a part of the satanic trinity: dragon, beast and false prophet. The dragon and beast are two different individuals, yet they look almost alike. There is only one difference: The dragon has crowns on his heads, the beast has crowns on his horns.

> And I saw three unclean spirits like frogs come out of the mouth of the dragon, and out of the mouth of the beast, and out of the mouth of the false prophet. For they are the spirits of devils, working miracles, which go forth unto the kings of the earth and of the whole world, to gather them to the battle of that great day of God Almighty.—Rev. 16:13, 14

This is the goal of this prophecy, the great Battle of Armageddon, when the power of Antichrist is broken and Satan is cast into the bottomless pit for one thousand years. This event marks the end of Daniel's visions because that is when the kingdoms of this world become the kingdom of Christ and the saints.

Revelation deals with the saints. The end for Antichrist and his nations is not the end for the saints, so Revelation carries the story much farther into the future. The "end" in Revelation is a thousand years after the "end" in Daniel.

> And then shall that Wicked [One] be revealed, whom the Lord shall consume with the spirit of his mouth, and shall destroy with the brightness of his coming: even him, whose coming is after the working of Satan with all power and signs and lying wonders, and with all deceivableness of unrighteousness in them that perish; because they received not the love of the truth, that they might be saved.
>
> And for this cause God shall send them strong delusion, that they should believe a lie: that they all might be damned who believed not the truth, but had pleasure in unrighteousness.—II Thess. 2:8-12

Revelation tells about Antichrist and the Tribulation Saints. Paul tells about Antichrist and the church before the Rapture. Antichrist will not be "revealed" as Satan till the Rapture; but he will come as a man and deceive the world before the Rapture. Many church members have the truth, but they do not have a love of the truth and therefore are easily deceived.

Deceit is the outstanding feature of the rise of Antichrist. When the disciples asked Jesus, "What shall be the sign?" the first thing He said was, "See that ye be not deceived."

Paul said his coming would be with all deceivableness of unrighteousness. Revelation speaks of Satan "which deceiveth the whole world." There is only one way to avoid being deceived; that is to know and love the truth. You will not be deceived if you know what to expect.

The term Antichrist is found only in I and II John. There it is anyone who denies Christ. His name is not revealed, so each Bible writer has his own name for him.

The Little Horn (Dan. 7:8; 8:9)
A Vile Person (Dan. 11:21)
The Assyrian (Isa. 10:5)
The Chaldean (Hab. 1:6)
Gog and Magog (Ezek. 38)
The Man of Sin (II Thess. 2:3)
The Beast out of the sea (Rev. 13:1)

Here is the man who completely represents Satan. From the time of his rise, all earthly doings revolve around him. He will continue to grow in power and arrogance till Christ comes. His destruction is the climax of Daniel's prophecies. He is the fulfillment of Satan's two compelling ambitions: to be the prince of this world and to be the god of this world—to rule and to be worshipped. Daniel makes two statements about world conditions at the time that Antichrist makes his appearance.

And in the latter time of their kingdom when the transgressors are come to the full, a king of fierce countenance, and understanding dark sentences, shall stand up. And his power shall be mighty, but not by his own power: and he shall destroy wonderfully, and shall prosper, and practise, and shall destroy the mighty and the holy people.—Dan. 8:23, 24

1. "When the transgressors are come to the full." Jesus referred to this particular time as the harvest (Matt. 13:20). The harvest is the end of the growing season. The judgment will be a harvest. God will judge only a finished work. He will allow evil to come to a harvest. The time of trouble such as never was will be due to a time of evil such as never was; but everything will be in its order. Daniel's reference to transgression is not to moral conditions (which may be bad enough) but to

the spread of bad government. Those who are attempting to enslave the world and who use violence, lies, confiscation of property and rigged courts will reach the utmost limit of their potential.

2. "He shall destroy wonderfully." This could be rendered: "He shall destroy wonderful things." When nations have acquired the ability to destroy the earth and are reaching for the stars, to conquer them would involve the destruction of wonderful things. How much more wonderful things could you get? We are dealing with the ultimate.

The prophet Habukkuk has more to say about the conditions at the time of the rise of Antichrist. He is so important that his destruction is thought of as synonymous with the establishing of the kingdom. Daniel has four visions running parallel. They do not all begin with the same event, but they all end with the destruction of Antichrist or the establishing of the kingdom or both.

THE NATIONS

In the first one, the ten toes of the image represent the nations dominated by Antichrist. The stone cut out without hands destroys the toes of the image. Then the stone becomes a great mountain and covers the earth. This is explained in these words:

> In the days of these kings shall the God of heaven set up a kingdom, which shall never be destroyed: and the kingdom shall not be left to other people, but it shall break in pieces and consume all these kingdoms, and it shall stand forever.—Dan. 2:44

Here the destruction of Antichrist's dominion and the setting up of the kingdom of God are considered as one event. Antichrist himself is not seen in this vision, but the visions are progressive. What is omitted in one is included in the next.

In the next vision (Daniel 7) the symbols are changed, but the theme is the same. The four great empires of history are reviewed in brief, but most of the vision concerns the last days of the age when Antichrist appears. The vision looks forward to the time that "the judgment shall sit, and they shall take away his [Antichrist's] dominion, to consume and to destroy it unto the end."—Dan. 7:26.

> The kingdom and dominion, and the greatness of the kingdom under the whole heaven, shall be given to the people of the saints of the most high, whose kingdom is an everlasting kingdom, and all dominions shall serve and obey him.—Dan. 7:27

Here again, the destruction of one and the setting up of the other are considered as one event. This being true, the coming of the kingdom awaits the coming of Antichrist. This raises Antichrist to a place of tremendous importance in prophecy. All the prophets treat him in this light.

In the third vision, the prophecy starts at a different time but it ends in the same place. In this vision the kingdom does not appear, but the contemporaneous event, the destruction of Antichrist, does; and cross reference is made to the first vision at the place where it mentions the kingdom. The stone was cut out without hand and became a great mountain and filled the whole earth.

The third vision says "He [Antichrist] will be broken WITHOUT HAND."—Dan. 8:25.

The whole verse reads: "And through his policy also he shall cause craft to prosper in his hand; and he shall magnify himself in his heart, and by peace shall destroy many: he shall also stand up against the Prince of princes: but he shall be broken without hand."

Here the setting up of the kingdom is not mentioned, but it is implied. "He shall stand up against the Prince of princes." When Christ comes to set up His kingdom He will be the King of kings and the Lord of lords. It is at His second coming that Christ meets Antichrist in the Battle of Armageddon and it is because of His victory there that He establishes His kingdom.

This fact is referred to in the fourth vision. There the kingdom is not mentioned directly but, again, it is implied. The scene is the glorious holy mountain where the kingdom is to be established. "For the law shall go forth of Zion, and the word of the Lord from Jerusalem."—Micah 4:2.

> And he shall plant the tabernacles of his palace between the seas in the glorious holy mountain; yet he shall come to his end, and none shall help him.—Dan. 11:45

The establishing of the kingdom, therefore, is dependent on the rise and reign of Antichrist. This is one reason for the important place Antichrist has in the prophecies of the last days.

THE JEWS

The return of the Jews is a prelude to the everlasting kingdom of David.

> Thus saith the Lord God, Behold, I will take the children of Israel from among the heathen, whither they be gone, and will gather them on every side, and bring them into their own land: and I will make them one nation in the land upon the mountains of Israel: and one king shall be king to them all.—Ezek. 37:21, 22

This situation comes as a result of a great battle. The nations assembled against Israel under the leadership of Gog (Satan) and Magog (Antichrist) are suddenly and miraculously destroyed.

CHRONOLOGICAL HARMONY
The Church, The Nations, And The Jews

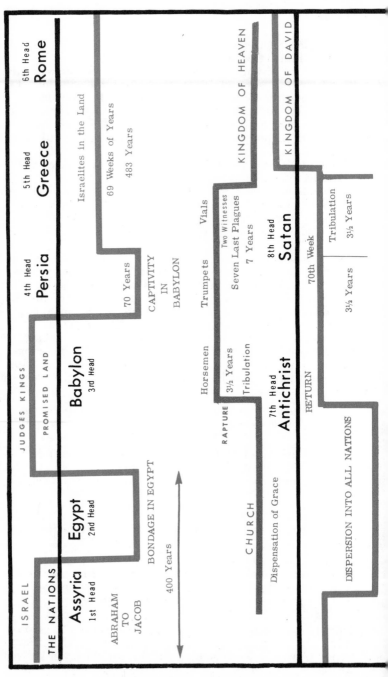

Ezekiel gives the results of the battle as follows:

> And thou, son of man, thus saith the Lord God; Speak unto every feathered fowl, and to every beast of the field, Assemble yourselves and come; gather yourselves on every side to my sacrifice that I do sacrifice for you, even a great sacrifice upon the mountains of Israel, that ye may eat flesh, and drink blood. . . . Ye shall eat fat till ye be full, and drink blood till ye be drunken, of my sacrifice which I have sacrificed for you. . . . And I will set my glory among the heathen [Gentile nations], and all the heathen shall see my judgment that I have executed, and my hand that I have laid upon them. So the house of Israel shall know that I am the Lord their God from that day forward. . . . Then shall they know that I am the Lord their God, which caused them to be led into captivity among the heathen: but I have gathered them into their own land, and have left none of them any more there. Neither will I hide my face any more from them: for I have poured out my spirit upon the house of Israel, saith the Lord God. —Ezek. 39:17-29

So, the redemption of Israel and the destruction of Antichrist and his forces are also synonymous terms.

THE CHURCH

In Revelation the defeat of Antichrist is the prelude to the kingdom. John saw the resurrected saints reign with Christ, but that was only after Satan had been chained. This, in turn, is the direct result of his defeat at the so-called Battle of Armageddon.

The wording of Revelation is very similar to that of Daniel and Ezekiel. The difference is that Daniel is talking about the future of the nations, Ezekiel the future of the Jews, and Revelation the future of the church.

> And I saw an angel standing in the sun; and he cried with a loud voice, saying to all the fowls that fly in the midst of heaven, Come and gather yourselves together unto the supper of the great God. That ye may eat the flesh of kings, and the flesh of captains, and the flesh of mighty men, and the flesh of horses, and of them that sit on them, and the flesh of all men, both free and bond, both small and great.
>
> And I saw the beast [Antichrist], and the kings of the earth, and their armies gathered together to make war against him that sat on the horse and against his army.—Rev. 19:17-19

This scene in Revelation comes after the coming of Christ (chap. 19:11) and before the kingdom (chap. 20). So the three events—the coming of Christ, the defeat of Antichrist and the setting up of the kingdom—come so close together that they may be considered as one event.

In the Olivet Discourse Jesus is answering the question:

"What shall be the sign of thy coming?" There are two main signs. The first is the persecution of the Tribulation Saints, which according to Revelation is the work of Antichrist (Rev. 12, 13).

The second is the abomination of desolation standing in the holy place. This, according to Daniel and Paul, is the presence of Antichrist in the temple.

> And he shall confirm the covenant with many for one week: and in the midst of the week he shall cause the sacrifice and the oblation to cease, and for the overspreading of abominations he shall make it desolate, even unto the consummation, and that determined shall be poured upon the desolate.—Dan. 9:27
>
> Who opposeth and exalteth himself above all that is called God, or that is worshipped; so that he as God sitteth in the temple of God shewing himself that he is God.—II Thess. 2:4

These things are a prelude to the coming of Christ. Even the Rapture (our gathering together unto Him—II Thess. 2:1) awaits the coming of Antichrist. So, where there is prophecy, there is Antichrist. He connects with the future of the nations, the Jews and the church.

THE MEANING OF "ANTICHRIST"

The word "Antichrist" is found only in I and II John. There he is anyone who denies Christ, but John recognizes that there is to be an individual coming in the last days who will oppose Christ and will, therefore, be Antichrist. We have taken a name out of John and applied it to a man who, in prophecy, is called by other names. Each writer has his own name for him: the little horn, the vile person, the Assyrian, the Chaldean, Gog and Magog, the man of sin, the son of perdition, the beast.

Some of these are names, some are symbols, but sometimes the symbol becomes a name. The prefix "anti" may also have the meaning of 'similar to' as in antitype, but in John it means 'against.' The little horn will stand up against the Prince of princes. The beast will "open his mouth in blasphemy against God, to blaspheme his name, and his tabernacle, and them that dwell therein. And it was given unto him to make war with the saints."—Rev. 13:6, 7.

There is no prophecy that intimates that Antichrist will be like Christ, or that he claims to be Christ, or that the world will worship him because they think he is Christ. Christ they would crucify; Satan they will worship. "And they worshipped the dragon that gave power unto the beast."—Rev. 13:4.

There is no Scriptural support to the theory that the Jews will accept Antichrist because they think he is Christ, or for any other reason. The Jews will return and possess their land, not with Antichrist's help, but in spite of him. Antichrist will always be against the Jews. He confirms the covenant only to bring them under his power. The deal lasts only three and a half years.

The use of many names for Antichrist may have significance. His actual identity seems to be somewhat of a mystery. "Here is wisdom. Let him that hath understanding count the number of the beast: for it is the number of a man; and his number is Six hundred, threescore and six."—Rev. 13:18.

"For it is the number of a man" means his number indicates a certain man. He will deceive the world on a grand scale. Only those with Scriptural understanding will recognize him for what he is. There is a mystery connected with his rise. "Whose coming is after the working of Satan with all power and signs and lying wonders."—II Thess. 2:9.

This will be Satan's masterpiece of deceit and is probably what is meant by Rev. 12:9: "And the great dragon was cast out, that old serpent, called the Devil and Satan, which deceiveth the whole world."

Although we do not know Antichrist's name, we know many things about him. Special note is made of his eyes, his big mouth and his fierce countenance. We have already mentioned his attitude toward God, Christ, the saints, and the Jews. There may be some differences here, because there will be a radical change at the Rapture. If Antichrist is to deceive the whole world, he will have to come as the savior of the world. This may be the secret of his immediate success. The only reason given as to why the world will worship him is his ability to make war. "And they worshipped the beast saying, Who is like unto the beast, and who is able to make war with him?"—Rev. 13:4.

THE LITTLE HORN

The prophets have only a little to say about a new world empire. The idea of a revival of the Roman Empire is a conclusion drawn from an interpretation, rather than from direct and positive statements. The positive statements are made primarily concerning a man. The point that we should recognize now is that the new order, when it comes, will be the possession of one man and will assume more or less his own character.

This man will be a conqueror. He will therefore have a realm over which he reigns, a realm which he has mastered by the force of arms and by craft. We know he will have a kingdom because we are told that the Devil gave him his throne and power and great authority. Other prophecies indicate the limits of this empire; but in all of them it is the man, more than the empire, that is in view. The fact is, the physical limits of the empire are not of so great significance as its economic and religious ramifications. We are beginning to realize today how small a country, in a political sense, may dominate the world in an economic and religious sense.

The final actual area controlled by Antichrist may not be large as compared to the whole earth. Yet, when that portion of the earth passes into the personal hands of Satan, who holds spiritual sway over the whole earth, the impact upon all countries will be tremendous. In fact, so much so that the whole world—that is, people in all parts of the world—will be induced to worship Antichrist and receive his mark.

Rapture a Dividing Point

In thinking of the rise and exploits of this man of prophecy, we should separate the events before the Rapture from those weird and satanic operations in the final days of man's dominion over the earth. The special significane of the Rapture in this connection is not that it removes some people from the earth, but that the devil and his angels will then be cast out of heaven down to the earth, "having great wrath, because he knoweth that he hath but a short time."

It is then that the man of sin is "revealed." Then the world will experience the personal reign of Satan. Satan is the prince of this world and his reign, even though over a limited empire, politically speaking, will involve the whole earth. When Satan takes over in person, he will not set up an empire or a new order; he will take over one already formed. Therefore the forming of this new order will come before the revelation of Satan.

It is at this point that the name "Antichrist" takes on a double meaning. If we think of Antichrist as Satan in the flesh, then Antichrist will not be revealed until after the Rapture. But if we think of Antichrist as the little horn of Daniel who rises from a small beginning and by a process of conquering and power politics builds for himself a kingdom covering the territory of the former world empires, then we may look for him to arrive any time.

There is coming a time when this man also becomes Satan. He may, therefore, be said to die and be raised. He may be thought of as a different individual because he is now Satan in the flesh; or he may be thought of as the same man because he will retain his own personality, apart from that of Satan. When Christ comes again he will take the beast and the false prophet and cast them into the lake of fire; but Satan will be chained and cast into the bottomless pit. They are separate personalities. This is as mysterious as the Trinity of God and somewhat parallel to it; at least it is a counterfeit of it.

If Satan is to reign in person he must have a body. He cannot create one. Of Christ it was said: "A body hast thou prepared me." No body will be prepared for Satan. It will not be by birth that he will come into the world. He will have to make a deal with some man. The bribe will be the kingdoms of the earth. The price will be the man's body. Satan will possess it. It will appear to be a death, with Satan seeming to duplicate the resurrection that has just taken place on a large scale.

This will all take place immediately after the Rapture. But the man must be here before the Rapture. He will not have as much power, but he will be able to establish himself as a world figure and he will gain control of those nations which Satan gives him.

At the start it is the man, not the empire, that is the important thing. Satan is not particularly interested in an empire; he is the prince of this world anyway. But he is interested in a man whom he can deal with, a man whom he can possess, a man who will take on his character.

The new order will be a man who will arrange the kingdoms of his realm to suit himself and appoint their kings. The important thing is the man. The empire follows the man. Therefore, it is not the revival of an empire that we should look for, but the arrival of a man whose character, motives, methods and attitudes are after the manner of Satan.

There is no prophecy that states or remotely suggests that the Roman Empire is to be revived by the expansion of Italy. There is no prophecy that says the Roman Empire will be revived at all as it was at some given date.

Satan Has No Co-Workers

If Satan were going to establish himself on the earth in a new and more real way, a world war would be most in keeping with his nature. The reign of Satan over the whole earth will not bring peace, but war and strife. Thus it will be during most of the reign of Antichrist: war and rumors of war, the sea and the waves roaring.

Of course Satan can, for his own evil purpose, produce a false peace and a false sense of security. He is a great deceiver. It is when people cry peace and safety that great destruction will come upon them.

Chapter 11

THE PROPHECY OF HABAKKUK

Habakkuk tells us nothing about himself. We do not know who his parents were, where he lived or when. We do know that he was a bold and great prophet as well as an eloquent poet. His writings show us that.

> I will stand upon my watch, and set me upon the tower, and will watch to see what he will say unto me, and what I shall answer when I am reproved.—Hab. 2:1

The Lord had shown Habakkuk a vision of the last days, beginning at a time just before the rise of Antichrist and extending into the time of tribulation. It is this feature that makes Habakkuk unusually interesting now. He is the one prophet that saw in some detail the conditions that prevail before Antichrist comes and, therefore, could be the cause of his rise.

However, Habakkuk did not like what he saw and tried to change it. He thought such things were too terrible for a merciful God to allow, and he tried to do something about it. He made a formal complaint before God, arguing that some modification should be made in the interest of God's own integrity.

Then Habakkuk said: "I will stand upon my watch, and set me upon the tower, and watch and see what he will answer to my complaint." (That is the meaning.)

The Lord answered him, but the answer was not what Habakkuk expected.

> And the Lord answered me, and said, Write the vision, and make it plain upon tables, that he may run that readeth it.
> For the vision is yet for an appointed time, but at the end it shall speak, and not lie: though it tarry, wait for it; because it will surely come, it will not tarry.—Hab. 2:2, 3

"Write the message and make it plain." Few prophecies in the Bible are so strongly emphasized. Habakkuk has a special place in the time of the end. His book contains vital information found nowhere else. Instead of beginning his prophecy at the time of the appearance of Antichrist, as the others do, Habakkuk starts BEFORE the rise of Antichrist.

Prophecy has a special place in the program of God. It is God's prepared weapon against Satan in the day of Satan's power. No miracle in the Bible is as sensational as prophecy when it is being fulfilled. All of Satan's power and signs and lying wonders will but serve to enforce God's claims when they are fulfilling His Word.

God has no other way. He has staked everything on His revealed Word. But to make His plan work, God must have messengers. They must be instructed before they can instruct others.

"That he may run that readeth it." To run is to proclaim a message. In those days there were no means of communication except by word of mouth. The king sent messengers, or runners, to inform the people of his wishes, "And behold the angel that talked with me went forth, and another angel went out to meet him; and he said unto him, Run."—Zech. 2:3, 4.

Daniel saw this situation, the time when prophecy would be unsealed, because its time has come. "Many shall run to and fro and knowledge shall be increased." Merely running does not increase knowledge. Those who run must have a message. They must teach.

Knowledge will be increased because the Bible will be opened up as never before. God has kept in reserve a vast storehouse of information so vital that it will shake the world, even in the face of Antichrist. But knowledge is not increased automatically. It takes teachers. Somebody has to proclaim it. Many will run.

Habakkuk has the message that will speed the messengers forth. This is the first detailed prophecy to be fulfilled. It will start the ball rolling.

"For the vision is yet for an appointed time." But in the end, that is, in the end time, it shall speak. This prophecy is written especially for a certain time. It will not take its place in God's plan till that time comes. Then watch out! for it will shake the church as well as the world. If it seems to tarry, watch, for it will come on time.

What is this vision that will be so important in the time of fulfillment? The first two chapters of Habakkuk have only one subject: Antichrist.

> Behold, his soul which is lifted up is not upright in him: but the just shall live by his faith. Yea also, because he transgresseth by wine, he is a proud man, neither keepeth at home, who enlargeth his desire as hell, and is as death, and cannot be satisfied, but gathereth unto him all nations, and heapeth unto him all the people.—Hab. 2:4, 5

"He is a proud man." Habakkuk uses no symbols. The book is a poem and at times a certain poetic license is used, such as, "Thou didst ride upon thine horses and thy chariots of salvation."—Hab. 3:8.

Habakkuk does not repeat word for word what the other prophets have said, but he says the same things in his own words, sometimes adding details not found elsewhere. He starts with world conditions, goes from there to the rise of a particular nation, and ends with a man. The man becomes the central figure. In this respect he is like the other prophets.

"Neither keepeth he at home." This is explained by the rest of the verse. It does not mean that he goes out nights; it means that he is not content to be the dictator of only one country. He is ambitious. He wants to rule all countries. He raises an army and starts out. It may not take much of an army at the start, because he will have satanic power and possibly help from sources not visible now.

Twice, Germany has tried to become a world power, and other nations would try if they had any promise of success. Antichrist will succeed, because among other things, he will seem to be a savior of the world.

Now we will turn to the first chapter and take it from the beginning.

> The burden which Habakkuk the prophet did see. O Lord, how long shall I cry, and thou wilt not hear! even cry out unto thee of violence, and thou wilt not save! Why dost thou shew me iniquity, and cause me to behold grievance? for spoiling and violence are before me: and there are that raise up strife and contention.
>
> Therefore the law is slacked, and judgment doth never go forth: for the wicked doth compass about the righteous; therefore wrong judgment proceedeth.—Hab. 1:1-4

Habakkuk here describes what he saw that caused him so much concern. At first it was not a man nor even a country, but a condition, a situation or a system, that was spreading itself over the world causing great misery. Notice the words Habakkuk uses to describe this new kind of conquest.

Violence, iniquity, grievance, spoiling, strife, contention—these are the very words you would use to describe Communism. It started with violence and it uses riots, strikes, uprisings, plots, murders, in fact, every known means of undermining legitimate governments.

That is the first phase of their cold war. The next phase is the confiscation of property. The people are robbed (spoiled) of their holdings, put through rigged court trials, and sent to concentration camps. Their accusers are their judges so there is no such thing as a fair trial. It would be difficult to put into words, even today, a more accurate or concise statement of what happens when the Communist gangsters take over a country. It has happened over and over again and is still going on.

The law is slacked, judgment never goes forth, the wicked compass about the righteous, and wrong judgment, or complete injustice, prevails.

This has happened in so many places that we have lost all count. Whole countries, once happy and prosperous, are lost behind the Iron Curtain. Habakkuk saw this situation spreading like a cancerous sore over the entire world, until it seemed to him that the entire world would be lost and God's program of redemption would be brought to an abrupt end. (This is what nearly everybody will think before it is over.)

To Habakkuk the world was becoming totally dark, with no possibility of the light of God ever shining through. Yet, what Habakkuk saw is exactly what has happened in country after country. Every year new territory is added to the Communist world program. But we only slow it down; we do not stop it. The terror that Jesus mentioned, caused by world wars and commotions, would be upon us if just one country got out of control, anywhere in the world.

Habakkuk was dealing with a world-wide situation. Now, for the first time since Habakkuk, any war anywhere could bring on a terrifying condition. We got quite concerned about some guns in Cuba aimed at us; but the difference between guns in Cuba and guns in Russia is only about fifteen minutes.

The alternate to being Red is what Habakkuk saw coming. The crisis, when it comes, will be a time of final decision. It will change things as they never have been changed before. This is especially true of the church, and that is why special messengers will be needed.

The only people who can witness in a time like this are people who know what God intends to do—people who understand the prophetic Scriptures. It is hard to put this in words because there are no words to express an experience that has never been faced before by the world or by the church.

> Behold ye among the heathen, and regard, and wonder marvellously: for I will work a work in your days, which ye will not believe, though it be told you.—Hab. 1:5

"Behold ye among the nations." Now God speaks. This is characteristic of the end time. God has been silent for centuries, and people have the impression that He never will do anything; but that is not the case. When the time comes God will act.

When God speaks, He speaks to or for the benefit of His people. At the time of this prophecy, God's people are among the nations (called the heathen in the Old Testament). It is a mistake to think that all Old Testament prophecy is only about the Jews. The prophets deal with the whole world, including the New Testament saints. God does not have two separate programs, one for the Jews and one for the rest of the world. He has one program which includes the Jews, the saints, and the world.

"In your days" means that this relief from oppression, or the threat of it, will come in the normal lifetime of the people who are the victims. Jesus put it in another way. He said, "This generation shall not pass till all these things be fulfilled." However, it will be so unexpected that they will be literally "stupefied by astonishment." If they did not see it, they would not believe it.

One reason why this will be so unbelievable is that Antichrist's coming is after the working of Satan. Satan will give him his throne and power and great authority. Nothing short of this could cope with the weapons that are in the hands of the nations today.

We have been shown the background; now comes the event. This is what Daniel saw: the rise of the little horn.

> For, lo, I raise up the Chaldeans, that bitter and hasty nation, which shall march through the breadth of the land, to possess the dwelling places that are not theirs.
> They are terrible and dreadful: their judgment and their dignity shall proceed of themselves.—Hab. 1:6, 7

Now we are dealing with (1) a nation and (2) a man. As to the nation, Daniel told the general location and Habakkuk the character of the people. An important point to remember is: Daniel, Ezekiel and Habakkuk all start with the land and end with a man. We have already noted this in Daniel.

Ezekiel also starts with the land, the land of Magog (Ezek. 38:2), but soon the land is forgotten and only the man is in view.

The land is important only as a starting place for Antichrist. He must start with a small country. Daniel calls it a LITTLE horn. (The ten horns are nations.) But he soon becomes more stout than his fellows.

Habakkuk starts with a nation which he calls the Chaldeans. The prophets used historical names when they did not know the final names. The ancient country became a type of the final one. However, it is not the ancient country but the final one that Habakkuk describes.

"I will raise up the Chaldeans, that bitter and hasty nation." "They are called hasty as being vehement and impetuous in attack and rapid in movement."—*Pulpit Commentary*. The Germans had a name for it: Blitzkrieg—lightning war.

"Which shall march through the breadth of the land," or "which marcheth through the breadths of the earth." This explains their general character. This is what they are prone to do. There is only one nation in Europe today that could be so described. Twice Germany has done exactly that. So, Germany will be a good country to watch for future developments. Germany is also in a good geographical position to fulfill Daniel.

> And out of one of them came forth a little horn, which waxed exceeding great, toward the south, and toward the east, and toward the pleasant land.—Dan. 8:9

Antichrist will move in three directions—south, east, and toward Palestine. To do this, he would have to start in the northwest. Germany was half in and half out of the Roman Empire, so it could come out of the head of the beast and still be another horn (Dan. 7:8).

> Their horses also are swifter than the leopards, and are more fierce than the evening wolves: and their horsemen shall come from far; they shall fly as the eagle that hasteth to eat.—Hab. 1:8

The Revised Version uses the plural (they) down to the tenth verse, and then changes to the singular (he). The Hebrew is singular after the sixth verse. We are dealing with a nation and a man, the man becoming more important all the time, until finally the nation disappears and the man becomes a world figure.

His horsemen fly. They come by air with great speed, and they come from far. The question could arise: How far is far? Distances on earth are becoming very short. We are reaching for the moon and on into space. Soon the moon will not be very far. Satan is the prince of the power of the air. He has principalities and powers (organized governments). We may soon find out just what is meant by the power of the air.

It is this seemingly supernatural element in the rise of Antichrist that will make all the difference. His "horsemen" come by air; that makes them airmen. They come not only from a great distance, but with extreme speed. This would have to be speed in comparison with enemy planes and missiles. Today, that would be almost supernatural speed, because we are reaching the limits of human speed.

Daniel says he will destroy wonderful things. The wonderful things are here, but to destroy them would require something still more wonderful. The United States and Russia have reached a stalemate; neither one can destroy the other and still remain intact. Both would be destroyed because they are about equal in strength. In time other nations may reach the same equality.

But Antichrist will be superior to such an extent that there will be no defense. There is a significance in the simile, "As the eagle that hasteth to eat." An eagle swoops down from the sky at great speed. It drops almost straight down on its prey.

> They shall come all for violence: their faces shall sup up as the east wind, and they shall gather the captivity as the sand.
> And they shall scoff at the kings, and the princes shall be a scorn unto them: they shall deride, every strong hold; for they shall heap dust, and take it.—Hab. 1:9, 10

He will come upon his enemies with a great show of violence. His face will look toward the east. That is the meaning of "he shall sup up as the east wind." That eastward movement is again noted. It seems to put the nation somewhere in the western part of Europe.

"He shall scoff at the kings." Nations with atomic power will present no problem to him, for he will have a superior weapon. A hundred years ago that might have been a bomber, but what would it be today? It is impossible to conceive such power in the hands of one man. Antichrist would have no means of developing such power, or weapons of that magnitude, without being detected. The only alternative is that his coming is after the working of Satan with all power and signs and lying wonders.

"He will heap dust and take it." The R.V. is stronger: "He will heap UP dust and take it. He will take a stronghold by throwing dust at it! The best the commentators can do with that is to say that he will throw up a pile of dust and hide behind it. But the commentaries were written before anybody knew anything about radio active dust.

This is not a defensive measure. Antichrist is on the march. He is conquering whole countries. He is "gathering the captivity as the sand." Dust is his weapon of conquest. Today scientists could tell us the exact nature of that dust. They are trying to make it. If his horsemen come from far, they may bring the dust with them, and that will give Antichrist absolute control. The empire that he will set up will eventually include the four empires of Daniel, but his influence will be world wide and that influence will be great.

> Then shall his mind change, and he shall pass over, and offend, imputing this his power unto his god.—Hab. 1:11

"Then shall his mind change." There are other translations: "Then he sweepeth on as the wind." He is like a tempestuous wind that sweeps all before it. It corresponds to Daniel's prediction that he will pull up three horns by the roots. "Imputing this his power unto his god." Again Daniel makes a similar statement. Daniel says it will be "not by his own power." His power comes from Satan. Eventually this will be acknowledged. Revelation says they will worship the dragon which gave power to the beast.

Up to this point God has been explaining to Habakkuk how he will overcome the course that has been spreading itself over the earth. Now Habakkuk speaks.

> Art thou not from everlasting, O Lord my God, mine Holy One? we shall not die. O Lord, thou hast ordained them for judg-

ment; and, O mighty God, thou hast established them for correction.

Thou art of purer eyes than to behold evil, and canst not look on iniquity: wherefore lookest thou upon them that deal treacherously, and holdest thy tongue when the wicked devoureth the man that is more righteous than he?

And makest men as the fishes of the sea, as the creeping things, that have no ruler over them?

They take up all of them with the angle, they catch them in their net, and gather them in their drag: therefore they rejoice and are glad.

Therefore they sacrifice unto their net, and burn incense unto their drag; because by them their portion is fat, and their meat plenteous.

Shall they therefore empty their net, and not spare continually to slay the nations.—Hab. 1:12-17

"We shall not die." Habakkuk identifies himself with God's people and speaks as though he were living at the time of fulfillment. This is quite common practice. Our hope, says Habakkuk, is in the fact that God is from everlasting and His purpose cannot fail, even though things may seem hopeless at times.

"Thou hast established [him] for correction." The Chaldean (Antichrist) is a rod in God's hand to correct the injustices that Habakkuk saw and complained about. Afterward, God will deal with Antichrist. Isaiah calls Antichrist the Assyrian and says, "O Assyrian, the rod of mine anger, the staff in their hand [the Assyrians] is mine indignation."—Isa. 10:5.

God will also punish Israel by the same rod. That is what Isaiah is especially concerned about. The principle is the same: God uses one evil power to punish another one. Isaiah says, "He thinketh not so." Antichrist does not realize that he is carrying out God's program and that God is using him to carry out His own purpose.

Habakkuk's question "Why?" is the question we all ask. Why does God allow these things? We get the answer, as Habakkuk did, by looking at the goal. This goal is stated in 2:14: "For the earth shall be filled with the knowledge of the glory of the Lord, as the waters cover the sea."

Now follows a summary of the activities of Antichrist to the time of the end, when he will gather all nations against the Lord. The nations are like fish. Antichrist empties his net, then goes out for more. "He gathereth unto him all nations, and heapeth unto him all people."—2:5.

This is the harvest. God allows evil to run its full course and come to its natural harvest. Then it will be judged. So, Habakkuk concludes: "The Lord is in his holy temple: let all the earth keep silence before him."—2:20.

THE LESSON OF HABAKKUK

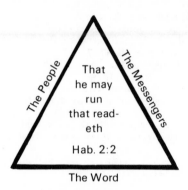

The Word

God said to Isaiah, "Whom shall I send, and who shall go for us?" That is always the question. There are three essentials:

1. The Word
2. A People who are hungry for the Word
3. Messengers of the Word

Chapter 12

EGYPT

The history of Egypt is bound up with the history of the Jews. In fact, Israel was born in Egypt. The future of Egypt also involves the Jews, especially in the process of their return. When the Jews entered the promised land for the first time to establish a nation there, they came out of Egypt.

When the great mass return takes place, that is, when all the Jews of the world return at one time in complete fulfillment of prophecy, many of them, if not most of them, will come from Egypt or through Egypt. This is a strange prophecy in the light of present-day world affairs. There are almost no Jews in Egypt now. Something is going to happen to change this situation and that is the most interesting feature of the prophecies concerning Egypt.

Egypt's role in the fulfillment of prophecy is not only large, but strange. Israel was born in Egypt and Israel will be born again in Egypt. That is, the nation will be born in Egypt before it returns to Palestine.

The present partial return of the Jews does not fulfill the prophecies concerning the great mass return except those which deal with the restoration of the land.

If the nation is to be born in Egypt and if the Jews, for the second time, are coming out of Egypt, then the time must come when the Jews will return to Egypt. Egypt's treatment of the Jews at that time is so shameful that Egypt will be severely punished.

We will start with Jeremiah 46.

This chapter is not the beginning of the story. It is, in fact, the end; but it tells something about Egypt which we must know at the start.

> Who is this that cometh up as a flood, whose waters are moved as the rivers? Egypt riseth up like a flood, and his waters are moved like the rivers; and he saith, I will go up, and will cover the earth; I will destroy the city and the inhabitants thereof. Come up, ye horses; and rage, ye chariots; and let the mighty men come forth; the Ethiopians and the Libyans, that handle the shield; and the Lydians, that handle and bend the bow.—Jer. 46:7-9

All the nations round about Israel who will try to destroy the Jews and prevent their return will be severely punished. The severity of the punishment indicates that the provocation will be very grave. Jeremiah lists many of these nations and tells about the punishment which will be meted out to them. The first one is Egypt.

The feature that we are interested in now is the amazing growth of Egyptian power across Africa and the great world importance that Egypt will attain in the last days.

Jeremiah follows the standard prophetic method of starting with some event or situation of his own time (verse 2) and using it as a spring board to jump immediately into the future scene. And also, following the standard prophetic practice, Jeremiah states plainly that he has passed into the future with his prophecy. He does this in verse 10.

> For this is the day of the Lord God of Hosts, and a day of vengeance, that he may avenge him of his adversaries: and the sword shall devour, and it shall be satiate and made drunk with their blood: for the Lord God of hosts hath a sacrifice in the north country by the river Euphrates.

The day of the Lord, in prophecy, always refers to that time leading up the Second Coming of Christ.

It has been said that prophecy is a mingling of the near and the far. That is not quite the case. The near and the far are definitely separated. When there is a passing from the near to the far, the prophet indicates where the change takes place or, at least, indicates that a change has taken place and that he is now talking about the far distant future.

"The Day of the Lord" is one of the terms the prophets use to indicate that their prophecy is concerning the last days before the return of Christ.

When we are dealing with Old Testament prophecy there is always the question of *when?*—when will it be fulfilled? Is it a prophecy concerning the immediate future, or does it concern the last days?

There is a rule that we can apply: *If a prophecy has not been totally fulfilled in the past, then there will be a future complete fulfillment.*

Many times commentaries will put all these prophecies concerning nations, cities and Bible lands into the past; then they have to warp either the prophecy or the history or both to make them fit. The prophets used a number of means to show the general time of fulfillment. One of these is to state plainly, "In the day of the Lord," or, "This is the day of the Lord." Sometimes it is shortened to "that day" or "at that time" or "in the last days" or some similar expression.

Jeremiah plainly states that this is a prophecy concerning the day of the Lord. "For this is the day of the Lord God of hosts."—vs. 10.

What Jeremiah saw concerning the future of Egypt astonished him and he expressed that astonishment. He said, "Who is this that cometh up like a flood, whose waters are moved as the rivers?" He answered, "Egypt," and I think if we wanted to convey the tone of his voice we would have to put several exclamation points after Egypt. The king of Egypt said, "I will go up and conquer the earth, I will destroy the city and the inhabitants thereof."

Jeremiah saw Egypt becoming so powerful as a nation that it will think it can conquer the world. Of course, Egypt will not get very far in that conquest. She will be met and defeated decisively by a superior power.

Daniel tells the story in his 11th chapter, but in this connection he does not mention Egypt. He says, "the king of the south."

Why would Daniel say "king of the south" when he means Egypt? Daniel knew about Egypt and even calls Egypt by name in this same chapter.

Apparently, when Daniel says "king of the south" he is talking about a federation of countries of which Egypt is the head. These will probably be African countries. There could be a number of federations before the time comes that these countries form one confederacy under Egypt.

Obadiah mentions one of them. He says: "How are the things of Esau searched out! How are his hidden things sought up!" This probably refers to oil or other riches that will be discovered in the Arab countries—possibly gold.

Obadiah continues: "All the men of thy confederacy have brought thee even to the border"—the border of Israel. This seems to be happening now, but Obadiah is talking about a time that is still somewhat future.

Meantime Egypt is going to become so great that there will be principalities, there will be princes and governors; it is going to be a mighty confederacy. Jeremiah mentions the nations that will be in this confederacy which Daniel calls the king of the South.

ETHIOPIA. On the map, Ethiopia is the southernmost country that may be considered a part of prophetic lands. It is the oldest continuing government in the world and has great prophetic significance because of its connection with the Jews, especially at the time of their return.

LIBYA. In ancient times this land was called Put.

ALGERIA. The ancient name is Lud or Ludim. There were no actual boundaries. The names referred simply to a general location. Today our maps would show them as independent countries with very definite borders.

The prophecy takes in a territory from Ethiopia to Algeria

covering a large part of the Sahara. Jeremiah is showing the
countries that will be confederate with Egypt in the day when
Egypt reaches its full power. Isaiah has something to say about
Egypt in the last days, a prophecy which we will examine in
some detail.

The reason why Egypt figures so prominently in prophecy
is her treatment of the Jews in the time of their extremity.
The Jews now in Palestine will be banished to Egypt; or, at
least, an attempt will be made to exterminate them, and many
of them will escape to Egypt. They will be driven out of Israel
with no place to go but Egypt. Egypt will also be a dumping
ground for Jews from many other countries.

We assume this to be the work of Antichrist because there
is no other character capable of doing what Antichrist will do
to the Jews.

Moses, at the end of his long discourse concerning the future
of the Jews, said: "And the Lord shall bring thee into Egypt
again with ships, by the way whereof I spake unto thee, Thou
shalt see it no more again: and there ye shall be sold unto
your enemies for bondmen and bondwomen, and no man shall
buy you."—Deut. 26:68.

The Jews will probably be expected to die in the desert sands
and probably many of them will. That is when God goes into
action.

Egypt is a country of contrasts. The cities in the northern
part of Egypt are unusually prosperous and wealthy; but along
the Nile, all the way to the Sudan, live some of the poorest
people in the world. The Aswan Dam may change some of this.
A great lake will be formed south of Aswan and the water will
be used to irrigate the land. The land is fertile enough but there
is no rain. Isaiah suggests that they will build canals and ponds
out in the desert that will support a large number of people.
Isaiah says they will be full of fish. But something else is happening in Egypt of extreme prophetic importance. The report
of Egyptian and Russian oil missions reads as follows:

Oil

Existence of a huge oil basin extending from Libya's Sirte
Basin to Suez Gulf is upsetting the old belief of existence of a
separating belt between Libya and Egypt's Western Desert.
Egyptian General Petroleum Corp. sources said that the studies
open prospects for "vast oil reserves in Western Desert area."

Researchers took into account all previous geological and
seismological studies of the area in drawing their conclusion.
They divide Egypt into three main oil basins: (1) the northern
basin extending from Libya's Sirte Basin in west to north Sinai in
east, including northern part of Western Desert and Nile Delta;

(2) southern basin extending from Coufir Basin in Libya covering Nile valley, southern part of both Western and Eastern deserts; (3) the basin comprising both coasts of Suez Gulf and extending south to the Red Sea.

Also Water

OCCIDENTAL TAPS VAST UNDERGROUND WATER RESERVOIR AT KUFRA—The proven water reserves in Libya are estimated to be in the neighborhood of a quadrillion barrels—equivalent to a 200-year flow of the Nile River. Occidental regards this huge underground water discovery, which could turn Libya into the most fertile country in North Africa, as the most important event in Libya since the discovery of oil. The Kufra Oasis Agricultural development scheme was one of the extra benefits offered by Occidental in order to obtain Libyan Concessions.

It almost immediately initiated research and water exploration activities which culminated in September 1968 in the discovery of a major water well with a daily production of 100,000 barrels. The development scheme, now proceeding at an accelerated pace, involves (a) the improvement of traditional farming methods employed in the area, and (b) the reclamation of about 62,500 acres of desert land. The company expects to spend about $50 million on agricultural development in the area over the next five years. Occidental estimates that for every man put to direct agricultural work in the Kufra area, enough work would be generated during the next 10 days for 30 men in related industries such as food processing, transportation, warehousing and other activities.

Other extremely large oil deposits have been discovered in the Sahara. These countries of North Africa are extremely rich in natural resources. There is enough water under ground to make the Sahara, in the words of Isaiah, blossom as the rose. If these countries should get together and form one united republic, it would be one of the greatest powers on earth. It is no wonder that Egypt and those countries think that someday they could conquer the world.

It is quite probable that the Jews from many countries around the world would be forced out of their homes and made to go to Egypt quite some time before the massacre of the Jews in Israel, because Isaiah says that in that day five cities in the land of Egypt will speak the language of Canaan (Hebrew). This shows to what extent the Jews will overrun Egypt and what their influence will be there.

However, very little time will elapse between the time that the Jews are forced out of Israel and the time of their return.

The Egyptians hate the Jews and will treat them shamefully. There will be a great slaughter of Jews in the deserts of Egypt. Ezekiel says:

> And all the inhabitants of Egypt shall know that I am the
> Lord, because they have been a staff of reed to the house of
> Israel. When they took hold of thee by thy hand, thou didst
> break, and rend all their shoulder: and when they leaned upon .
> thee, thou brakest, and madest all their loins to be at a stand. There-
> fore thus saith the Lord God: Behold, I will bring a sword upon
> thee, and cut off man and beast out of thee.—Ezek. 29:6-8

How can you lay a desert waste? How can you make a
desert desolate? Egypt right now, outside of a few cities, is
one of the poorest countries on earth. The only part of Egypt
that can support any life at all is along the Nile River. People
living along the Nile can get just enough food to exist so they
are always hungry. How can you lay a country like that waste?
Ezekiel assumes that Egypt will be prosperous and the desert
will blossom as the rose. There may be a lot of desert left but
enough of it will be reclaimed to make the country prosperous.

Ezekiel continues.

> And the land of Egypt shall be desolate and waste; and they
> shall know that I am the Lord: because he hath said, The river
> is mine, and I have made it. Behold, therefore I am against thee,
> and against thy rivers, and I will make the land of Egypt utterly
> waste and desolate, from the tower of Syrene even unto the border
> of Ethiopia.
> No foot of man shall pass through it, nor foot of beast shall
> pass through it, neither shall it be inhabited forty years. And I
> will make the land of Egypt desolate in the midst of the coun-
> tries that are desolate, and her cities, among the cities that are
> laid waste, shall be desolate forty years: and I will scatter the
> Egyptians among the nations, and will disperse them through the
> countries.
> Yet thus saith the Lord God; At the end of forty years will
> I gather the Egyptians from the people whither they were scat-
> tered: And I will bring again the captivity of Egypt, and will
> cause them to return into the land of Pathros, into the land of
> their habitation: and they shall be there a base kingdom. It shall
> be the basest of the kingdoms; neither shall it exalt itself any
> more above the nations: for I will diminish them, that they shall
> no more rule over the nations.—Ezek. 29:9-15

Egypt appears in various prophecies all the way through the
reign of Antichrist. It is mentioned as a nation right up to the
time of the so-called Battle of Armageddon, so the destruction
of Egypt must take place approximately at the time of the coming of Christ. The forty years mentioned by Ezekiel would run
on into the Millennium.

What makes this prophecy the more exciting is that it is
beginning to happen. The Jews have fulfilled the first part of
this prophecy by returning and restoring the land. The second
part may not be far away. The process of the return of the

Jews is in progress now and Egypt must be prepared to fulfill her part of the prophecy.

The nineteenth chapter of Isaiah has more of the story; in some respects it is more complete. It tells what will happen as the result of the Jews being in Egypt and the result of Egypt's bad treatment of the Jews while they are there.

> The burden of Egypt. Behold, the Lord rideth upon a swift cloud, and shall come into Egypt; and the idols of Egypt shall be moved at his presence, and the heart of Egypt shall melt in the midst of it.—Isa. 19:1

Notice the mention of idols. Here is one of the strangest prophecies in the Bible and it runs all through the prophecies concerning the last days. There is to be a return to idolatry. Even the Jews will again make idols for themselves to worship. Isaiah says that every man will make is own idols and set them up to worship. It seems that the Antichrist will promote the worship of idols.

> And I will set the Egyptians against the Egyptians: and they shall fight every one against his brother, and every one against his neighbour; city against city, and kingdom against kingdom. And the spirit of Egypt shall fail in the midst thereof; and I will destroy the counsel thereof: and they shall seek to the idols, and to the charmers, and to them that have familiar spirits, and to the wizards.
>
> And the Egyptians will I give over into the hand of a cruel lord; and a fierce king shall rule over them, saith the Lord, the Lord of hosts. And the waters shall fail from the sea, and the river shall be wasted and dried up.—Isa. 19:2-5

Egypt is going to have some bitter enemies in that day and they will take advantage of the peculiarities of the Nile. Most rivers have tributaries. The Mississippi, for instance, starts very small up in the northern part of Minnesota. It is just a little stream that grows bigger as it flows south because of the other streams flowing into it.

But the Nile has no tributaries, no streams flow into it after it reaches the border of Ethiopia. It rises in two lakes, Lake Victoria in Africa and Lake Tana in Ethiopia. It would require only a simple engineering feat at these two sources to bring Egypt to complete ruin.

"And I will set the Egyptians against the Egyptians; and they shall fight every one against his brother" (vs. 2). This is a special feature of the Battle of Armageddon which takes place at the time of the coming of Christ when all the nations are gathered against Jerusalem to battle.

Ezekiel says: "And I will call for a sword against him throughout all my mountains, saith the Lord God: every man's sword shall be against his brother."—Ezek. 38:21.

Zechariah talking about the same event says: "And it shall come to pass in that day, that a great tumult from the Lord shall be among them; and they shall lay hold every one on the hand of his neighbour, and his hand shall rise up against the hand of his neighbour."—Zech. 14:13.

And Haggai says: "And I will overthrow the throne of kingdoms and I will destroy the kingdoms of the heathen (nations). I will overthrow the chariots and they that ride in them: and the horses and their riders shall come down, every one by the sword of his brother."—Haggai 2:22.

> The paper reeds by the brooks, by the mouth of the brooks, and every thing sown by the brooks, shall wither, be driven away, and be no more. The fishers also shall mourn, and all they that cast angle into the brooks shall lament, and they that spread nets upon the waters shall languish.
>
> Moreover they that work in fine flax, and they that weave networks, shall be confounded. And they shall be broken in the purposes thereof, all that make sluices and ponds for fish.—Isa. 19:7-9

It is difficult to fit this prophecy into Egypt as it is today, but the Aswan Dam could change everything and produce the very conditions that the prophecy calls for. The discovery of oil and water could also help to produce this change.

> And the land of Judah shall be a terror unto Egypt, everyone that maketh mention thereof shall be afraid in himself, because of the counsel of the Lord of hosts, which he hath determined against it. In that day shall five cities in the land of Egypt speak the language of Canaan, and swear to the Lord of hosts; one shall be called, The city of destruction.—Isa. 19:17, 18

The land of Judah is a terror unto Egypt right now, but it is nothing compared to what it will be when God delivers the Jews from Egyptian oppression. Prophecy indicates that the great mass return of the Jews will be, for the most part, through Egypt because it is in Egypt, probably in the desert places, that God will plead with Israel and bring them again into the bond of the covenant (Ezek. 20:36, 37).

Here is a prophecy of a revival of a dead language, a thing that never has happened before in the world. When Ezekiel said this, it was the most unlikely of fulfillment of any prophecy in the Bible: yet it has happened, and we have seen it happen. The Jews in Egypt will speak Hebrew.

> In that day shall there be an altar to the Lord in the midst of the land of Egypt, and a pillar at the border thereof to the Lord.—Isa. 19:19

We do not know the nature of this altar to the Lord or the

pillar that is to be erected on the border of Egypt as a witness
to the Lord. But we do know that, in Egypt, the children of
Israel will turn to the Lord, for they must repent and acknowledge their sins and that their troubles are due to the fact that
they left the Lord, before they can be allowed to return to their
land from all the nations of the earth (Deut. 30:1-4).

> And it shall be for a sign and for a witness unto the Lord of
> hosts in the land of Egypt; for they shall cry unto the Lord
> because of the oppressors, and he shall send them a saviour, and
> a great one, and he shall deliver them. And the Lord shall be
> known to Egypt, and the Egyptians shall know the Lord in that
> day, and shall do sacrifice and oblation; yea, they shall vow a
> vow unto the Lord, and perform it.
>
> And the Lord shall smite Egypt; he shall smite and heal it;
> and they shall return even to the Lord, and he shall be intreated
> of them, and shall heal them. In that day shall there be a highway
> out of Egypt to Assyria, and the Assyrian shall come into Egypt,
> and the Egyptian into Assyria, and the Egyptians shall serve with
> the Assyrians.
>
> In that day shall Israel be the third with Egypt and with
> Assyria, even a blessing in the midst of the land: Whom the Lord
> of hosts shall bless, saying, Blessed be Egypt my people, and
> Assyria the work of my hands, and Israel mine inheritance.—Isa.
> 19:20-25

Chapter 13

THE TIME FACTOR

DATING A PROPHECY

To understand any prophecy it is absolutely necessary that you place it in the right time. In the Old Testament the decision usually is between past and future. The Hebrew verb has no future tense, so, in the original all prophecy is written in either the present or past tense. When the context very decidedly calls for it, the versions usually use the future tense; but, because the text is in the past tense, it does not necessarily mean that the prophecy is not for a future time.

One rule is: *If a prophecy has not been fulfilled perfectly in the past, then there will be a future fulfillment.*

Nothing is gained by warping a prophecy a little, or disregarding certain features to make it fit some past situation. It is usually necessary, then, also to change history a little bit. An illustration may be noted in the oft-repeated expression: "And they shall know that I am the Lord." The grand purpose of prophecy is to call attention to God and His Word.

When the great Old Testament prophecies come to pass, that is exactly what will happen. Prophecy is the grand evangelizing catalyst in the end time. Therefore, if a prophecy ends with these significant words, you may put it down as being future. More Old Testament prophecy is aimed at the end time than is usually supposed.

The prophets very consistently indicate the general time of the prophecy either by associating it with some known event, or, more frequently, stating the time in so many words, such as, in that day, at that time, in the last days, etc. There are many variations. These expressions do not refer back to what has been said before. They are indicators that the prophet is referring to that future, but, to him, unknown, time of the fulfillment of all prophecy.

"The end" never means the cessation of all things. It always refers to the consummation of the prophecy, the final focal point, the end of the particular program to which the prophecy points.

The Rapture is the focal point of much prophecy. The many prophecies that point to the Rapture must come before the Rapture. The time of the prophecy in reference to the Rapture may be easily determined. The rule is: *If a prophecy could not be fulfilled after the Rapture, it must come before.*

This is a more accurate test than might be supposed. The time between the Rapture and the Return is very short to contain all the things that must happen in that limited time. The prophesied details are many—so many, in fact, that a day-by-day chronology could almost be set up.

The Rapture is a rescue from a day of calamity, which Paul calls "sudden destruction." Other expressions are: nation against nation, take peace from the earth, famine, earthquake, pestilence, stars fall from heaven, fire, heat, demons, the sea and the waves roaring, affliction such as never was.

This is not the time of building great and wealthy cities. It is not the time of a city like great Babylon enriching the nations. It is not the time for building the temple or spreading the knowledge of the glory of the Lord over all the earth.

Sodom and Gomorrah were destroyed, but they were built and they prospered some time before they were destroyed. The same must be true of the great cities and world prosperity that will be destroyed immediately after the Rapture. First comes the building, then the destruction. The Rapture comes in between.

Satan will deceive the whole world, but it is by peace and security that he deceives. Destruction deceives no one.

THE END OF THE AGE

In the King James Version, end of the age is translated end of the world. The Greek word *aion* is correctly translated *world* in many places, but it carries the idea of the world at a given time. The dictionary meaning is age, or dispensation. The marginal rendering in the R.V. is *consummation of the age.*

Many students have distinguished seven ages or dispensations. This division of time has some advantages. It helps us to understand how God has dealt with men in the past and how He will deal with them in the future, but it may easily be misused. God deals with men under seven different world conditions.

There is a pattern of new starts and judgments, seven in all.

SEVEN NEW BEGINNINGS
SEVEN JUDGMENTS

1. Adam—Gen. 1:7
   Expulsion from the Garden—Gen. 3:22-24
2. Seth—Gen. 4:25
   The Flood—Gen. 6-8
3. Noah—Gen. 9:2
   Confusion of Tongues—Gen. 11
4. Abraham—Gen. 12:1-3
   Bondage in Egypt—Ex. 1:7-14

5. Moses—Ex. 3:1-12
   Dispersion (complete in A.D. 70)
6. Holy Spirit—Acts 2
   Day of the Lord—II Thess. 2:1-3; II Pet. 3:10
7. Christ—Rev. 20:1, 2
   Gog and Magog—Rev. 20:7-9

Jesus referred to the end of a dispensation when He said, "As it was in the days of Noah." That was the end of a dispensation. The dividing of time into seven dispensations is helpful in many ways, but the Bible does not so divide itself. It is a man-made division or outline and can be carried to an extreme that actually contradicts the Bible teaching. It should be used with caution and never carried beyond the limits of a man-made outline.

THE BIBLE DIVISIONS

The Bible divisions are the Old Covenant and the New Covenant, or Testament. The Old Covenant goes back to Adam and includes all the Old Testament saints, Jew and Gentile. The Law is a part of the Old Covenant. Enoch, as well as Elijah, was in the Old Covenant. But, inasmuch as the so-called Dispensation of Law is the final one in the Old Testament, we think of it as the one that will come to a consummation in the last days. The New Covenant is the same as the Dispensation of Grace, but it comes as a parenthesis within the Dispensation of Law. There are seven years of the old yet to run. We call this Daniel's Seventieth Week.

In this way, both Old and New Covenants or Testaments, may be brought to a close at about the same time. When the disciples asked Jesus, "What shall be the sign of the end of the age?" He included in His answer the end of both the old and the new dispensation.

The end of this age, the Dispensation of Grace, covers a period of time. There will be a succession of events, sometimes differing greatly in nature. The world will pass through three distinct periods which we must know and be able to recognize if we are to place the prophecies in their proper order.

No prophecy can be understood if it is placed in the wrong time. Many prophetic teachers do not recognize this principle and so are apt to quote prophecies that have no reference to the present time. For instance, you may hear this verse quoted as referring to the present dilemma in which the nations find themselves:

"And there shall be signs in the sun, and in the moon, and in the stars; and upon the earth distress of nations, with perplexity; the sea and the waves roaring."—Luke 21:25.

"Distress" means a huddling together, like the United Nations. "Perplexity" means no way out. This seems like a perfect description of the world situation. But the accompanying signs are not present. The time of this prophecy is just before the Second Coming of Christ. The nations are gathered around Jerusalem. It is easy to get mixed up in a foreign war and then find there is no way out; but this prophecy applies to a situation much worse and much more universal than what we have today.

The present world situation will get worse and even seem to reach an impasse, but there will be a way out. It may not be a good way, but it will bring about a temporary peace and safety. The world will settle down and seem to prosper. Nothing is ever gained by taking a prophecy out of its context and applying it to some other time. Therefore, we must understand the times if we are to understand the prophecies.

This age ends with the Resurrection; however, the Resurrection is not all in one piece. Enoch and Elijah and Moses were translated or raised; and a large number, possibly all the Old Testament saints, came out of their graves at the resurrection of Christ.

The First Resurrection

After the Rapture, there will be a resurrection of the Tribulation Saints. Revelation 20:5 says that they are in the First Resurrection. The Rapture is also a part of the First Resurrection. They are both parts of one event.

The mention of the First Resurrection implies that there will be a resurrection after the Millennium. But now we are interested in what Revelation calls the First Resurrection, which includes the Rapture and the resurrection of the Tribulation Saints, who are saved after the Rapture during the first part of the reign of Satan on earth.

Therefore, the First Resurrection includes two classes of people: (1) those who are raised from the dead or translated at the Rapture and (2) those who are saved after the Rapture and killed by Antichrist (Rev. 6:9-11; 7:9-17; 13:4-8; Matt. 24:7-14).

So, the first thing we must understand is that the Rapture does not end this dispensation. The Dispensation of Grace runs for a short time after the Rapture, while the Tribulation Saints are being gathered. There will be a great revival after the Rapture, brought on, partly, by the Rapture itself. It is the resurrection of the Tribulations Saints that brings this dispensation to a close and begins Daniel's Seventieth Week. In fact, it is at this very time that we find the twelve tribes named for the first time in the New Testament (Rev. 7:4-8).

That brings both the old and new dispensations to an end at about the same time. The Olivet Discourse (Matt. 24; Luke 21) gives us the end of both ages in one view and with the events placed in order. Matthew has most to say about the end of the new dispensation, while Luke is more concerned with the old.

Three Time Zones

World Crisis	Fulfilled Prophecy	"As in the days of Noah"
THE NATIONS Spread of Communism Wars and commotions All hope gone	THE NATIONS World common market Building of great cities Expansion of Egypt Destruction of Communism	THE NATIONS Peace and security Great prosperity
THE CHURCH A time of terror Many false christs	THE CHURCH A new Church Satanic signs and wonders Spread of the Gospel over the world Preparation of the "Bride"	THE CHURCH Wealth and indifference "Where is the promise of His coming?" Exaltation of man
THE JEWS The land restored A partial return Trouble with the Arabs RISE OF ANTICHRIST	THE JEWS Crisis in Israel Complete return Temple rebuilt	THE JEWS Return to idolatry THE RAPTURE

Before the Rapture, we can distinguish three time zones that are quite different:

The first time zone is a build-up to a world crisis—the greatest crisis since the Tower of Babel. The whole world will seem to be exploding at once with trouble everywhere. It will be a time of terror, partly due, perhaps, to the fantastic weapons that might be thrown into the conflict. Another cause of terror could be disasters that seem to have some supernatural source. Things which cannot be explained can cause more fear than natural plagues. There may be some preliminary warnings of the coming of the man of sin whose coming is with satanic power and signs and lying wonders.

The second time zone is a time of fulfilled prophecy. The time of trouble and terror will come to an abrupt end by the appearance of a world figure that Bible students will recognize as Antichrist, but which many church leaders will hail as a sort of savior. Then will come a demonstration of deceit on a grand scale. He will produce a hypnotic effect on the world. There will be a sense of well-being and security. Before the Rapture, Antichrist's policy will be deceit. The world will not recognize him as Satan.

The new world common market will bring a wealth never before experienced. This alone would be enough to deceive people, with "We never had it so good!" Great cities will be built. The temple in Jerusalem will rise again in all its grandeur.

There will be great religious activity. Satan's greatest ambition is to be worshipped. Many false Christs will almost demoralize the existing church. The false Christs will seem to have all the answers. The present-day church program could not cope with a situation of this kind. It will be poor, blind, and naked.

On the other hand, the gospel will be carried to the ends of the earth, so that every kindred, tongue, people and nation will know about God, Christ, and the gospel. An apostate church could not do this. There will have to be a new movement, outside the old established denominations.

An immense amount of prophecy will be fulfilled during this time, some of it in a very sensational manner, for instance, the miraculous return of the Jews. These are prophecies that could not be fulfilled in any other time zone. This will be God's answer to the signs and wonders of Antichrist and will probably be the biggest factor in the spread of the gospel.

The third time zone will be like the days of Noah. We will pass gradually into this time zone. Prosperity will bring apostasy and indifference. During the time of great miracles, the coming of Christ will be momentarily expected. Then things will quiet down and there will be no thought of His appearing. Unbelievers, especially those in the church, will again take the initiative and scoff: "Where is the promise of His coming? everything has returned to normal!"

The world will be plunged into idolatry and unspeakable sin, even as it was in the days of Noah (Isa. 2:10-22).

The tribulation follows immediately. In fact, the Rapture is a rescue from the tribulation and judgment. The Dispensation of Grace does not end for three and a half years. The gospel is still preached, but this time from heaven (Rev. 14:6). It is the unhindered reign of Satan.

There is one common factor that runs all the way through. It is Antichrist's attempt to become the god of this world. Before the Rapture, as has already been stated, Antichrist's policy will be deceit. After the Rapture he will use force. Deceit as to his nature will no longer be possible. Now the world will worship him as Satan (Rev. 13:4).

The seven last plagues (trumpets and vials) are judgment without mixture of grace. No one is said to be saved. At this time God will purge the earth of the results of sin. This ends with the return of Christ.

You will notice that the events in each time zone are harmonious.

THE END OF THE AGE

Build-Up to a World Crisis

1. Spread of Communism
2. Wars, Rumors of Wars, and Commotions
3. A Time of Terror
4. A Host of False Christs
5. All Hope of Survival Gone
6. RISE OF ANTICHRIST

Time of Fulfilled Prophecy

1. Satanic Power, Signs and Lying Wonders
2. A New Church
3. A World Common Market
4. Building of Great Cities
5. Crisis in Israel
6. Complete Return of the Jews
7. Building of the Temple
8. Expansion of Egypt
9. Growing Importance of the Middle East

As the Days of Noah

1. The Earth at Rest
2. Peace and Prosperity
3. In the Church, Wealth and Indifference
4. "Where Is the Promise of His Coming?"
5. Return of Idolatry
6. Exaltation of Man
7. *THE RAPTURE*

Tribulation

1. Satan Takes Over the Earth
2. The Mark of the Beast
3. Peace Taken from the Earth
4. Famines and Pestilences
5. Earthquakes and Falling Stars
6. Gospel Preached to All Nations
7. A Great Company Saved
8. Many Martyrs
9. 144,000 Israelites Sealed
10. RESURRECTION OF THE TRIBULATION SAINTS

The Seven Last Plagues

1. Purging of the Heavens and the Earth
2. The Three Woes
3. Gathering of the Armies at Armageddon
4. *THE RETURN OF CHRIST*

THE DAY OF THE LORD

"The Day of the Lord" is a common expression in the prophetic Scriptures. There are variations having somewhat similar meanings, or referring to about the same time: that day, the last days, the time of the end, the end of the days, afterward, the Day of Christ (N.T.), and others. The Day of the Lord refers to a more specific time than some of the other expressions.

The Day of the Lord corresponds very closely with Daniel's Seventieth Week, the last seven years before the return of Christ. It starts about the time the Dispensation of Grace ends. That makes it correspond with the trumpets and vials of Revelation. The descriptions of the events of the Day of the Lord in the Old Testament correspond exactly with the seven last plagues (trumpets-vials) of Revelation.

Sometimes when the prophet says, "In the day of the Lord," he means some time during the Day of the Lord; for instance, the last half of the Day of the Lord called Jacob's trouble. The Day of the Lord comes at a time when the Lord is dealing again with the Jews as a nation, so, usually, the Jews or the nations around Israel are in view.

The Day of Christ comes at the same general time, but the saints rather than the Jews are in view.

A great deal of confused thinking has been caused by a failure to recognize the fact that the Rapture comes a few years before the end of the Dispensation of Grace. There must be time for the Tribulation Saints in the Dispensation of Grace. Sometimes people think we are teaching a Mid-tribulation Rapture, but this is not the case. The tribulation comes after the Rapture and before Daniel's Seventieth Week. The Rapture is first; the tribulation follows.

It is called the Day of the Lord because it is the day that God rises up to judge the earth. "The great day of his wrath is come and who shall be able to stand?" We must distinguish between the purpose and the method. The purpose is the redemption of everything good. The method is the destruction of everything bad.

All redemption involves purging. "Without the shedding of blood there is no remission of sin." The only purging agents are blood and fire. The world has rejected the blood. Fire is the only alternative. Fire consumes that which cannot be redeemed and purges that which can.

God will judge the earth by fire. Many people will live through it; there are still nations here when it is all over. You will notice that feature in the descriptions of the Day of the Lord. The judgments of the Day of the Lord are only a part of the whole process of redemption. It might be well to have in mind the whole process when we consider this part of it.

The Purposes Are:

1. The purging out of the results of sin.
2. Preparation for the coming Kingdom
   (especially in reference to the Jews).
3. Conditioning of the human race for eternity

The Whole Process Includes:

1. The sacrifice for sin (the cross).
2. The choosing of a Bride, a royal people
   (future kings and priests).
3. Preaching of the gospel to every creature.
4. The judgment of the nations (the Day of the
   Lord) and the salvation of Israel.
5. The 1000 year reign (to restore the population
   and set up a perfect world).
6. A final cleansing of the nations.
7. The tabernacle of God is with men.

The Time

After the Dispensation of Grace, the old dispensation is resumed for a period of seven years. This period of seven years is called Daniel's Seventieth Week. The term "end of the age" sometimes refers specifically to the end of the age of grace. Jesus so applied it. When the disciples asked, "What shall be the sign of thy coming and of the end of the age?" Jesus separated them as to time.

After telling of the beginning of the signs, He said, "The end is not yet" (the end of the age is not yet). Then, after describing in some detail the events of the tribulation for the saints, He said, "Then shall the end come." That is the end of the age, for that is what He was talking about.

Then Jesus goes into the matter of the end of the Old Testament age which ends with His Second Coming. So, we have two periods of time: the end of the age of grace and the Day of the Lord, one following the other.

The Day of the Lord is not the entire time between the Rapture and the Return of Christ. The tribulation for the saints has to come in there also.

The Old Testament prophets also recognized the time of the end which comes before the Day of the Lord. Joel tells of a coming revival which began at Pentecost, but which will be completed in a mighty outpouring of the Spirit before the great and terrible day of the Lord.

"And I will show wonders in the heavens and in the earth, blood, and fire, and pillars of smoke. The sun shall be turned into darkness, and the moon into blood, before the great and the terrible day of the Lord come."

Joel mentions the sun being turned into darkness and the moon into blood BEFORE the great and terrible day of the Lord comes. These are the features of the tribulation out of which come the Tribulation Saints:

> And I beheld when he had opened the sixth seal, and, lo, there was a great earthquake; and the sun became black as sackcloth of hair, and the moon became as blood.—Rev. 6:12

OBADIAH tells of the experiences of the Jews when they try to escape. This is the second step in the return. The great mass return must come after this persecution by Antichrist.

Obadiah mentions the time of this persecution. He says: "For the day of the Lord is near upon the nations."—Verse 15. This experience comes before the Day of the Lord. So, again, we have a period of fulfilled prophecy before the Day of the Lord.

ZEPHANIAH deals almost exclusively with the Day of the Lord. That is the subject of his book. But Zephaniah also recognizes a situation that exists before the Day of the Lord.

> And it shall come to pass at that time, that I will search Jerusalem with candles, and punish the men that are settled on their lees; that say in their heart, The Lord will not do good, neither will he do evil. Therefore their goods shall become a booty, and their houses a desolation; they shall also build houses and not inhabit them; and they shall plant vineyards and not drink the wine thereof. The great day of the Lord is near, and hasteth greatly, even the voice of the day of the Lord. — Zeph. 1:12-14

There is to be a time of peace and quiet when they will say "peace and safety." They will build and they will plant. They will make great plans for the future. They will say, "We never had it so good." It will be a time of great world prosperity and a false sense of security. This is the time when the Day of the Lord is near, when sudden destruction will come upon them.

There is only one Day of the Lord. This must be true because Jesus said, "For in those days shall be affliction, such as was not from the beginning of the creation unto this time, neither shall be."—Mark 13:19.

This is the day of affliction, or tribulation, for Israel, especially the last half of it. Daniel's Seventieth Week, the Day of the Lord, and the seven last plagues are all different phases of one program.

It should be noted that the expression "Day of the Lord" is sometimes used in a restricted sense applying to the very last part of the process which actually is the Battle of Armageddon and the events immediately leading up to it; for instance, Malachi 4:5, 6: "Behold, I will send you Elijah the prophet before the coming of the great and dreadful day of the Lord: and he shall turn the heart of the fathers to the children and the heart of the children to their fathers, lest I come and smite the earth with a curse."

The Jews are involved in the Day of the Lord. First, because they are a nation in prophetic lands and, second, because they have a special place in the program.

THE DAY OF THE LORD

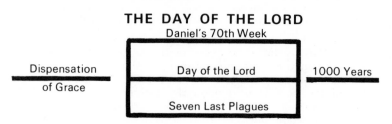

Daniel's Seventieth Week is the last seven years before the coming of Christ.

The Day of the Lord ends with the coming of Christ.

The seven last plagues come just before the coming of Christ to reign. In fact, the seventh plague (the seventh trumpet and vial) ushers in the coming of Christ. Therefore, they must all come at the same time. We have here, then, three different aspects of one process.

In the Day of the Lord, most of the saints are in heaven. If any are on the earth, they are sealed or otherwise protected. The remaining subjects of redemption are the Jews (the nation of Israel), the nations (those of the nations that pass through the judgments), the earth (It is to be made new after being purged by fire).

The saints in heaven have charge of the redemption of the earth and the judgment of the nations. They are the actors in Revelation. They have charge of the plagues.

So, we have three subjects of redemption and we have three groups of people and three names that refer to their work.

1. The Jews (Daniel's 70th Week)
2. The Nations (The Day of the Lord)
3. The Saints (The Trumpets and Vials)

In each case redemption is involved, fulfilling God's covenant with Noah.

Daniel's 70th Week brings redemption to Israel.

The Day of the Lord prepares the nations for the reign of Christ (Rev. 20:4).

The Seven Last Plagues—Trumpets and Vials—purge out the results of sin and prepare the earth for the reconstruction during the Millennium, when the earth will be made perfect as it would have been if Adam had not sinned.

All three are in Revelation, but there the earth is the primary subject. For more information on the judgment of the nations we have to go into the Old Testament. The Day of the Lord refers primarily to the nations. Special attention is paid to those nations that have persecuted the Jews in their hour of trials, thus adding to their affliction.

The Nature of the Day of the Lord

The great day of the Lord is near, it is near, and hasteth greatly, even the voice of the day of the Lord; the mighty man shall cry there bitterly.

That day is a day of wrath, a day of trouble and distress, a day of wasteness and desolation, a day of darkness and gloominess, a day of clouds and thick darkness.

A day of the trumpet and alarm against the fenced cities, and against the high towers.

And I will bring distress upon men, that they shall walk like blind men, because they have sinned against the Lord: and their blood shall be poured out as dust, and their flesh as the dung.

Neither their silver nor their gold shall be able to deliver them in the day of the Lord's wrath; but the whole land shall be devoured by the fire of his jealousy: for he shall make even a speedy riddance of all them that dwell in the land.—Zeph. 1:14-18

Zephaniah begins abruptly with the announcement of universal judgment on the whole world. "I will utterly consume," literally, "taking away, I will make an end" (vs. 2). This is reflected in the 18th verse: "He shall make a speedy riddance," or more accurately, "He shall make an end, yea, a speedy end."

This does not mean that everything will cease to exist or that all people will die. There will be an end to the present world condition. An earthquake can completely destroy a city, yet it will be built up again. When it is all over, people are still here, for Zephaniah says:

For my determination is to gather the nations, that I may assemble the kingdoms, to pour upon them mine indignation, even all my fierce anger: for all the earth will be devoured with the fire of my jealousy. For then will I turn to the people a pure language, that they may call upon the name of the Lord, to serve him with one consent.—Zeph. 3:8, 9

For more complete details see Revelation, chapters 8, 9 and 16. You will note that when there is loss of life, the plague afflicts no more than one-third of the earth at once. People always live through it. In fact, it says that they will seek death and death will flee from them (Rev. 9:6).

Of course many people will die, but in the end there are still people on the earth so that the population may be speedily restored. In the Millennium, Christ and the saints will reign over the nations. They must still be here.

Babylon in the Day of the Lord
Isaiah 13:1-22

The Babylon in view in Isaiah 13 is not ancient Babylon, for none of the things related here happened to the Babylon of Nebuchadnezzar. Note the following items:

The Time

Howl ye: for the day of the Lord is at hand; it shall come as a destruction from the Almighty.—Isa. 13:6.

The whole time covered by the Day of the Lord is in view here, but the destruction of the city comes near the end of this time. The destruction of Babylon comes just before the Battle of Armageddon. Revelation puts it just before the return of Christ. It comes under the seventh plague. Revelation says concerning it:

True and righteous are his judgments: for he hath judged the great whore, which did corrupt the earth with her fornication, and hath avenged the blood of his servants at her hand.... And I heard as it were the voice of a great multitude, and as the voice of many waters, and as the voice of mighty thunderings, saying, Alleluia; for the Lord God omnipotent reigneth. —Rev. 19:2, 6

The Battle of Armageddon follows this scene (Rev. 19:11-21).

The Participants

1. The Nations

The burden of Babylon, which Isaiah the son of Amoz did see. Lift ye up a banner upon the high mountain, exalt the voice unto them, shake the hand, that they may go into the gates of the nobles. I have commanded my sanctified ones. I have also called my mighty ones for mine anger, even them that rejoice in my highness.

The noise of a multitude in the mountains, like as of a great people; a tumultuous noise of the kingdoms of nations gathered together; the Lord of hosts mustereth the host of the battle.

They come from a far country, from the end of heaven, even the Lord, and the weapons of his indignation, to destroy the whole land.
—Isa. 13:1-5

The Battle of Armageddon is the climax of the Day of the Lord. All of God's people are present. All the nations are gathered together from the ends of the earth; every nation under heaven will be represented. There is a great noise on the mountains as they gather.

2. *The Saints*

The saints will return with Christ. The exact order of events is:

The Destruction of Babylon by an earthly power. (This is in contrast to the destruction wrought by the seven plagues.)

The Return of Christ. (He comes while the nations are gathering and before the actual Battle of Armageddon which takes place around Jerusalem.)

The Establishing of the Kingdom. (This will take some time.) The stone that struck the image grew until it covered the earth (Dan. 2:35).

The Cause

And I will punish the world for their evil, and the wicked for their iniquity; and I will cause the arrogancy of the proud to cease, and will lay low the haughtiness of the terrible.—Isa. 13:11

It is difficult for us to imagine, in this day when the Christian influence is everywhere, the extent of sin and evil that Satan will bring upon the world. Even now, to wipe out organized crime in some cities would be equivalent to destroying the city. What would it take to wipe Hinduism out of India? The judgments are against the sinners, not against their victims, although the victims suffer. The causes of sin must be destroyed and the results of sin purged out.

The Destruction of Babylon

Behold, I will stir up the Medes against them, which shall not regard silver; and as for gold, they shall not delight in it.

Their bows also shall dash the young men to pieces; and they shall have no pity on the fruit of the womb; their eye shall not spare children.

And Babylon, the glory of kingdoms, the beauty of the Chaldees' excellency shall be as when God overthrew Sodom and Gomorrah.

It shall never be inhabited, neither shall it be dwelt in from generation to generation; neither shall the Arabian pitch tent there; neither shall the shepherds make their fold there.

But the wild beasts of the desert shall lie there; and their houses shall be full of doleful creatures; and owls shall dwell there, and satyrs shall dance there.

And the wild beasts of the islands shall cry in their desolate houses, and dragons in their pleasant palaces; and her time is near to come, and her days shall not be prolonged.—Isa. 13:17-22 (Compare this with Rev. 18.)

We do not know who these Medes are that are used to destroy Babylon. They evidently will have some kind of atomic power because Revelation indicates a "fallout" (Rev. 18:10).

In ancient times the Medes were a people dwelling east of Babylon. They became a part of the Persian Empire. The prophet uses this name to refer to a people that are yet to come into prominence.

Babylon will be a glorious city, the greatest city ever built and the most influential. Habakkuk calls Antichrist the Chaldean. Babylon will be the glory of his empire and his greatest achievement. One other city will be almost as great. It is called Tyre in prophecy (Ezek. 26, 27, 28).

This prophecy has never been fulfilled; it is not true of the present site of ancient Babylon. That country is yet to become the very center of the earth. Who controls it now controls the very center of the earth. It is the most vital spot in the world. Ships based on the Persian Gulf would command all the routes to the Far East. Nations will fight for this advantage. For one nation with world ambitions to control the Indian Ocean would upset the world balance of power and throw the world into chaos. Russia knows this. So does the United States.

The events of the last days of the age await the rebuilding of Babylon. It will be one of the greatest of all the signs and possibly the most sensational.

Judgment with a Purpose

The Day of the Lord is no ordinary judgment. It is not a calamity that comes as a result of natural causes, or the acts of men. It is not, for instance, the atomic bomb. It is not even divine retribution on a wicked generation.

It is the consummation of redemption. These judgments are a part of redemption. They are closely superintended by innumerable saints operating from heaven. Their purpose is the cleansing of the earth from the results of sin.

During the reign of Christ that is almost immediately to follow, the earth will be transformed into a grand paradise. The prophet says: "The earth will blossom as the rose." The rubbish has to be cleaned up and burned before the garden can be planted.

God cursed the ground for man's sake; now the curse is about to be lifted, for it cannot remain on the earth while Christ reigns. The results of the curse are weeds, pests, sickness-producing germs, flies, mosquitoes—everything that mars God's otherwise perfect creation.

Nothing will escape the fires of this judgment. They will cleanse every portion of the earth from the lowest depth to the rarest atmosphere. What science has been trying to do with only limited success, the agents of God will do in seven years. This is a necessary part of the redemption of the earth. The meek shall inherit the earth, but it will be a cleansed, perfected, glorified earth. The plagues will purge the earth and destroy everything bad. The reign of Christ will restore all things.

People who live through this judgment will either be redeemed during the Millennium or destroyed at the end of it.

TIMES OF THE GENTILES

And they shall fall by the edge of the sword, and they shall be led away captive into all nations: and Jerusalem shall be trodden down of the Gentiles, until the times of the Gentiles be fulfilled. —Luke 21:24

Jesus is talking about the events of His second coming. All the Jews will be back in Palestine, the temple will be built, and Antichrist will be making his final attempt to rule the world, this time from Jerusalem. The great Battle of Armageddon will be impending. The time will be the last half of Daniel's Seventieth Week, a period of three and a half years. It is during this time that Jerusalem will be trodden down by the Gentiles.

"When ye shall see Jerusalem compassed with armies." The siege of Jerusalem actually begins with the Abomination of Desolation; it will end with the Battle of Armageddon. The armies will mobilize at Armageddon and for three and a half years Jerusalem will be under Gentile influence. It is not easy to comprehend all that is happening at this time because there are factors involved that do not obtain in ordinary wars. The battle is for the possession of the whole earth.

At this time we are nearing the consummation of the battle of the earth which began in the Garden of Eden. Satan's defeat will be decisive, and he is as a stag at bay. "Woe to the inhabiters of the earth and of the sea! for the devil is come down unto you, having great wrath, because he knoweth that he hath but a short time."—Rev. 12:12.

The gathering of the armies is Satan-inspired for the express purpose of preventing the reign of Christ and the saints.

> And I saw three unclean spirits like frogs come out of the mouth of the dragon, and out of the mouth of the beast, and out of the mouth of the false prophet. For they are the spirits of devils, working miracles, which go forth unto the kings of the earth and of the whole world, to gather them to the battle of the great day of God Almighty.—Rev. 16:13, 14

Even though the abomination is in the temple and Jerusalem is trodden by Gentiles, it is still a Jewish city and the capital of the nation of Israel. The 144,000 are on Mount Zion; the two witnesses are withstanding Antichrist with fire and plaguing the earth by not allowing rain to fall. Antichrist's troubles are centering in Jerusalem. He must either take over Jerusalem completely, drive out the Jews and get rid of the temple and the 144,000 who have the seal of God's protection, or he will lose the battle of the earth. Antichrist is thus forced to assemble the nations against Jerusalem. This gives point to the wording of Zechariah's declaration, "I will gather all nations against Jerusalem to battle."

"And Jerusalem shall be trodden down of the Gentiles, until the times of the Gentiles be fulfilled." This is probably one of the most misinterpreted prophecies in the Bible. The term *times of the Gentiles* has been taken out of its context and given a meaning not found anywhere in the Bible. It is this practice that makes prophecy so hard to handle; we have to unlearn so much that we have been taught. We continually have to choose between the wild pronouncements of expositors and the plain teaching of Scripture.

Jesus is merely saying that Jerusalem will be trodden down by Gentiles until their time is up—not from the time of Nebuchadnezzar, who is not in view here at all, but from the time of the beginning of Antichrist's invasion.

Jesus was not talking about some long period of time, beginning supposedly with Nebuchadnezzar and ending when the Jews are all back in Palestine and Jerusalem is an all-Jewish city. Jerusalem will be an all-Jewish city long before the invasion by Antichrist.

The four world empires of prophecy, which began with Nebuchadnezzar and which will continue until the saints possess the kingdom, are nowhere in Scripture called the times of the Gentiles. In this part of the Olivet Discourse, Jesus is certainly not talking about the four world empires of Daniel. He is talking about the siege of Jerusalem by Antichrist and says that Jerusalem will be trodden down by Gentiles until their time is fulfilled. Revelation 11:2 states that the length of this time is 42 months or 3 1/2 years: "But the court which is without the temple leave out, and measure it not; for it is given unto the Gentiles: and the holy city shall they tread under foot forty and two months." The times of the Gentiles, then, is the last 3 1/2 years before the return of Christ, the last half of Daniel's Seventieth Week, or the time of Jacob's trouble (Jer. 30:7).

THE FULNESS
OF THE GENTILES

For I would not, brethren, that ye should be ignorant of this mystery, . . . that blindness in part is happened to Israel, until the fulness of the Gentiles be come in.—Rom. 11:25

The fulness of the Gentiles is not the same as the times of the Gentiles. The gospel was taken first to the Jews and when the Jews rejected it, Paul said, "Lo, we turn to the Gentiles." From that time on the gospel has been primarily a Gentile process. The Jews, as a whole, have not received the gospel. But the time is coming when this dispensation will be brought to an end. God will start dealing with the Jews in a very aggressive manner to bring them to repentance and to an acknowledgment of Christ, their Saviour.

And I will pour upon the house of David, and upon the inhabitants of Jerusalem, the spirit of grace and of supplications; and they shall look upon me whom they have pierced, and they shall mourn for him, as one mourneth for his only son, and shall be in bitterness for him, as one that is in bitterness for his firstborn. —Zech. 12:10

Then the fulness of the Gentiles will have come.

Time of the End

The end in Bible prophecy usually means the goal, the time of the fulfillment of the prophecy. The disciples asked Jesus, "What shall be the sign of thy coming and of the end of the age?" In the Bible there is no such thing as the end of the world, in the sense that all things cease to be.

The Year-Day Theory

The Bible does not say day when it means year unless it specifically so states. In one place in Ezekiel God says, "I have appointed thee a day for a year." That was because Ezekiel would not be expected to lie on his side for 430 years, but that does not mean that every time God says day He means year. If it did, then God could not say day and mean day.

TIMES AFTER THE RAPTURE

After the Rapture, it would seem that everything is timed. There are two important time periods each 3 1/2 years long. The

first closes the Dispensation of Grace and the second closes the
Dispensation of Law, which we call Daniel's Seventieth Week. In
between there is another period of 3 1/2 years which is the first
half of Daniel's Seventieth Week.

The first of these three is a time of tribulation for the saints,
which comes immediately after the Rapture. Revelation calls it
the Great Tribulation. The gospel is preached during this time and
people are saved. At the end of this 3 1/2 year period all the saints
that have been killed by the Antichrist will be raised from the
dead. They appear in heaven in Revelation 7. This same chapter
also lists for the first time in the New Testament the 12 tribes
of Israel, indicating that Daniel's Seventieth Week is about to begin.
Daniel's Seventieth Week is a continuation of the Old Testament
Dispensation of Law, and it cannot start until the Dispensation
of Grace is over. The Tribulation Saints are in the First Resurrection (Rev. 20: 4, 5).

3 1/2 Years, Tribulation
of the Saints

This period is stated as 1260 days (Rev. 12:6); a time, and
times, and half a time (Rev. 12:14; Dan. 7:25); and 42 months
(Rev. 13:5). Antichrist continues to persecute the saints for 42
months. This is not the length of time of the existence of Antichrist,
which is more than that, but the amount of time he persecutes
the saints after the Rapture.

3 1/2 Years, Tribulation for Israel

There is also coming a time of tribulation for Israel, which
is also 3 1/2 years long. It is the last half of Daniel's Seventieth
Week. This could not very well come at the same time as the tribulation of the saints because the conditions are entirely different.
The whole of Daniel's Seventieth Week is a time of tribulation but
the last half is especially severe. It is called the time of Jacob's
trouble, but Jeremiah says, "He shall be saved out of it" (Jer.
30:7). Revelation gives this period of the tribulation for Israel as
42 months (Rev. 11:2). If it were not for the power of the two
witnesses, probably no Jews would be saved.

Daniel: Three Periods

Daniel also mentions three periods of approximately 3 1/2 years
each (Dan. 12:5-12). The first is in Daniel 12:7: "And I heard the
man clothed in linen, which was upon the waters of the river, when

he held up his right hand and his left hand unto heaven, and sware by him that liveth for ever that it shall be for a time, times, and an half; and when he shall have accomplished to scatter the power of the holy people, all these things shall be finished." This is the symbolic way of saying 3 1/2 years. Then follow two more periods of approximately 3 1/2 years. The last period, which is the more important, is mentioned first.

> And from the time that the daily sacrifice shall be taken away, and the abomination that maketh desolate set up, there shall be a thousand two hundred and ninety days.
> Blessed is he that waiteth, and cometh to the thousand three hundred and five and thirty days.—Dan. 12:11, 12

THREE PERIODS OF 3 1/2 YEARS

The only differences between the length of the times given here in Daniel and those given elsewhere are the time required to seal the 144,000 and the time required for the 7th trumpet.

The purpose of prophecy is not to pinpoint the time to the very minute; in fact, that would be impossible in many cases because events do not move that fast. For instance, you might say that a war lasted four years, but the exact time of the start might be either when the first shot was fired or when the declaration of war was issued. Even so, the end of the war might be considered as either when the last shot was fired, or when the armistice was made, or when the treaty of peace was signed. This might make a difference of a few days or even months.

In all prophecies, these times are about the same length, but there may be some slight variation between some relating to the Jews, and some to the nations. For instance, to the saints, the Second Coming of Christ may be when He comes in the clouds with His saints as recorded in Revelation 19. But to the nations, the Second Coming may be when He destroys Antichrist. (Daniel saw it that way.) And to the Jews, the Second Coming will be when He comes suddenly to His temple, according to Malachi. These events will be a few days apart. Ezekiel's time of 2520 years (Ezekiel 4) may even run to the formal establishing of the kingdom. Daniel's final "week" could begin and end with any number of important events which will happen during that time. The last week of 7 years is divided into two parts, though they may not be exactly equal. Daniel 7 says, "in the midst of the week." This would not have to be the exact center down to the day but somewhere near the middle.

And so, a difference of a few days, or weeks, in two different reckonings would only mean that we have a different starting or stopping point for each particular situation. The fact remains that Daniel was shown three separate, unequal periods of about 3 1/2 years each. (The same three periods may be determined by a study of Revelation. In Revelation the viewpoint is different because it is the operation of the saints that is being considered; in Daniel we are thinking from the standpoint of the nations and Israel.)

In Chaper 12 of Daniel, then, we have three unequal periods of about 3 1/2 years each. We have already discovered that the first period (vs. 7) is the length of time Antichrist persecutes the saints. This is exactly the same length as that given in Revelation 12 and 13, for in both cases it is the saints that are involved.

In chapter 12 of Daniel, then, we have three unequal periods in both Daniel and Revelation; this first period is 1260 days, or 3 1/2 prophetic years.

Next is mentioned the last of the three periods of 3 1/2 years, the one that begins with the Abomination of Desolation. This period starts in the middle of Daniel's 70th Week and runs to the end of that "week." The exact number of days is 1290. During this period the two witnesses prophesy for 42 months (1260 days or 3 1/2 years).

Revelation 11:3 says, "I will give power unto my two witnesses, and they shall prophesy a thousand two hundred and three score days, clothed in sackcloth." Three and a half years is also the length of time Jerusalem will be trodden under foot by the Gentiles. This period would have to be the last half of Daniel's 70th Week. It is the second woe. (The third woe is the 7th trumpet.) So the 1260 days take us up to the blowing of the seventh trumpet. Some time would be required for the events under the 7th trumpet.

1335 Days

Between these two extremes is a second period, which, according to verse thirteen, lasts 1335 days. We are not told the exact events that mark the boundaries of this middle period of 3 1/2 years, but it may start with the sealing of the 144,000 which takes place about 3 1/2 years after the Rapture.

Some of the events covered by these three periods of time may be thought of as occurring somewhat instantaneously; others would take time. The Rapture, the resurrection of the Tribulation Saints, the return of Christ in glory, even the setting up of the Abomination of Desolation, might be pinpointed to the day. But the sealing of the 144,000 takes some time, for the four angels hold in check the four winds of the earth saying, "Hurt not the earth, neither the sea, nor the trees, till we have sealed the servants of our God in their foreheads." If this sealing were instantaneous, there would be no need to hold back the wind till the sealing was completed. (The winds are the forerunners of the plagues.) The Battle of Armageddon will also take time; likewise, the setting up of the kingdom.

The only differences between the length of the times given here in Daniel and those given elsewhere are the time required to seal the 144,000 and the time required for the 7th trumpet.

2300 DAYS

Dan. 8:10-14

How long shall be the vision concerning the daily sacrifice, and the transgression of desolation, to give both the sanctuary and the host to be trodden under foot? And he said unto me, Unto two thousand and three hundred (2300) days; then shall the sanctuary be cleansed.—Dan. 8:13, 14

This 2300 days would amount to about 6 1/2 years. There is a 10 1/2 year period between the Rapture and the return of Christ. The last 7 years correspond to Daniel's 70th Week. During the first 3 1/2 years, Antichrist is engaged in getting rid of the saints. Then he turns his attention to the Jews. We do not know exactly when these 2300 days start, or where they end. We are informed here only of the total length of time in which the temple will be subject to desecration. Jesus referred to this when He said: "When ye therefore shall see the abomination of desolation, spoken of by Daniel, the prophet, stand in the holy place. . . ."—Matt. 24:15.

1000 YEARS—MILLENNIUM

Revelation 20

The Millennium is a time of reconstruction. The plagues, the earthquakes, the great hail, and the fire have destroyed the works of man. The earth is in ruins. It will require seven years just to bury the dead after that great Battle of Armageddon (Ezek. 39:9). Then will begin the work of reconstruction under the personal supervision of Christ.

"For he must reign, till he hath put all enemies under his feet."—I Cor. 15:25. This work of reconstruction will be carried on until perfection has been achieved. Long life will be restored during those days; but death, the last enemy, will still prevail until the end of the 1000 years (Isa. 65:20). The 1000 years will bring the world to a state of perfection, as it would have been if Adam had not sinned.

> The desert shall rejoice, and blossom as the rose. It shall blossom abundantly, and rejoice even with joy and singing: the glory of Lebanon shall be given unto it, the excellency of Carmel and Sharon, they shall see the glory of the Lord, and the excellency of our God.
>
> Strengthen ye the weak hands, and confirm the feeble knees. Say to them that are of a fearful heart, Be strong, fear not: behold, your God will come with vengeance, even God with a recompence; he will come and save you. Then the eyes of the blind shall be opened, and the ears of the deaf shall be unstopped.
>
> Then shall the lame man leap as an hart, and the tongue of the dumb sing; for in the wilderness shall waters break out, and streams in the desert. And the parched ground shall become a pool, and the thirsty land springs of water: in the habitation of dragons, where each lay, shall be grass with reeds and rushes. And an highway shall be there, and a way, and it shall be called The way of holiness; the unclean shall not pass over it; but it shall be for those; the wayfaring men, though fools, shall not err therein.
>
> No lion shall be there, nor any ravenous beast shall go up thereon, it shall not be found there; but the redeemed shall walk there: and the ransomed of the Lord shall return, and come to Zion with songs and everlasting joy upon their heads: they shall obtain joy and gladness, and sorrow and sighing shall flee away."
> —Isaiah 35

The reconstruction period is 1000 years. The kingdom is everlasting. The 1000 years is not the length of the kingdom; it is the length of time that Satan is chained.

There is no record nor suggestion that the earth is to be destroyed by fire at the end of the Millennium. It is God's purpose to redeem the earth, not to destroy it. That which is redeemed is not destroyed. The reign of Christ for 1000 years will not end in such failure that His kingdom will have to be destroyed by fire. Instead, we are told that He will deliver it up to God a perfect work (I Cor. 15:24-26).

A New Heaven and a New Earth

The new heaven and the new earth are not the result of some unrecorded catastrophe, happening between the 20th and 21st chapters of Revelation. They are the result of the process of redemption and the reign of Christ for one thousand years. It is unthinkable that the redemptive work of Christ, culminating in the reign of Christ, should result in such failure that total destruction would be necessary. No previous dispensation has been that bad.

This is retrospect on the part of John. "Old things are passed away; behold, all things are become new." With the final cleansing of the earth and the judgment of the great white throne, redemption is complete. For a thousand years Christ and the saints have been working at the task of restoring all things. The result is recorded in this verse (Rev. 21:1).

This completes the story of redemption that began in the Garden of Eden. Every effort of man to restore the earth has failed. Every civilization has in it the germs of its own destruction. There is one hope and only one, the blessed hope (Titus 2:13).

Imagine, if you can, the conditions on this earth after the seven last plagues and the Battle of Armageddon. Then imagine the changes that would come in a thousand years of reconstruction under the personal supervision of Christ. If you could imagine that, then you would see what John saw—"a new heaven and a new earth; for the first heaven and the first earth were passed away."

There is nothing in the word "pass" or in the word "away" that suggests any kind of destruction. We speak of our loved ones as having passed away. They have passed into a new realm and eventually are forgotten here. Passed away is a redemptive expression. Paul, after his conversion, said, "Old things are passed away, behold, all things are become new." The same is true of the redeemed earth. "The former things are passed away." "Behold, I make all things new."

And there was no more sea. This does not mean that there will be no more water but that the land and the water will be more evenly divided, doing away with all barren land and making every spot on the earth like the Garden of Eden. This change in the earth's surface will probably be one of the results of the mighty earthquakes so frequently mentioned in the prophecies concerning the last days.

Again, this is retrospect. John was summing up. He had seen the world as it is today. He had seen the destruction in the Day of the Lord—the earthquakes, the falling stars, the fire, and the hail. He had seen every wall fall to the ground and the mountains moved into the sea, bringing whole new continents into being. He had seen the surplus water disappear.

Regeneration is restoration to the original state. The heavens and the earth as they were before the Fall are described in Genesis.

This was also a remaking, as the earth has been here for a long time. We may learn something of the restored heaven and earth by looking at the former one.

> And God said, Let there be a firmament in the midst of the waters, and let it divide the waters from the waters. And God made the firmament, and divided the waters which were under the firmament from the waters which were above the firmament: and it was so. And God called the firmament Heaven . . . And God said, Let the waters under the heaven be gathered together into one place, and let the dry land appear: and it was so. And God called the dry land Earth; and the gathering together of the waters he called Seas.—Gen. 1:6-10

The word for seas in both the Hebrew and the Greek may be used of bodies of water, large or small. The meaning must be gathered from the context. The original seas could have been large enough for whales and still not be larger than the Mediterranean. On the other hand, there could have been a great number of seas, all connected. Whole new continents could rise in the oceans and still there would be plenty of water.

When John said "there was no more sea," he could have meant that the great oceans were filled with new expanses of land so that we would have the "seas" of Genesis rather than the "sea" or ocean of the present time.

If, then, there was less water at the first and more dry land, where was this extra water? Genesis tells us. The firmament called heaven is the sky—the atmosphere above the earth. This firmament was in the midst of the waters so that it divided the waters from the waters. Genesis suggests that the division was somewhat equal. This water that was above the sky was not then upon the earth. Instead of being three quarters water and one quarter land, the surface of the earth might have been more land than water. The animals that God created could easily have migrated to all parts of the earth where their remains have been found.

Even the remote islands of the sea could have been connected to main land, as must have been the case. Great changes have taken place on the earth since those days of re-creation.

God sums it all up in Revelation 21:5 when He speaks from the throne saying, "Behold, I make all things new." After the Millennium there will be a change, because the program of redemption is complete. The seat of government will be the Holy City. The saints will enter their "long home," but there will be nations on the earth forever.

The kingdom of David is an everlasting kingdom. "And they shall dwell in the land that I have given unto Jacob my servant, wherein your fathers have dwelt; and they shall dwell therein, even they, and their children, and their children's children forever: and my servant David shall be their prince forever."—Ezekiel 37: 25.

"And he shall reign over the kingdom of David forever and of his kingdom there shall be no end."—Luke 1:33.

It has been supposed by some that the Millennium is the final dispensation after which everything will be burned up; but the reign of Christ and the saints will not end in such dismal failure. Judgment fires burn only those things that cannot be redeemed. The thousand years is not the length of the kingdom. It is the time that the saints will reign while Satan is chained.

"But Israel shall be saved in the Lord with an everlasting salvation: ye shall not be ashamed nor confounded world without end." —Isa. 45:17.

Chapter 14

SPECIFIC TIMES

Times are never set for the church before the Rapture, and times are never set for Israel in such a way that they would reveal the time of the Rapture. After the Rapture times are freely set.

The Israelites have never been outside their land, but the time has been set for their return.

430 YEARS—BONDAGE IN EGYPT

Before the Israelites ever saw Egypt, their exodus from Egypt, including the date, had been foretold; indeed it was foretold before there were any Israelites. Even before the birth of Isaac, God told Abraham about the bondage, the return, and exactly how long it would be.

> When the sun was going down, a deep sleep fell upon Abram; and, lo, an horror of great darkness fell upon him. And he said unto Abram, Know of a surety that thy seed shall be a stranger in a land that is not theirs, and shall serve them; and they shall afflict them four hundred years; and also that nation, whom they shall serve, will I judge: and afterward shall they come out with great substance. And thou shalt go to thy fathers in peace; thou shalt be buried in a good old age. But in the fourth generation they shall come hither again: for the iniquity of the Amorites is not yet full.—Gen. 15:12-16

A generation was then considered a hundred years. This was apparently thirty years after Abraham's entrance into the Promised Land. So the entire time from Abraham's entrance into Palestine to the Exodus was to be 430 years. This was not an approximate time, but an exact date.

> Now the sojourning of the children of Israel, who dwelt in Egypt, was four hundred and thirty years. And it came to pass at the end of the four hundred and thirty years, even the selfsame day it came to pass, that all the hosts of the Lord went out from the land of Egypt.—Ex. 12:40,41

70 YEARS CAPTIVITY IN BABYLON

The second time the Israelites were forced to leave their

land is called the Captivity. This refers specifically to Judah, inasmuch as the ten northern tribes had been scattered over Assyria some time before the Fall of Jerusalem. More than one invasion of Judah was required to complete the captivity, and so the captivity took place over a period of about twenty years. It was during this time that Jeremiah predicted that they would serve the king of Babylon seventy years and then return to their own land. The time of the return was set and announced before they went into captivity.

> Therefore thus saith the Lord of hosts; Because ye have not heard my words, behold, I will send and take all the families of the north, saith the Lord, and Nebuchadrezzar the king of Babylon, my servant, and will bring them against this land, and against the inhabitants thereof, and against all these nations round about, and will utterly destroy them, and make them an astonishment, and an hissing, and perpetual desolations.
>
> Moreover I will take from them the voice of mirth, and the voice of gladness, the voice of the bridegroom, and the voice of the bride, the sound of the millstones, and the light of the candle. And this whole land shall be a desolation and an astonishment; and these nations shall serve the king of Babylon seventy years. —Jer. 25:8-11
>
> For thus saith the Lord, That after seventy years be accomplished at Babylon I will visit you, and perform my good word toward you, in causing you to return to this place.—Jer. 29:10

Although during Jeremiah's lifetime his warnings went unheeded, his prediction of a seventy years' captivity was taken very seriously. The sacred historian added it to the record of the Fall of Jerusalem.

> And them that had escaped from the sword carried he away to Babylon; where they were servants to him and his sons until the reign of the kingdom of Persia: to fulfill the word of the Lord by the mouth of Jeremiah, until the land had enjoyed her sabbaths: for as long as she lay desolate she kept sabbath, to fulfill threescore and ten years.
>
> Now in the first year of Cyrus king of Persia, that the word of the Lord spoken by the mouth of Jeremiah might be accomplished, the Lord stirred up the spirit of Cyrus king of Persia, that he made a proclamation throughout all his kingdom, and put it also in writing, saying, Thus saith Cyrus king of Persia, All the kingdoms of the earth hath the Lord God of heaven given me, and he hath charged me to build him an house in Jerusalem, which is in Judah. Who is there among you of all his people? The Lord his God be with him, and let him go up.—II Chron. 36:20-23

Daniel was taken captive in one of the raids and lived in Babylon during the entire seventy years. He was a student of Jeremiah and when the seventy years were up, Daniel became very much concerned about what was going to happen, apparently reading into the prophecy much more than was there. As a result, the angel was sent to Daniel to inform him of a further period of 70 sevens of years that were yet to be accomplished before Israel could look for complete redemption.

Isaiah's prophecies were much more detailed, even calling Cyrus by name: "That saith of Cyrus, He is my shepherd, and shall perform all my pleasure: even saying to Jerusalem, Thou shalt be built; and to the temple, Thy foundation shall be laid."—Isa. 44:28.

Jeremiah's prophecy is the only one mentioned in connection with the return, although from the proclamation of Cyrus it is apparent that the controlling factor was the prophecy of Isaiah.

That which made Jeremiah's prophecy stand out so strongly in the minds of the leaders was the time element. The time element is the most powerful detail of any prophecy; therefore, the time element of all prophecy is of extreme importance.

The most successful and troublesome false religions of our day are those that started by setting dates. Even though they were wrong, the fact that they claimed to know a date gave them an advantage over all others. In a false religion honesty and consistency are not virtues; nevertheless they serve to illustrate how these prophecies that reveal times have the greatest impact upon the minds of hearers. Those times that are hidden, we should not try to pry into; but those that are revealed, we should understand thoroughly, for "the secret things belong unto the Lord our God: but those things which are revealed belong unto us and to our children for ever."—Deut. 29:29.

2520 YEARS WORLDWIDE DISPERSION

Both Daniel and Ezekiel foretold the number of years the Jews would be scattered among the nations. Daniel has a period of 490 years, divided into three parts (see Daniel chapter 9); Ezekiel has two periods, one of 390 years and one of 40 years, making a total of 430 years.

The Qumran Commentaries (Dead Sea Scrolls) attempt an explanation of these figures. Although they rightly supposed that the length of the Dispersion was forecast in these prophecies, they fell into the common error of trying to make all prophecy culminate in their time. They tried to make the 430 years fit into the 490-year period and treated them as a reinterpretation of Jeremiah's seventy years.

However, the seventy years was an exact time. At the end of that period of captivity in Babylon, Palestine again became a Jewish homeland, and all who so desired could return. The prophecy of the seventy years' captivity was literally fulfilled by their return, as was recorded by Ezra and by Nehemiah.

But the return after the Babylonian Captivity was only a partial return, for many of the Jews remained in Babylon. Palestine never again became independent until this century. Throughout the years it was always a captive country so that the Jews never again had a reigning king. Successively, Palestine was dominated by Persia, Greece, Syria, and Rome. Finally, the Jews were scattered once more among all countries, where they have remained until this day. For the first time in over 2500 years, there is today an independent Jewish state in Palestine.

Whenever the Israelites were outside their land, times were set for their return. But in the case of the return of the captives, there is a complication. In 536 B.C. some of them went back, and prophecy follows the returned Jews down through the advent and rejection of Christ to the promised kingdom. But there is also the story of the other dispersion, which has always existed since the Fall of Jerusalem (586 B.C.) and which became complete again in A.D. 70. Because there are two lines of history, there are also two lines of prophecy: one about the Jews that returned to Palestine about 536 B.C.; the other about the Jews that were scattered among the nations, were later joined by those from Palestine, and are yet to return to their land.

In the Scriptures, therefore, one line of prophecy follows the Jews who returned. This includes the rebuilding of Jerusalem and its wall, the rejection of Christ, the temporary lapse during the Dispensation of Grace and the experiences with Antichrist, and the end of iniquity. Daniel's prophecy of the 70 weeks concerns these Jews who returned.

Ezekiel was told about those who did not return. How long their dispersion would be was revealed, but it was told in such a way that it would not influence its fulfillment nor point to the time of the Resurrection. Because of the fact that the return of the Jews is closely associated in time with the Resurrection, the time element must be somewhat veiled.

Ezekiel's Dramatized Prophecy

Ezekiel's account, then, of the number of years of dispersion is an acted-out prophecy which amounts almost to an enigma (Ezek. 4).

> Then the spirit entered into me [Ezekiel]... and said unto me.... Thou also, son of man, take thee a tile, and lay it before thee, and portray upon it the city, even Jerusalem: and lay siege against it, and build a fort against it, and cast a mount against it; set the camp also against it, and set battering rams against it round about.

Moreover take thou unto thee an iron pan, and set it for a wall of iron between thee and the city; and set thy face against it, and it shall be besieged, and thou shalt lay siege against it. This shall be a sign to the house of Israel.

Lie thou also upon thy left side, and lay the iniquity of the house of Israel upon it: according to the number of the days that thou shalt lie upon it thou shalt bear their iniquity. For I have laid upon thee the years of their iniquity, according to the number of the days, three hundred and ninety days; so shalt thou bear the iniquity of the house of Israel.

And when thou hast accomplished them, lie again on thy right side, and thou shalt bear the iniquity of the house of Judah forty days; I have appointed thee each day for a year. Therefore thou shalt set thy face toward the siege of Jerusalem, and thine arm shall be uncovered, and thou shalt prophesy against it. And, behold, I will lay hands upon thee, and thou shalt not turn thee from one side to another, till thou has ended the days of thy siege. —Ezek. 3:24; 4:1-8

Ezekiel was told to take a tile and portray upon it the city of Jerusalem and lay siege against it by lying on his left side for 390 days. Each day was to represent one year of the iniquity of Israel. Next Ezekiel was told to lie on his right side for 40 days, each day for a year. Evidently these years were to begin with the siege of Jerusalem, for the Lord said, "Son of man, behold, I will break the staff of bread in Jerusalem: and they shall eat bread by weight and with care; and they shall drink water by measure and with astonishment: that they may want bread and water, and be astonied one with another, and consume away for their iniquity."—Ezek. 4:16, 17.

The purpose of this prophecy is stated frankly—to show how long the Jews will be scattered among the nations: "I have laid upon thee the years of their iniquity, according to the number of the days" (vs. 5), "I have appointed each day for a year" (vs. 6). "Even thus shall the children of Israel eat their defiled bread among the Gentiles, whither I will drive them" (vs. 13). This dramatized prophecy has only one announced purpose—to show that the length of time the Jews will be scattered among the nations is 390 years plus 40 years (vss. 5, 6).

But the iniquity and the dispersion of Israel and Judah did not end either in 390 years, nor in 40 more years. The fact is these figures from Ezekiel 4 simply do not point to any experience in the dispersion of the Jews. It is evident, therefore, that some other conditions or factors must be applied. Those conditions may be found in Leviticus 26:18: "If ye will not yet for all this hearken unto me, then I will punish you seven times more for your sins." Evidently there were to be two periods of punishment. The length of time of the first punishment is not given in Leviticus. (In Jeremiah and Daniel it is expressly given as seventy years, Jer. 29:10, Dan. 9:2.) The Lord does say that if after that first period they do not leave their sins and turn to God, the balance of the punishment will be multiplied by seven.

Ezekiel's 430 Days

Ezekiel laid siege to Jerusalem for a total of 430 days (390 plus 40), indicating 430 years of the determined punishment for Israel and Judah. If we subtract 70 from the 430 (they were punished in Babylon 70 years), we have a balance of 360 years. According to Leviticus 26:18, God told Moses that these 360 years would be multiplied by seven. The number of years of world-wide dispersion for Israel is therefore 360 times 7 or 2520 years.

When will the 2520 years of punishment for Israel end? All dates must be considered approximate, but they are near enough for our purpose. The captivity began about 606 B.C. and was complete about 586 B.C.—that is, the process of taking Palestine and the Jews captive took about twenty years. Seventy years from Nebuchadnezzar's first captivity in 606 B.C. saw the first return of the captives (536 B.C.), and seventy years from the final captivity of Nebuchadnezzar in 586 B.C. saw the final return (516 B.C.); therefore the return also took about twenty years. The prophecy of the 2520 years could start any time within that twenty-year period. It is so arranged that we cannot set actual dates in advance.

Assyrian records set the time of the Fall of Jersualem at 586 B.C. The first return, seventy years from that date, would bring us to 516 B.C.; 2520 years from 516 B.C. would bring us to about A.D. 2004. We do not know what event will mark the end of this time. It could be sometime after the return of Christ. Before the return of Christ, there will be a temple built, for Malachi says, "The Lord, whom ye seek, shall suddenly come to his temple."—Mal. 3:1.

Regarding the return of the Jews to Palestine, there is a vast field of prophecy, involving a large number of countries. This return will require some time. Some very sensational developments (almost unbelievable, in fact) lie ahead.

God was speaking of those events when He told us through Habakkuk, "I will work a work in your days, which ye will not believe, though it be told you."—Hab. 1:5.

From these figures in Ezekiel 4 no dates for the Resurrection or the return of Christ can be set. But these 2520 years are beginning to run out, and the events scheduled are beginning to take place. The time prophesied is about up. The Jews are beginning to return, and Palestine is returning to productivity. Two world wars have had only one tangible result—Palestine becoming what Ezekiel called it, the center of the earth.

This is sufficiently accurate for our purpose. For the full understanding we will have to wait the event; but it will undoubtedly come, as did the going out of Egypt, "on the selfsame day" that the time is up.

This prophecy of the 2520 years concerns all Israel, those who returned and those who did not. It does not take note of the partial return under Ezra and Nehemiah, nor the partial return that is in progress now. Those partial returns are foretold in other places.

490 YEARS
Daniel's 70th Week

During the Babylonian Captivity, the nation of Israel was divided into two kingdoms: on the north, ten tribes, sometimes called Israel and sometimes called Ephraim, because Ephraim was the largest of the ten tribes; and on the south, two tribes of Juda and Benjamin, called Judah, from which we get the name Jew.

Israel went into captivity first. The Israelites were scattered throughout the Babylonian Empire. Later the Jews were taken into the same country as captives. After seventy years the Jews were allowed to return to Palestine. Some of them took advantage of the opportunity, but not all. Many remained in Babylonia.

In A.D. 70, about forty years after the crucifixion of Christ, all the Jews of Palestine were scattered over the face of the earth, the same as the ten tribes. In the dispersion they lost all tribal identity and so were fused into one nation, just as Ezekiel said they would be (Ezekiel 37:15-22). They are all known today as Jews or Israelites.

It was only during the days of the divided kingdom that there was any distinction made between Jew and Israelite. The prophets did not always distinguish between the two nations. They spoke of the whole house of Israel, meaning all twelve tribes. Today there is no difference. The prophecy of Ezekiel has been fulfilled. There is no such thing as the Ten Lost Tribes. The Book of James was addressed to the twelve tribes scattered abroad.

Because of the fact that in Ezekiel's day the nation was in two parts (some in Palestine, and some scattered), there were two lines of prophecy, one for each group. (Ezekiel's prophecy of 2520 years disregards the return after the exile and follows that part of the nation that remain scattered.)

On the other hand, Daniel was told about the future of those who returned. The number of years involved was 490. It is called 70 weeks. In the original it reads 70 sevens. Neither the Hebrew nor the English has a word meaning 7 years. We have a word for 10 years, a decade; and we have a name for 100 years, a century. But we have no word for 7 years, so the word "week" is used to mean a period of 7 years. This would make 70 sevens or 490 years.

> Seventy weeks are determined upon thy people and upon thy holy city, to finish the transgression, and to make an end of sins, and to make reconciliation for iniquity, and to bring in everlasting righteousness, and to seal up the vision and prophecy, and to anoint the most Holy.—Dan. 9:24

To accomplish these things, 70 weeks of years (490 years) are determined (vs. 24). A study of this prophecy indicates that the 70 weeks will run until the Second Coming of Christ. Of course it is obvious, if we consider the almost 2,000 years since Christ's birth, that this prophecy must refer to far more than 490 years. Therefore, the prophecy is not explainable if the entire 490 years are to run consecutively without a break. But if you put the Dispensation of Grace into this period as a parenthesis, then you can figure out exactly 490 years until the events that take place at the coming of Christ in glory.

Divisions of the 70 Weeks

> Know therefore and understand, that from the going forth of the commandment to restore and to build Jerusalem unto the Messiah the Prince shall be seven weeks, and three-score and two weeks: the street shall be built again, and the wall, even in troublous times.—Dan. 9:25

Next the angel proceeds to break down the seventy weeks into three smaller periods and indicates what each one represents.

From the going forth of the commandment to restore and to build Jerusalem . . . : the street shall be built again, and the wall. The 490 years are to start with "the going forth of a decree to restore and build Jerusalem." But the decree of King Cyrus did not involve any rebuilding of the city. It simply states, "The Lord God of heaven . . . hath charged me to build him an house at Jerusalem."—Ezra 1:2. This clearly is not the decree intended. Likewise, when Ezra and his companions left Babylon and came to Jerusalem in the seventh year of Artaxerxes, still no command had been given to build again the walls of Jerusalem. (This was about 458 B.C.) But to Nehemiah, in the twentieth year of the reign of Artaxerxes, there was a command given to build the wall of Jerusalem. This brings us to about 445 B.C. It is possible that none of these is the command referred to by the angel but another command from God that is not recorded. These dates serve only to show the general time.

Seven weeks, and threescore and two weeks. Sixty-nine weeks of years (483 years) from 458 B.C. would bring us to the year A.D. 25. If, however, we start with 445 B.C., it would bring us to A.D. 38. No one can fail to be struck with the fact that these dates are very near the most sacred date of all history—that of the crucifixion of our Lord.

The End of the Age

And after threescore and two weeks shall Messiah be cut off, but not for himself: and the people of the prince that shall come shall destroy the city and the sanctuary; and the end thereof shall be with a flood, unto the end of the war desolations are determined.—Dan. 9:26

Daniel divides the 490 years into three parts as follows: 7 weeks (49 years); 62 weeks (434 years); 1 week (7 years), divided "in the midst" (vs. 27).

Seven weeks would see the street and wall built again. (This is recorded by Nehemiah.) Sixty-two more weeks would bring us to the "cutting off" of Messiah. Crucifixion was a Roman form of punishment unknown to the Jews of Daniel's day, and not specifically mentioned in the Old Testament. But crucifixion is referred to in the Old Testament in no uncertain terms, as, for instance, in Psalm 22. The rejection and "cutting off" of Messiah brings us to the end of the first 69 weeks (7 weeks and 62 weeks).

One week. The last division of the 490 years given here is one "week" (or 7 years). The events of this week, the 70th Week, did not take place immediately after the crucifixion. Between Daniel's 69th and 70th weeks, the Dispensation of Grace intervenes. The Jewish nation was side-tracked and a new dispensation was begun, dominated by the Gentile Church, for "blindness in part is happened to Israel until the fulness of the Gentiles be come in" (Rom. 11:25).

Daniel's 70th Week, then, is the last seven years before the return of Christ in glory. (In Revelation it corresponds to the seven last plagues, Rev. 15 and 16.)

This verse and the next one (vs. 27) are made more difficult because of the condition of the text and the difficulty of getting a good translation. The versions all differ; the general meaning, however, is clear.

Messiah shall be cut off but not for himself probably means

that He was alone in His hour of trial. (At this point we skip to the end of the age.)

The prince that shall come is certainly Antichrist because Jesus referred to this passage and applied it to the end of the age (Matt. 24:15). The destruction of the city and the sanctuary brings us to the very point of the coming of Christ.

And the end thereof shall be with a flood. This is thought not to be a literal flood but an overrunning of armies. But there will also be a flood, for there will be a very great earthquake so that the Mount of Olives will divide in the middle and a great valley will appear. This will open up an underground river which will flow out of Jerusalem in two directions and will flood much land (Zech. 14:8; Ezek. 47:1-5).

The Covenant Confirmed

> And he shall confirm the covenant with many for one week.
> —Dan. 9:27a

He shall confirm the covenant is sometimes rendered, he shall make a firm covenant. But this has little support and does not make as much sense. "The covenant" is undoubtedly God's covenant with Israel concerning the land. It is this covenant that Antichrist confirms, thus trying to assume God's position as the protector of the Jew.

With many. Antichrist confirms God's covenant not with all the Jews, nor with Israel as a nation, but with "many." How much of the nation is involved is not said. The charge is not made that Israel as a nation officially accepts the overtures of Antichrist. The "many" may perhaps be leaders and men in power. They, the many, are alone made responsible, but for their disloyalty to God, the nation suffers.

Whatever may come from a "deal" with Antichrist, the benefits are short-lived, for in the middle of the "week," Israel will feel Antichrist's iron hand.

THREE AND ONE-HALF YEARS TRIBULATION FOR ISRAEL

> In the midst of the week he [Antichrist] shall cause the sacrifice and the oblation to cease, and for the overspreading of abominations he shall make it desolate.—Dan. 9:27b.

According to this statement, the 70th Week, or seven years, will be divided "in the midst"—into two halves of about 3 1/2 years each.

The last half of the 70th Week is "the time of Jacob's

trouble" (Jer. 30:7). By this time, Antichrist has infiltrated to the point of almost complete control. Such infiltration would not have been possible if he had not been allowed to "confirm the covenant." God will not prevent Antichrist from entering Palestine; instead, God will use Jacob's trouble for His own purpose, namely, the deliverance of Israel: "He shall be saved out of it" (Jer. 30: 7).

The pattern for the time of Jacob's trouble is the same as for the tribulation for the saints. The length of time is the same (3 1/2 years). But the two events do not take place simultaneously, for when the tribulation for Israel begins, the tribulation of the saints, mentioned in Revelation 7, is over. The purposes of the two tribulations are the same—to bring people to God through Christ—but the method of tribulation will be adapted to the peculiar conditions encountered. In both cases there will be tribulation accompanied by messengers from heaven. But in the case of Israel, the result will be different. Today the gospel is effective on only a part of its hearers; then, all Israel will be saved (Rom. 11:26).

During the tribulation of the Jews, instead of messengers flying in the midst of heaven having the everlasting gospel to preach (Rev. 14:6), there will be two witnesses sent from heaven, who will be easily recognizable because of their work. These two witnesses will duplicate the acts of Moses and Elijah and then will re-enact Jesus' death, resurrection, and ascension.

To the Jews the coming of these witnesses will be a sure sign, for they know that Elijah must first come. The disciples asked Jesus, "Why say the scribes that Elias must first come?" (Mark 9:11). The prophet Malachi said, "Behold, I will send you Elijah the prophet before the coming of the great and dreadful day of the Lord: and he shall turn the heart of the fathers to the children, and the heart of the children to the fathers, lest I come and smite the earth with a curse."—Mal. 4:5, 6.

The two witnesses will operate for 3 1/2 years. Revelation 11:2, 3 says, "The holy city shall they (the Gentiles) tread under foot forty and two months." During this time the forces of Antichrist will be "softening up" the Jews, preparatory to the great invasion called Armageddon. These 3 1/2 years are the "times of the Gentiles" mentioned by Jesus (Luke 21:24).

Chapter 15

CHRONOLOGICAL LIST OF PROPHETIC EVENTS

There is a natural, sensible, logical order of events. There is a time when world events are leading up to a world dictator, a world church and a common market. This is a time of unrest, uncertainty, wars and commotions. Some prophecies are fulfilled during this time.

Then there is a time of peace and prosperity, when the world dictator is in charge of world movements, commerce and trade. Great cities are being built and new countries are coming into being and old countries are becoming prosperous. This is the time of the exaltation of man.

Then there will follow a time of calamity, peace taken from the earth, wars between races and nations, great signs in the heavens and earthquakes in many places. Satan will be revealed in his true light.

The next era will see the judgments of God on the nations. This will be a time of purging, with fire the principal agent. Satan will build up to his final defeat.

Then, after the destruction will come the reconstruction—the reign of Christ and His saints, followed by the eternal state.

So, if you put prophecies scheduled for one time zone into some other time zone, confusion will result. In fact, confusion has already resulted from this very practice. We must distinguish the time; then the prophecies fall into place.

One time zone will sometimes blend into the following time zone without any drastic change. As, for instance, the rise of Antichrist may come in a time of wars, commotions, and confusion, and gradually result in a time of peace and prosperity. To begin with, Antichrist will probably be viewed by most of the world as a savior of the world, although the Bible usually pictures him in his real character.

It is impossible to list with chronological accuracy all the prophecies within a time period, because so many of them are happening at the same time. They have to be listed one after another. Some of the time periods are short and the events many. The important thing is to get each prophecy into its own time period (see page 152).

We have given the key references. In the following list the time periods are chronological. Events within a time period may or may not be happening at the same time.

Chronological List

BACKGROUND FOR ANTICHRIST

Wars and Rumors of Wars   Matt. 24:6

There have always been wars. This would not be a sign unless wars were widespread and rumors of wars were coming from all parts of the world at once.

Commotions   Luke 21:9

Terror is an accompanying sign.

False Christs, Deceit   Luke 21:8

One false teaching is: "The time draweth near."

The church always seems to be in a state of apostasy, but revivals always come—if not from the old church, at least from a new movement. This will probably happen again on a worldwide scale.

The Latter Rain   James 5:7, 8; Joel 2:28-32

The whole world must hear the gospel. The gathering around the throne after the Rapture includes people from every kindred, and tongue, and people, and nation (Rev. 5:9). The final apostasy (II Thess. 2) would have to come after this world-wide preaching of the gospel, because it comes during the time in which Antichrist is deceiving the world. This may take a little time.

Falling Away (Apostasy)   II Thess. 2:1-3

This falling away emphasizes the false teachings that the Day of the Lord is at hand. The truth is: All prophecy must be fulfilled regardless of how much time it takes. This apostasy is the final one and is the result of Antichrist's program of deceit. Any apostasy that is not connected with Antichrist is not the one mentioned in this chapter.

PEACE AND PROSPERITY

Rise of Antichrist   II Thess. 2:9, 10; Dan. 7:8; Dan. 8:23; Rev. 13:1

Many prophecies reflect the prosperity and riches of that day; it is almost beyond conception. Buildings are decked with gold, and churches are in need of nothing. Satan will deceive the world with wealth.

The return to idolatry is almost beyond belief, yet is mentioned in many prophecies. It has been supposed that the Jews have been cured of idolatry. But they will return to it in the days just preceding the coming of Christ.

Peace and Safety I Thess. 5:3

Nature of Antichrist Dan. 8:23-25
Antichrist's nature changes after the Rapture, when Satan takes over his body. He then becomes a part of the satanic trinity.

Names of Antichrist (Antichrist's actual name is not revealed. Each writer has his own name for him.)

The Assyrian	Isa. 10:5
Gog and Magog	Ezek. 38:2
The Little Horn	Dan. 7:8
The Chaldean	Hab. 1:6
Man of Sin	II Thess. 2:3
Beast	Rev. 13:1

Others are mentioned.

Direction of Movement Dan. 8:9
This applies to the time of his rise.
Antichrist will bring peace out of war, and security out of chaos.

Rebuilding of Babylon Isa. 13:17-22; Jer. 50:23-46; Jer. 51:1-58; Rev. 18:1-20
Babylon was located on the Euphrates River about 150 miles north of the Persian Gulf. It was an important city in the dawn of history, and it will be again in the time of the end. Its importance in the future is indicated by the large amount of space given to it in both the Old and New Testaments. Its destruction marks the end of purely human government.

The great importance of Babylon may be due to the fact that any great power having a base on the Persian Gulf would be in command of all the Far East as well as the Middle East; and would be in a position to dictate terms of prosperity to the whole world. This is exactly what Babylon does.

Revival of Ancient Bible Lands

This group of prophecies is among the most amazing; and

so will be the most sensational when they happen. The prophet is usually concerned with the destruction of these places, but they have to be built before they can be destroyed. In the report of the destruction, many details are included that indicate the great future wealth of these lands. Except for Babylon, the cause of the judgment is usually their treatment of the Jews in their hour of crisis.

Moab   Jer. 48; Isa. 15 and 16
Moab and Edom were southeast of Palestine, across the Dead Sea. They are now occupied by Jordan. Great changes are due there.

Edom   Jer. 49:7-22

Damascus   Isa. 17; Jer. 49:23-27

Elam   Jer. 49:34-39
This is a most remarkable prophecy. Elam is situated east of Babylon in what is now Iran, around the Persian Gulf. The prophecy shows that Elam will become a powerful country. Again this shows what great changes will come from the conquest of Iran and Iraq.

Egypt   Jer. 46:7-28; Ezek. 29, 30, 31, 32
Egypt plays a very important prophetic role, especially in connection with the Jews. The route of the return in through Egypt. Egypt will become so strong that she will have visions of world conquest (Jer. 46:8). There will be an Egyptian Empire or Confederacy (The King of the South) reaching across Africa from Ethiopia to Algeria. Lydia and the Lydians (Ludim) were located in what is now Algeria.

Tyre   Ezek. 26, 27 to 28:19
This city will be built by Antichrist and be his capital. He is the Prince of Tyrus. The city was in two parts, and will be again. One part was on the mainland, and one part on an island just off the mainland.

Ethiopia   Isa. 18; Dan. 11:43
Ethiopia contains two peoples: Jews (Falashas) and African Ethiopians. They have possession of the original Ark of the Covenant, and therefore will be the leaders in the great return of the Jews. The ark (Ensign) will be taken from Ethiopia to Mt. Zion at the time of the return.

Prosperity, Riches, Idolatry   Isa. 2:10-22; Rev. 3:14-18; Rev. 17, 18

Return of the Jews

Partial Return   Ezek. 35 to 36:5; Obadiah
The purpose of the partial return is to prepare the land for the mass return. The partial return (now in process) fulfills only those prophecies that concern the land and the opposition of the Arabs.

Great World-wide Persecution   Deut. 28:63-68; Ezek. 37:1-14

Expulsion to Egypt (Wilderness)   Deut. 28:68; Ezek. 20:33-44

Palestine Taken Over by Arabs for a Prey   Ezek. 36:5

War in Ethiopia   Isa. 18

The Ensign Appears   Isa. 18:3; Isa. 11:12
The Ensign of prophecy has all the features of the Ark of the Covenant. The Ark will rest again on Mt. Zion, and people will visit it until after the return of Christ (Jer. 3:16).

State of the Jews Prior to the Return   Jer. 30:17; Ezek. 37:1-14; Isa. 1:2-24

Repentance of the Jews   Deut. 30:1-3; Ezek. 20:33-38
The Jews must repent and turn to God, the God of their fathers, before they can completely possess their land. They will not accept Christ at this time.

Miracles of the Return   Isa. 11:15, 16

Great Mass Return of the Jews   Isa. 11:11-16; Ezek. 36:7-38
This will include all the Jews from all lands (Ezek. 36:10).

Arabs and Strangers Driven out of Israel   Isa. 11:14

Tabernacle of David Rebuilt   Amos 9:11
The Tabernacle housed the Ark while the temple was being built.

Temple Rebuilt   Ezek. 41, 42, 43
Ezekiel's Temple will be built after the Return and before the Coming of Christ—probably before the Rapture, during the time of world prosperity. It must be here before the Return of Christ (Mal. 3:1). The Temple mentioned by Haggai (2:9) will probably be built during the reign of Christ.

Prosperity in Israel   Isa. 3:16-23; Ezek. 38:11, 12
     This prosperity will lead to great sin and idolatry (Mal. 1 and 2).

THE RESURRECTION (Rapture)

The Shout, Voice and Trumpet   I Thess. 4:16; Rev. 4:1; Dan. 12:1
     The voice is the voice of the archangel.

Impending World Calamity   Matt. 24:21, 22; Luke 21:36; Dan. 12:1; Isa. 26:20, 21

Dead in Christ Raised   John 5:25; I Cor. 15:23, 52; I Thess. 4:16, 17; Dan. 12:2; Psalm 17:15

Living Saints Caught Up   I Thess. 4:16, 17; Rev. 12:5; Zeph. 2:3

Satan and Host Cast out of Heaven   Rev. 12:7-10; Dan. 8:10-13; Ezek. 28:18

Revelation of the Man of Sin (Satan in the flesh)   Rev. 12:9; II Thess. 2:3, 8, 9; Rev. 13:3, 4; Rev. 17:8; Ezek. 28:12-19

Judgment in the "Kingdom"   Matt. 13:41; Dan. 12:2

Separation of the Wheat and Tares   Matt. 13:40-43

Separation of the Fish in the Net   Matt. 13:49

Some Taken, Some Left   Luke 17:34-37; Matt. 24:40, 41

Some Cast Out, Some Left Out   Matt. 25:1-13; Matt. 22:13; Luke 13:25-28

THE TRIBULATION PERIOD
As Seen from Heaven

Saints in Heaven   Rev. 4 and 5
     Elders, Beasts (Living Ones), Horsemen, Angels

The Great Reunion   II Thess. 2:1

Thrones Set Up   Rev. 4:4 (Rev. 20:4)

Christ Takes the Sealed Book   Rev. 5:7

The Seals Are Opened   Rev. 6
    The opening of the seals represents the redemption of the earth. The process includes, first, purging; second, reconstruction. The purging takes place during the opening of the seals. The restoration comes during the reign of Christ and the saints. This takes 1000 years.

Wrath Mixed with Grace   Rev. 7:9-17; Hab. 3:12, 13

The Four Horsemen Sent Out From Heaven   Rev. 6:1-8

Gospel Preached to All Nations   Rev. 14:6; Matt. 24:14

Peace Taken from the Earth   Rev. 6:4; Matt. 24:7

Famine   Rev. 6:5, 6; Matt. 24:7

Pestilence   Rev. 6:8; Matt. 24:7

Earthquakes, Falling Stars   Rev. 6:12-17; Matt. 24:7

A Great Multitude Saved   Rev. 7:9-17
    These are the Tribulation Saints saved after the Rapture.

144,000 Israelites Sealed   Rev. 7:4-8
    These are also Tribulation Saints, but they have not been killed because Antichrist is making an agreement with the Jews at this time. The 144,000 remain on the earth and are sealed against the coming plagues.

As Seen from the Earth

Antichrist's Deadly Wound Healed   Rev. 13:3

Antichrist Reigns with Full Power   Rev. 13; Rev. 17; Dan. 8:
    23-25

Persecution of the Tribulation Saints   Rev. 13; Dan. 7:25

The False Prophet   Rev. 13:11-18

The Mark of the Beast   Rev. 13:16-18

Antichrist's Church   Rev. 17

Wars of Antichrist   Dan. 11

Egypt Destroyed   Ezek. 29:9-13

Egyptians Go into Captivity   Ezek. 29:9-13

Sudden Flood from the Sea   Amos 9:6; Ezek. 27:34; Jer. 47:2
The last three items could come in the Day of the Lord, close to the end.

End of the Gospel Age   Matt. 24:14.

THE DAY OF THE LORD

Day of the Lord   Zeph. 1:14-18; Joel 2:1-10

70th Week—Seven Years   Dan. 9:27

Covenant with Antichrist   Dan. 9:27; 11:28
This is Antichrist's attempt to nullify God's Covenant with Israel.

Seven Last Plagues   Rev. 8, 9, 16
Inanimate: Fire on land, sea, rivers, air. Animate: Evil Spirits from the bottomless pit. Christ and the saints from Heaven.

Christ Takes Legal Possession   Rev. 10:1-7

Satan Gathers the Nations   Rev. 16:13-16; Ezek. 38:1-17; Joel 3:9-16; Zech. 14:1-3

Travel by Air   Isa. 5:26-30

Jacob's Trouble   Jer. 30:7

Two Witnesses   Rev. 11:1-12
This is a witness to Israel. The two witnesses duplicate the life, death, resurrection and ascension of Christ. The purpose is to condition the Jews to receive Christ.

No Rain for 3 1/2 Years   Rev. 11:6
The Return of Christ follows immediately.

Abomination of Desolation   Dan. 9:27; Matt. 24:15; II Thess. 2:4
The two witnesses oppose this operation of Antichrist.

Satan's Armies March Down Palestine   Isa. 10:28-34

Jerusalem Besieged   Luke 21:20-24; Rev. 19:17-21; Zech. 14:1-3

Jews Dispersed Among the Nations   Luke 21:24; Zech. 14:2
    This dispersion takes place just before the return of Christ. There will be a regathering of the Jews after the return of Christ (Isa. 66:19-21).

Babylon Destroyed   Rev. 18; Jer. 51

Great Earthquake and Hail   Rev. 16:21; Ezek. 38:19-23

Marriage Supper   Rev. 19:7, 8; Ps. 45

Signs of Christ's Coming   Matt. 24:29-31; Luke 21:25-27

RETURN OF CHRIST

Saints in Heaven Called Together   Matt. 24:31; Mark 13:27

In the Clouds   Acts 1:9-11; Rev. 1:7

With His Saints   Rev. 19:14; Jude 14; Zech. 14:5

Jews Saved from Destruction   Zech. 14:3; Obadiah 17-21

Armies of Antichrist Destroyed   Ezek. 39:1-6; Rev. 19:17-21; Zech. 14:12-15; Hag. 2:22

Antichrist Killed   Ezek. 28:1-10
    Satan, as Antichrist, will die like a man; but Satan is more than man. His "spirit" will be cast alive into the lake of fire (Rev. 19:20).

Israel Redeemed   Zech. 12:10-14; Ezek. 36:24-38; 39:25-29

Fall of Many Nations   Isa., chapters 14 to 23; Jer., chapters 46 to 51; Ezek. 25 to 32

Scarcity of Men   Isa. 4:1; Isa. 13:12

Symbolism of the Ark Fulfilled   Jer. 3:16

Judgment of the Unsaved Dead Begins   Rev. 11:18

Judgment of Living Nations   Matt. 25:31-46

Satan Chained   Rev. 20:1-3

MILLENNIAL KINGDOM

Kingdom Established   Micah 4:1-5; Dan. 2:44, 45

Nations Serve the Lord   Zech. 14:16-21; Rev. 21:24

Wars Cease   Isa. 2:4

Jews Regathered from Many Nations   Isa. 66:19-21

Egypt Restored   Isa. 19:22-25

Kingdom of David   Ezek. 37:21-24; II Sam. 7:16

Earth Made New   Rev. 21:1, 5; Isa. 65: 17-25
    This is the culmination of a process that takes 1000 years.

Animal Kingdom   Isa. 11:6-9

New City   Rev. 21:9-27; 22:1-5
    This is the new heavenly city that only the saints with im-
mortal bodies may inhabit. There will also be a new earthly
Jerusalem (Isa. 60:14-22). The heavenly Holy City seems to give
light to the New Jerusalem on earth (Isa. 60:19, 20).

New Temple   Rev. 21:22
    There will be a new earthly temple, but few details are
given; in fact, no details are possible that we would understand
today (Hag. 2:9; Zech. 6:12, 13).

New River   Rev. 22:1
    This river is in the Holy City, the home of the saints. There
will also be a new river on the earth. It comes out of the New
Jerusalem and flows in two directions. It will be noted for the
abundance of fish (Ezek. 47:1-12).

New Heavens   Rev. 21:1; Isa. 66:22

New Covenant   Jer. 31:31-34

Satan Loosed   Rev. 20:7

Gog and Magog   Rev. 20:8
    This is the name given to Satan when he operates on the
earth as a man. Satan does this twice: once before the return
of Christ (Ezek. 38:2) and once at the end of the Millennium.

Satan Cast into the Lake of Fire   Rev. 20:10

Judgment of the Unsaved Dead Comes To an End   Rev. 20:11-15
This would take some time and may have been going on all during the Millennium.

ETERNITY
The Earth

The Everlasting Kingdom   Dan. 7:27
This kingdom is on the earth, under the whole heaven. It takes the place of the kingdom of the beast. "The kingdoms of this world are become the kingdoms of our Lord, and of his Christ; and he shall reign for ever and ever."—Rev. 11:15.

The Ever-expanding Kingdom   Isa. 9:7
This envisages more territory than is available on the earth alone.

David to be King   Ezek. 37:24, 25; 34:23

Tabernacle of God to Be with Men   Rev. 21:3

Curse Lifted   Rev. 21:4; 22:3

No More Death   Rev. 21:4

No More Sea   Rev. 21:1

The Heavenly City

In the Sky   Rev. 21:10

Home of the Saved   Rev. 21:9, 27

Foundations   Rev. 21:14

Gates   Rev. 21:12, 21
The foundations represent the saints of the New Testament; and the gates, the saints of the Old Testament.

River of Life   Rev. 22:1

Tree of Life   Rev. 22:2
The tree of life is not said to grow again on the earth, but only in the Holy City. This makes the people on the earth dependent upon the Holy City.

Kings Forever   Rev. 22:5

CYCLOPEDIC INDEX

Abomination of Desolation
Pages 124, 166, 190.

Daniel mentions "the abomination of desolation" a number of times (8:13; 9:27; 11:31; 12:11), always in reference to Antichrist. In the Olivet Discourse Jesus said, "When ye therefore shall see the abomination of desolation, spoken of by Daniel, the prophet, stand[ing] in the holy place. . . ." Then Jesus goes on to tell about the signs of His coming again. Here Jesus referred to this "abomination of desolation" as something future, not past. He connected it with the persecution of the Jews by Antichrist, not Antiochus, as some have thought. Antiochus does not appear in prophecy. His acts had no prophetic significance and no lasting results. In importance he does not approach Adolph Hitler, whose persecutions do have prophetic significance and lasting results—he forced the Jews to return to Palestine—and so, for the first time since Daniel, we have an independant Jewish state in the Promised Land.

An abomination is a ceremonial pollution, especially an idol. The abomination of desolation might be read, "The idol that causeth desolation." It is an act of Antichrist in the middle of the Seventieth Week by which he attempts to set up an idolatrous worship in the temple at Jerusalem (II Thess. 2:4).

Abraham
Pages 17, 62.

Adam
Pages 49, 51.

Adam to the Flood
Page 17.

Africa
Pages 93, 138.

After the Rapture
Page 38.

Agents
Page 30.
God's agents in Redemption.

Ages of the Ages
Page 97.

Aion
Page 147.

Alexander the Great
Page 102.

Algeria
Page 139, Map, page 86.

Lydians (L u d i m) (Jer. 46:9; Ezek. 30:5 A.V.). North Africa, along the Mediterranean Sea. It was a part of the Roman Empire. In prophecy it is associated with Libya. It is today a part of the Arab world and so may be expected to participate in the prophesied federation of Arab states under Egypt, called in Daniel "the king of the south." "All the men of thy confederacy have brought thee [the Arabs] even to the border [of Israel]."—Obad. 7. This confederacy will be opposed to the Jews at the time of their return (Dan. 11:25; Ezek. 30:3-6).

All Things New
  Pages 24, 170.

Amman
  Map, page 70.

Angel(s)
  Page 53.
  With trumpets and vials—page 45.
  The word means "messenger"
  and is indicative of office rather
  than of nature. Thus, it may be used
  of Christ, the saints, or special
  created beings, or even of God Himself. The Angel of the Lord is the
  Lord (Gen. 22:11). The Hebrew word
  Malak is translated "angel" 111
  times, "ambassador" 4 times, and
  "messenger" 98 times. The corresponding Greek word *aggelos* is
  translated "angel" 181 times and
  "messenger" 7 times. In Revelation angel means agent and is the
  usual designation for the saints,
  who in the tribulation and judgment
  periods are the agents of God in redemption.

Animals
  Redeemed—page 57.
  Kingdom—page 192.

Anti
  Page 124.

Antichrist
  Pages 112, 117-127. Map, page
  110.
  One who denies Christ (I John 2:
  22). The word has come to be ap-
  plied to the great antagonist of
  Christ of the last days.
  Meaning—119, 124, 126
  Names—119, 185
    Little Horn—43, 113, 119, 125,
      132, 183, 44 (chart)
    The Assyrian—77, 119, 135, 183
    Vile Person—119
    Chaldean—119, 132
    Gog and Magog—119, 121, 192
    Beast out of the sea—119
  Deceit—151

Origin—113
Dominion—117, 120
Man and Satan—118
Rise—120, 134, 150
Nature—113, 114, 185
Moves in three directions—133
Never conquers the world—116
Infiltrated Israel—182
Reigns with full power—189
Troubles—105, 162
Antichrist and the church—189
Antichrist and the Jews—74, 82,
    88
War with the saints—46
Savior of the world—115, 125, 183
Destruction—80, 121

Antiochus Epiphanes
  See *Abomination of Desolation.*
  Reigned 175-163 B.C. Antiochus
  instituted a vigorous persecution of
  the Jews. It is said that he placed
  a sow in the temple and forced the
  Jews to worship it. Many commentaries apply portions of Daniel's
  prophecies to Antiochus; but Antiochus did not fulfill them completely. We therefore look for a complete
  fulfillment during the reign of Antichrist.

Apokalupsis
  Page 29 (Unveiling, revelation,
  appearing, coming).

Apostasy
  The English form of the Greek
  word for "falling away" (II Thess.
  2:3). The falling away of the church
  from the faith in the last days of
  this age.

Aqaba
  Map, pages 61, 70.

Arab, Arabia
  Pages 65, 76, 93. Map, page 86.
  Driven out of Israel—187
  Oppose return of Jews—65
  Arabia is largely desert at the
  present time, but it was not always
  so, and will not always be so. God
  has a way of saying last things first.

The Garden of Eden was on the Euphrates River just north of Arabia. Four rivers joined at the Garden. Two of them are still flowing— the Tigris (Hiddekel) and the Euphrates. The other two have gone underground. One was called Gihon. It went all the way to Ethiopia (which in ancient times seems to have been connected with Arabia). The other watered Arabia, which is called Havilah. A very significant statement is made about Havilah: "Where there is gold; and the gold of that land is good: there is bdellium and the onyx stone."—Gen. 2:11, 12. Bdellium may refer to a precious stone or to a gum tree. It could also refer to oil.

The most amazing feature of the prophecies of these lands of the East is their come-back to wealth and power. There may be a gold rush in Arabia. The southeastern part of Arabia was once called "The Empty Quarter." A start has been made to explore it systematically; not only the surface, but specimens of soil far beneath the surface. The immediate purpose is oil but most anything can happen. (See *Jordan*.)

Ararat

A mountain in Eastern Turkey where Noah's ark rested after the Flood. Its discovery by air has been claimed. It may be one of the sensational features of the last days.

Ark (Noah's)

Page 31.

Ark of the Covenant

Pages 78, 90, 191, See *Ensign*.

The Ark was a box made of acacia wood about 5 feet long, 3 feet high, and 3 feet wide. It was overlaid, inside and out, with pure gold. There was a crown of gold around the top which held in place the cover, called the Mercy Seat. The Cherubim were an integral part of the Mercy Seat. Each cherub with its spread-out wings was beaten out of one piece of pure gold. They faced each other as they looked down upon the Mercy Seat.

Four golden rings were set in the four corners of the Ark, and through these rings were placed two poles with which the priests carried the Ark in its journeys. The poles also were overlaid with gold. The word for Mercy Seat means "to atone" or "to cover." In the New Testament it is rendered, "propitiation." God's mercy can be known only in Christ and on the ground of atonement. On the Day of Atonement, the High Priest entered within the veil, with the blood of a sin offering. This was sprinkled on the Mercy Seat once and before it seven times. Christ was offered once for all. That one atonement was perfect and complete. (Seven is the number of completeness.)

The Ark held the two tablets of the law, the basis of God's covenant with Israel. Later there was added a pot of manna and Aaron's rod that budded. The manna was symbolical of God's care and protection and the rod spoke of resurrection and everlasting life. Years later, when the Ark was brought to Solomon's temple, it contained only the stone tablets of the law.

When the Ark was at rest, it was kept out of sight in the Holy of Holies, the innermost part of the tabernacle. It could be seen once a year, and then only by the High Priest. When it was carried from place to place it was completely covered.

The Ark in Action

There was a majesty and glory connected with the Ark. It was the dwelling place of God in the Holy of Holies. It was built after the pattern of a heavenly Ark. On more than one occasion the glory and greatness of God were manifested in the Ark.

When the time came for the Children of Israel to cross the Jordan River into the Promised Land, the priests, bearing the Ark went before the people. When the feet of the priests touched the waters, the stream dried up and all the hosts of Israel crossed on dry land. The priests set the Ark down in the middle of the river bed and there it stayed until all the Israelites had safely crossed. Then the priests again took up the Ark, and when they reached the other side, the river resumed its normal course.

The Ark was not only the *symbol* of divine presence, but God actually was present with the Ark. To desecrate it even by touching it meant instant death. Carried forth to battle, it brought victory. It was the most wonderful, most powerful, possession any people ever had. No weapon formed against it could prosper. As long as the Israelites kept the covenant which the Ark represented, it was to them better than walls or fortifications. It meant that God himself would fight their battles for them.

The Israelites were in a precarious position after they crossed the Jordan and the river had resumed its course. Cut off from all possibility of retreat, with no supplies to feed the thousands of families, with no adequate fighting force, they faced a combination of the most powerful nations on the earth. Thirty kings were in federation against Joshua and his meager army.

Jericho was the first city in their line of march. It was the priests, not the army, that were delegated to take the city. The men of war were to march but not to fight. They were an escort for the Ark. In sol-

emn procession, announced by the blowing of trumpets, the Ark, the priests and the warriors paraded around the city. That is all. The walls fell down. The people fled. The Ark was victorious.

The supernatural power that surrounded the Ark was impressed at regular intervals upon the people. If a man so much as touched it without authority, he immediately dropped dead, as if he had touched a high tension wire. The glory of God was at times visible around it, and the place where it was kept, filled with smoke. If, however, the Israelites went into idolatry, the Ark lost its power.

There is a prophetic reference to the Ark in Jeremiah 3:16.

"And it shall come to pass, when ye be multiplied and increased in the land, in those days, saith the Lord, they shall say no more, The ark of the Covenant of the Lord: neither shall it come to mind: neither shall they remember it; neither shall they visit it; neither shall that be done any more."—Jer. 3:16.

The Ark is to be visited; it will be a tourist attraction of the first order. The time is specified: "At that time they shall call Jerusalem the throne of the Lord: and all the nations shall be gathered unto it, to the name of the Lord, to Jerusalem; neither shall they walk any more after the imagination of their evil heart. In those days the house of Judah shall walk with the house of Israel, and they shall come together out of the land of the north to the land that I have given for an inheritance unto your fathers."—Jer. 3:17-18.

This could be no other time than when the Jews are regathered and are living in Israel. It is after the coming of Christ, because Jerusalem is called the Throne of the Lord.

When Christ died the symbolism of the Holy of Holies was fulfilled and the veil of the temple was "rent in twain" exposing the Holy of Holies. It no longer had any prophetic significance. But the Ark was not there. The symbolism of the Ark applies to the Second Coming of Christ when His throne will be established in Jerusalem and "all the nations shall be gathered unto it."

When the symbolism of the Ark is fulfilled, it will no longer have prophetic importance. It must be, therefore, that the Ark of the Covenant will be in Jerusalem before the coming of the Lord.

Armageddon

Pages 47, 81, 83, 91, 94, 98, 100. Map, pages 61, 70. Chart, page 55. See *Battle of Armageddon.*

Armageddon, "Mount of Meggido," the Plain of Esdraelon, is the great Old Testament battleground. It was the scene of Barak's victory over Canaan and Gideon's victory over Midian. However, it is not the scene of the so-called Battle of Armageddon. It is the place of mobilization. The battle takes place at Jerusalem.

The so-called Battle of Armageddon is the final battle between Antichrist and the Lord at His second coming to take possession of the earth. Although there are many references to this battle, the word Armageddon occurs only in Revelation 16:16.

It is a gathering of all nations: "For I will gather all nations against Jerusalem to battle."—Zech. 14:2. At that time the nations will be divided into two groups: one under Antichrist and one independent. (See *Britain.*)

These two groups are indicated in Revelation at the place where Armageddon is mentioned. There are the armies under Antichrist:

"And I saw three unclean spirits like frogs come out of the mouth of the dragon, and out of the beast, and out of the mouth of the false prophet. For they are the spirits of devils, working miracles, which go forth unto the kings of the earth and of the whole world, to gather them to the battle of that great day of God Almighty."—Rev. 16:13-15.

Although Antichrist will have a limited kingdom, Satan exercises influence over the whole world. This does not make for a peaceful world. Satan's people fight. There is also a group which the spirit of Satan brings in, but not under the flag of Antichrist. They are called, in Revelation, "the kings of the east." "And the sixth angel poured out his vial upon the great river Euphrates; and the water thereof was dried up, that the way of the kings of the east might be prepared."—Rev. 16:12.

Jeremiah mentions the drying up of the waters of Babylon. "A drought is upon her waters; and they shall be dried up."—Jer. 50:38. Waters are used throughout prophecy to indicate people. The city called Babylon will be destroyed and the nation by the same name will be overthrown. On our maps today this land is called Iraq.

This opens the way for nations not connected with Antichrist directly to enter Palestine. The reason for the sudden convergence on Palestine by all nations, Ezekiel says, is to take a prey and a great spoil (Ezek. 38:12). This shows the great wealth of Palestine which will prevail under Jewish control. It will become the envy of the world.

Ezekiel lists the nations in each group. In the group under Gog, or Antichrist, there are two conspicuous omissions: Iraq and Egypt. Iraq will be wiped out with Babylon (Rev. 18) and the land dried up. It will not be a nation at the time of Armageddon.

Egypt will also be destroyed and the Egyptians scattered. (See *Egypt.*) So Egypt will not be a nation at that time.

Compare Ezek. 39:3, 4, 17-20 with Rev. 19:17-21. Also Ezek. 38:19-22 with Rev. 16:17-21. See also Joel 3: 1-16 and Psalm 2.

The Battle of Armageddon has a very definite date. It is at the return of Christ to reign. "Then shall the Lord go forth, and fight against those nations, as when he fought in the day of battle. And his feet shall stand in that day upon the mount of Olives which is before Jerusalem." —Zech. 14:3, 4.

It is difficult to realize how much the world will change before that time. The reign of Satan, the tribulation, the seven last plagues, the fire, earthquake and famine will take their toll. There will be no rain for three and a half years. Although Palestine will not be exempt from these judgments (except Mt. Zion), the kingdom of the beast will suffer most. There will be comparative prosperity in Palestine.

As with most wars, there are two causes for the Battle of Armageddon: the announced cause and the secret cause. The announced cause of the invasion of Palestine is to get food (Ezek. 38:11, 12). The other cause, the thing that moves Satan to act, is the impending return of Christ. The nations will take counsel together against the Lord, and against His anointed (Ps. 2:2).

Yet, in spite of all this show of power, God says: "Yet, have I set my king upon my holy hill of Zion." —Ps. 2:6.

It is also at this time that Christ will make His first official proclamation as the new King of the world. We have the full text of this proclamation:

"I will declare the decree: the LORD hath said unto me, Thou art my Son; this day have I begotten thee. Ask of me, and I shall give thee the heathen for thine inheritance, and the uttermost parts of the earth for thy possession. Thou shalt break them with a rod of iron; thou shalt dash them in pieces like a potter's vessel. Be wise now therefore, O ye kings: be instructed, ye judges of the earth. Serve the LORD with fear, and rejoice with trembling. Kiss the Son, lest he be angry, and ye perish from the way, when his wrath is kindled but a little. Blessed are all they that put their trust in him."—Ps. 2:7-12.

Armenians
Page 90 (Armenia—page 91).

Armies of Antichrist Destroyed
Page 191.

Arms of Silver
Page 102.

Ascend
Page 92.

Asia Minor
Page 91.

Assyria
Page 77. Map, page 61.

The people of Assyria were Semitic. In ancient times the great valley of the Euphrates shifted back and forth between the Assyrians and the Babylonians. The Assyrian Empire at its fullest extent covered most of the territory now known as the Middle East, including Turkey and Egypt.

The first prophetic empire and therefore a type of the final one.

Assyrian, the
Pages 77, 119, 185.
Antichrist—135.

Antichrist's name is unknown. In fact, there is some mystery about his identity (Rev. 13). Each prophet had his own name for him. Isaiah's favorite name was "the Assyrian." So it is possible that when Isaiah mentions Assyria prophetically, he is referring to Antichrist's Empire, the kingdom of the beast (Rev. 16: 10).

Assyrian—Antichrist

Sent Against Israel—*Isa. 10:5, 6;* Ezek. 38:8, 10-12.

God Uses Antichrist—*Isa. 10:7;* Ezek. 38:17; Zech. 14:2.

A Conqueror—*Isa. 10:8-11;* Rev. 17:12, 13; Dan. 8:9, 24; Dan. 11: 41-45.

God Will Punish Antichrist—*Isa. 10:12, 13;* Ezek. 38:21-23; Dan. 8:25.

Gathers Many People—*Isa. 10:14;* Hab. 1:15-17; Hab. 2:5; Isa. 14:16, 17.

Israel, God's Weapon—*Isa. 10:15-19;* Jer. 51:20-24.

Covenant with Antichrist Brings Disaster—*Isa. 10:20;* Dan. 9:27.

There will be a partial dispersion at the time of Armageddon; so, a final return of the remnant after the coming of Christ.

(The "anointing"—The Anointed One; The Messiah)—*Isa. 10:21-29;* Zech. 14:2; Ezek. 39:23-27.

God's Anger Will Result in the Destruction of the Enemy—*Isa. 10:32-34;* Joel 3:14-17; Rev. 19: 17-21.

Aswan Dam

Page 144. Map, pages 61, 86.

Atomic Power

Page 134.

Babylon

Pages 47, 82, 91, 105, 160. Map, page 61.

Destroyed—159, 191

In the Day of the Lord—158

Rebuilding—185

The name Babylon is derived from the root *Babel*, to confound. The early Babylonians were descendants of Cush. But the later Babylonians were Semitic. Babylon may refer either to the city or the Empire (Babylonia). The Babylonian empire was much smaller in extent than the Assyrian. It covered the Euphrates valley now known as Iraq. It was the first of four world empires of Daniel's visions.

There is nothing but sand now on the site of ancient Babylon (although there are some reports of activity there.) The rebuilding of that city will be one of the most sensational prophetic fulfillments. Our basic rule of interpretation is: *If a prophecy never has been fulfilled completely, then it is to be fulfilled.* The prophecies concerning Babylon were not fulfilled. Many of them are quoted in Revelation and applied to a future city and world religious system with its seat in Babylon. For instance, Rev. 18:2 says concerning a future city: "Babylon the great is fallen, is fallen, and is become the habitation of devils, and the hold of every foul spirit, and a cage of every unclean and hateful bird." This is taken directly from Isa. 21:9: "Babylon is fallen, is fallen, and all the graven images of her gods he hath broken unto the ground." Also compare Rev. 18:4-8 with Isa. 48:20, Zech. 2:7, Jer. 51:6.

Isaiah 13 could apply to nothing but the future Babylon. The time is stated as the day of the Lord and the signs of that day are mentioned: "Howl ye; for the day of the Lord is at hand; it shall come as a destruction from the Almighty.... For the stars of heaven and the constellations thereof shall not give their light: the sun shall be darkened in his going forth, and the moon shall not cause her light to shine.... And Babylon, the glory of kingdoms, the beauty of the Chaldees' excellency, shall be as when God overthrew Sodom and Gomorrah."

None of the prophecies concerning the fall of Babylon was fulfilled. Babylon was never so destroyed. It is not noted for doleful creatures. These things are all future. Babylon must be rebuilt.

The prophecies concerning Babylon imply tremendous changes in that part of the world. Not the least of these changes involves religion. Today Babylon is a part of the Arab world. The Arabs are Mohammedan. The new city will not be Mohammedan but the seat of a world-wide religion. It could include Mohammedanism, but Romanism is certainly involved. Babylon was the place of origin of many idolatrous religions. It was there that Satan tried to unite all such worship into one world religion. This would have given Satan almost complete and perpetual control of the world. Satan will almost accomplish this again at Babylon. After Babylon, the seat of Satan's religious activities was Pergamos, "where Satan's seat is" (Rev. 2:13); from there it went to Rome. From Rome it will return to Babylon; there it will be destroyed. The importance of Babylon may be realized from the amount of space given to it; two and a half chapters in Revelation—more than that given to any other subject.

Babylonian Empire
Pages 101, 109. Map, page 102.

Background for Antichrist
Page 184.

Battle of Armageddon
Pages 30, 83, 100, 118, 158, 159. See *Armageddon.*

Bear
Page 109.
Symbol of the Persian Empire.

Beast
(Antichrist) Pages 89, 118, 126.
Symbol of a world empire, also of the man that is the head of the empire. See *Little Horn, Antichrist.*

Beast (Living One)
Page 45.
The word beast in Rev. 4:6-9 should be translated "Living One." The word implies that these were dead but now have everlasting life.

Because
Reason for God's judgment of Arab states, page 66.

Before the Rapture
Page 150.

Beginning of the Kingdom of Heaven
Page 33.

Better Country
Page 26.

Bible
Pages 16, 17, 19, 20.

Bible Church
Page 38.

Bible Divisions
Page 148.

Bible Is Prophecy
Page 15.

Beirut
Map, page 70.

Bond of the Covenant
Page 74. See *Covenant.*

Bondage in Egypt
Page 172.

Book of Life
Page 48.

Bow
Word of God, page 46.

Brass

See *Trunk of Brass,* page 102.

Symbol of Judgment (Zech 6:1; Rev. 1:15; 2:18). Belly and thighs of brass, a symbol of the Grecian Empire (Dan. 2:32, 39).

Breaking the Seals

Page 189.

Bride of Christ

Pages 56, 21, 33, 36, 56.

Probably not limited to the saints of this dispensation, as both Old and New Testament saints appear in the Holy City, the home of the bride (Rev. 21:12-14).

Britain

Pages 63, 64, 93.

Roman soldiers entered England and even built some roads; so England was once a part of the Roman Empire. Whether or not England will be a part of the kingdom of the beast is a question. The prophecy is so worded that it could be. However, Great Britain is quite evidently a separate group. The final grouping of the nations will take place during the reign of Antichrist. Under him the nations will be divided as follows:

Group one: The Kingdom of the Beast. The Roman Empire, Persia (Iran), Babylonia (Iraq), Ethiopia. This is the territory covered by the four empires of Daniel's visions. Revelation 13 puts them together in the kingdom of the beast out of the sea; namely, the beast, the leopard, the bear, and the lion (Dan. 7). Ethiopia is added by name (Dan. 11:43). The same group is listed by Ezekiel 38; Ethiopia is also named. Ethiopia is named specifically because it was not in the four world empires. There will be some defections as indicated by Daniel 11.

Group two: The Kings of the East (Rev. 16:12). The only prophecy regarding these nations is

found here and in Ezekiel 38:13. The time of both prophecies is the same—the so-called "Battle of Armageddon." At that time there will be a group of nations banded together, independent of Antichrist's kingdom. The association will probably come long before that time. There is a suggestion of it in the Atlantic Pact, but it is not a fulfillment.

"Kings of the east" are not necessarily such nations as Japan, China, etc. The world is round and any place may be east. Such expressions in the Bible as king of the north, kings of the east are not to be interpreted according to their usage in this country. The viewpoint is Palestine, and Bible usage of these expressions applies them not to the direction these countries lie from Palestine, but the direction from which they would enter Palestine.

At the time mentioned in Revelation, all nations are converging on Israel. "For I will gather all nations against Jerusalem to battle." —Zech. 14:2. Antichrist will be in control of all territory around Palestine. Without his consent no armies could move through the Mediterranean. But the Euphrates will be dried up, Babylon will fall and that portion of Antichrist's empire will be wide open. The way will be prepared for this second group of nations to reach Palestine.

Ezekiel is more specific concerning the identity of these nations. "Sheba and Dedan, and the merchants of Tarshish, with all the young lions therefore, shall say unto thee, Art thou come to take a spoil?"—Ezek. 38:13.

Four is the world number and appears when the nations of the world are under consideration. In Revelation there are three spirits going out in three directions to gather the nations. Then there is the fourth group—*the kings of the east.*

In Ezekiel there are three groups (1) Meshech and Tubal; (2) Persia, Ethiopia, Libya; (3) Gomer, Togarmah and their bands. Then there is the fourth group made up of Sheba, Dedan, the merchants of Tarshish and the offshoots of Tarshish.

The important point here is the identity of Tarshish. It is usually thought to be England. However, Ezekiel was not referring to a city, but to a great world empire and association of nations strong enough to stand up to Antichrist. Tarshish would point to an Atlantic power. Another characteristic of this power is that it has offshoots, "young lions." According to this interpretation, the young lions would not be actual British possessions, but countries which were once British possessions and are then independent, but associated. This would include the United States, Canada, Australia and others.

If Tarshish refers to England, then England is not itself named, but only the merchants of Tarshish. The seat of empire could change without affecting the prophecy.

Brother
Page 94.
"Every man's sword shall be against his brother."

Bulgaria
Page 115. Map, page 86.

Cairo
Map, page 70.

Canaanite
Page 100.

Captivity in Babylon
Pages 172, 177.

Chaldea
Map, page 61.

Chaldean
Pages 119, 132, 185.

Chariots
Page 96.

China
Page 115.

Chittim (Kittim)
Map, page 61.
A name applying to the islands and coasts of the Mediterranean in a loose way, sometimes Cyprus.

Christ Takes Possession
Pages 53, 190.

Christ Will Come with His Saints
Page 47. Chart, page 44. See *Second Coming of Christ.*
In heaven—117

Chronological List of Prophetic Events
Page 183.

Chub
(Ezek. 30:5) A people confederate with Egypt in the Day of the Lord, not located specifically as yet.

Church
Pages 19, 26, 32, 34, 36, 37, 39, 40, 123. Chart, page 30.

Church and the Kingdom
Page 32.

Church Program
Page 151.

Clay
Pages 104, 105.

Common Market
Pages 17, 98, 114, 150, 183.

Commotions
Page 184.

Communism
Pages 38, 114, 115, 130, 131.

Dead Sea
Map, page 70.

The surface of the Dead Sea is 1290 feet below sea level, and in places it is 1200 feet deep. It is fed by the Jordan and several smaller streams, which pour into it 6 million tons of water a day. It has no outlet so all this water has to evaporate every day.

The sea contains a great store of chemicals which some day may be of great value. Some engineers have estimated that the money value of the chemicals in the Dead Sea will reach some 13 trillion dollars.

According to Ezekiel, the earthquake at the time of the coming of Christ will cause a great valley to extend east and west, and a river will flow out of Jerusalem across the desert. This river will freshen about one half of the Dead Sea, the other half will remain salt (Ezek. 47).

Very valuable, ancient writings called the "Dead Sea Scrolls" have been found in the caves near the Dead Sea. These writings date from about the time of Christ, from 175 B.C. to 225 A.D. A great deal of light is shed on the Old Testament, but nothing so far has been dis-

Elijah
Pages 34, 47, 149, 182.

Empire of Antichrist
Map, page 110.

End
Pages 118, 146.
Goal—15, 22, 97. See *Goal*.
End of the age—38, 146, 148, 152, 180

End of the World
There are three Greek words translated world:
Oikoumene which means earth, the inhabited world, sometimes specifically the Roman Empire.
Kosmos, the primary meaning of which is beauty. It refers to the physical earth and universe.
Aion. The dictionary meaning is age or dispensation. This is the word that is used when the end of the world is mentioned. A new dispensation began with the church and it will end with the first resurrection, which includes the Tribulation Saints.
There is no such thing in the Bible as the end of the Kosmos. That is everlasting, "world without end" (Isa. 45:17). The kingdom which Christ establishes on the earth will have no end (Luke 1:33).

England
Page 93. See *Britain*.
England was at one time a part of the Roman Empire, but it is not included specifically in the empire of Antichrist (the kingdom of the beast—Rev. 16:10). It may or may not be so included.

Enoch
Page 149.

Ensign
Pages 78, 185. See *Ark of the Covenant*.
The Hebrew *nes* is translated in the Authorized Version, *Ensign*, *Banner, Standard* and *Pole*. It is "not, in the English sense of the term, an arbitrary token to distinguish one band or regiment of Israel from another, but a common object of regard, a signal of observation, a rallying point to awaken men's hope and efforts. Moses called the altar of thanksgiving, after Amalek's defeat, *Jehovah Nissi*, 'Jehovah, my banner.' The altar is the pledge that Jehovah, in covenant with Israel, shall enable His people to defeat utterly Amalek and all his foes" (Fausset).

The Ark is a *nes*. It also is a pledge that Jehovah will enable His people to defeat their enemies. It was so regarded and used when they were in the act of possessing the Land. It was called the Ark of the Covenant. It represented the covenant of Jehovah with Israel. The covenant concerned temporal things—the Land, and the Kingdom. The decalogue was the basis of the covenant. So the two tablets of law were the only things officially placed in the Ark. God's covenant has not been cancelled. The Dispensation of Grace does not end that of Law, but interrupts it. There is to be a period of distinctly Jewish time, at least seven years long, after the close of the Dispensation of Grace. They will have a temple of some sort and a holy place. Jewish temple worship will be re-established. Jewish law will be in force. This is not to be an addition to the Dispensation of Law but a part of it. Daniel was told, "Seventy sevens [of years] are determined upon Israel." Sixty-nine are past. The Gentile Church comes in between the sixty-ninth and seventieth weeks of years. Seven years are still to run. Christ will appear as the Messiah, Redeemer and Deliverer of the Jews at the end of the seven years.

During this time the Jews will have a "nes," not a flag, but an object, a symbol of God's presence; for in connection with it God says, "I will hiss" and the Jews will rally around the ensign from all countries. The hiss was used to call the bees out of the hive. Like bees swarming out of the hives at the hiss of the keeper, so Israel will leave the countries of their adoption and come with speed swiftly at the call of the ensign when it is lifted up on Mount Zion. We are not told that the "nes" is the Ark but we are told that, after the coming of Christ and the "increase" begins, the Ark of the Covenant will no longer be visited (Jer. 3:16). Christ himself will take the place of the Ark. The Ark will still be there, but its symbolism having been fulfilled, its usefulness will end and it will be forgotten.

While it is true that an ensign is not necessarily the Ark, it is also true that the Ark is an ensign. Fausset's definition of the Hebrew *nes* could also be said of the Ark: "A common object of regard, a signal of observation, a rallying point to awaken men's hopes and efforts."

"When ye see the ark of the covenant of the Lord your God, . . . then ye shall remove from your place, and go after it."—Josh. 3:3. So when the ensign goes before them to Mount Zion the Jews will recognize the call, remove from their places and "go after it."

"And the ark of the covenant of the Lord went before them in the three days' journey, to search out a resting place for them. And it came to pass, when the ark set forward, that Moses said, Rise up, Lord, and let thine enemies be scattered; and let them that hate thee flee before thee. And when it rested, he said, Return, O Lord, unto the many thousands of Israel."—Num. 10:33, 35, 36. So, at the sign of the *nes,* regathered Israel will "fly upon the shoulders of the Philistines toward the west; they shall spoil them of the east [the Arabs] together." And when the regathering is complete and they are established in their land, and the *nes* is at rest on Mount Zion, then the Lord will "return unto the many thousands of Israel."

"The Glory is departed from Israel: for the ark of God is taken." —I Sam. 4:22. This was said when the Ark was taken by the Philistines. The Ark returned, however, and Israel reached its greatest glory under David and Solomon. At the end of Solomon's reign the glory departed, never to return until the ensign appears, when many of the miracles that accompanied the Ark will be repeated and the Land of Israel will become, under the Jews, a Land of Glory.

When the Ark was in action, it was accompanied by the blowing of trumpets. "The priests did blow with the trumpets before the ark of God."—I Chron. 15:24. "And seven priests shall bear before the ark seven trumpets of rams' horns."—Josh. 6:4. "And it came to pass, when Joshua had spoken unto the people, that the seven priests bearing the seven trumpets of rams' horns passed on before the Lord, and blew with the trumpets: and the ark of the covenant of the Lord followed them."— Josh. 6:8. So Isaiah speaks of a time when an ensign will be lifted up and a trumpet blown (Isa. 18:3). In the case of Joshua, the walls of Jericho fell down. In the case of Isaiah the invading armies are suddenly destroyed.

The Hebrew *nes* does not always refer to the same thing. It may have reference to Christ himself, or it may be a symbol of Christ. In Isaiah 11:10 the ensign is Christ. In Isaiah 11:12 the ensign is a symbol of Christ. In Numbers 21: 8, 9, it is translated "pole." It is the pole on which Moses raised the fiery serpent in the wilderness about which Jesus said, "Even so must the Son of Man be lifted up." Here the *nes* is the symbol of the crucifixion of Christ. The Ark had the same significance. Blood was sprinkled on the Mercy Seat once a year by the High Priest who offered a sacrifice for the sins of the people.

The Jewish law required two witnesses to establish a fact. There were two witnesses, the cherubim, on the Ark. They looked down on the Mercy Seat. They witnessed the covenant. The Ark was made after a heavenly pattern. God has two witnesses in heaven. Zechariah saw a vision in which Zerubbabel figured as the type of Christ who laid the foundation of the house (in atonement) and "his hands shall finish it."

That which Christ began He will come again and finish. "Then answered I, and said unto him, What are these two olive trees upon the right side of the candlestick and upon the left side thereof? Then said he, These are the two anointed ones, that stand by the Lord of the whole earth."—Zech. 4:11, 14.

On the mount of transfiguration two men, Moses and Elijah, appeared in glory with Jesus and talked with Him about what He would accomplish at Jerusalem (Luke 9:30, 31).

When the women entered the sepulchre after the resurrection of Jesus, "behold, two men stood by them in shining garments" (Luke 24).

At the time of the ascension of Jesus we are told that, "while they looked steadfastly toward heaven as he went up, behold, two men stood by them in white apparel" who said, "This same Jesus, which is taken up from you into heaven, shall so come in like manner as ye have seen him go into heaven." —Acts 1:10, 11.

Before this return of Christ, God will send to Israel two witnesses who will be killed and raised again the third day before all the people (Rev. 11).

The sacrifice of Christ did not fulfill all the symbolism of the Ark. The shedding of blood, so prominent in every part of Jewish worship was, with the law, the basis of the covenant. The Passover was without significance after the Lamb of God had been slain. The Holy of Holies was no longer a sacred place after the crucifixion. The veil of the temple was supernaturally rent in twain from top to bottom, exposing the Holy of Holies to view, showing that its significance was at an end. *But the Ark was not there.*

The Ark was not essential to worship, but it was essential to the successful conquest of the land. Its presence in the Holy of Holies was not considered necessary during the conquest of the land. In fact, during the entire history of Israel it was absent from the tabernacle or temple on the Day of Atonement more times than it was present. During thirty years of David's reign in Jerusalem, the Ark was not in the tabernacle of the congregation, which was at Gibeon, but in a special tabernacle, or tent, which David made for it in Jerusalem. Previous to that time, that is in the days of Saul, the Ark had been kept in the home of Abinadab in Kirjath-jearim (I Chron. 13:6, 7; I Chron. 16:1).

From the crossing of the Jordan to the building of the temple there is no record that the Ark remained in the Holy of Holies. (It was in the tabernacle in the days of Eli.) The Holy of Holies was the place of "rest" for the Ark, but the Ark could not rest until the conquest of the land was complete. It left its rest at the beginning of the conquest and entered into its rest again in the reign of Solomon when the conquest was complete, and the nation was at peace.

The temple was first conceived by David as a "house of rest for the Ark" (I Chron. 28:2). But David was a man of war. The Ark could not rest until the land was at rest.

So David said to Solomon, "My son, as for me, it was in my mind to build an house unto the name of the Lord my God: But the word of the Lord came to me, saying, Thou hast shed blood abundantly, and hast made great wars: thou shalt not build an house unto my name. . . . Behold, a son shall be born to thee, who shall be a man of rest; and I will give him rest from all his enemies round about: for his name shall be Solomon, and I will give peace and quietness unto Israel in his days. He shall build an house for my name."—I Chron. 22:7-10.

Its official name was, "The Ark of the Covenant of the Lord." First of all it had to do with the Covenant of God with Israel. This covenant was made with Abraham, renewed to Isaac, Jacob and the Children of Israel, and later to David, as an *everlasting covenant*. When David brought the Ark of the Covenant into the tabernacle he had erected for it, he gave to the chief musician a song to be used in praising God before the Ark. In this song David reviews the covenant in these words: "He is the Lord our God; his judgments are in all the earth. Be ye mindful always of his covenant; the word which he commanded to a thousand generations; even of the covenant which he made with Abraham, and of his oath unto Isaac; and hath confirmed the same to Jacob for a law, and to Israel

for an everlasting covenant, Saying, Unto thee will I give the land of Canaan, the lot of your inheritance."—I Chron. 16:14-18. "So he left there before the ark of the covenant of the Lord Asaph and his brethren, to minister before the ark continually, as every day's work required."—I Chron. 16:37.

The covenant was the promise that the Children of Israel would possess *forever* the land of Canaan. It was the Promised or Covenant Land. It still is. God has not forgotten His covenant. The Ark is the symbol of that covenant. In Isaiah, the ensign is the symbol of that covenant. Either God will raise up a new symbol to take the place of the Ark or the ensign is the Ark. But inasmuch as the symbolism of the Ark is to be fulfilled in the return of the Jews and the coming of Christ, it is more reasonable to suppose that the Ark itself "will go before them to search out a resting place for them."

The Ark had two distinct functions: in action and at rest. These two aspects were stated by Moses shortly after the Ark was made. First, the Ark in action: "And it came to pass, when the ark set forward, that Moses said, Rise up, Lord, and let thine enemies be scattered; and let them that hate thee flee before thee."—Num. 10: 35. This is the military aspect of the Ark. It is stated first. The conquest must come before the rest. So the Ark was accompanied by the blowing of trumpets and led the way into the Promised Land. The ensign performs the same office in connection with the return of the Jews and the possession of their land. The Ark was not only a symbol of victory to Israel, but it was also a sign of terror to their enemies.

"And it came to pass, when all the kings of the Amorites, which were on the side of the Jordan westward, and all the kings of the Canaanites, which were by the sea, heard that the Lord had dried up the waters of Jordan from before the children of Israel, until we were passed over, that their heart melted, neither was there spirit in them any more, because of the children of Israel."—Josh. 5:1.

"And when the ark of the covenant of the Lord came into the camp, all Israel shouted with a great shout, so that the earth rang again. And when the Philistines heard the noise of the shout, they said, What meaneth the noise of this great shout in the camp of the Hebrews? And they understood that the ark of the Lord was come into camp. And the Philistines were afraid, for they said, God is come into the camp."—I Sam. 4:5-7.

So the ensign is a signal "for the nations." "And he shall set up an ensign for the nations, and shall assemble the outcasts of Israel and gather together the dispersed of Judah from the four corners of the earth. . . . But they shall fly upon the shoulders of the Philistines toward the west; they shall spoil them of the east together. . . . And the Lord shall utterly destroy the tongue of the Egyptian sea; and with his mighty wind shall he shake his hand over the river . . . and make men go over dryshod."—Isa. 11:12, 14, 15.

"Then shall the Assyrian fall with the sword . . . and he shall pass over to his strong hold for fear, and his princes shall be afraid of the ensign, saith the Lord, whose fire is in Zion."—Isa. 31:8, 9.

"Go through, go through the gates; prepare ye the way of the people; cast up, cast up the highway; gather out the stones; lift up a standard [nes, ensign] for the people. Behold, the Lord hath proclaimed unto the end of the world,

Say ye to the daughter of Zion, Behold, thy salvation cometh; behold, his reward is with him, and his work before him. And they shall call them, The holy people, The redeemed of the Lord: and thou shalt be called, Sought out, A city not forsaken."—Isa. 62:10-12.

"Thus saith the Lord God, Behold, I will lift up mine hand to the Gentiles, and set up my standard [nes] to the people: and they shall bring thy sons in their arms, and thy daughters shall be carried upon their shoulders."—Isa. 49:22.

The ensign will be a factor in the Battle of Armageddon. Its presence in Zion is sufficient reason why Antichrist will not attempt to take Jerusalem until he can muster the armies of the whole world. "Set up the standard [ensign] toward Zion: retire, stay not: for I will bring evil from the north, and a great destruction."—Jer. 4:6.

The Jews will have no lasting peace in Palestine until after the coming of Christ. Because of the possession of the ensign, they will have strength and courage. They will not compromise with the Arabs, but will drive them out. As individuals they may be despised and persecuted in many countries, but as a nation they will be respected when the ensign is on Mount Zion. It will not be by force of arms that they will withstand the envy and hatred of the nations down to the very end, for Ezekiel describes them as "a land of unwalled villages and having neither bars nor gates" (Ezek. 38:11). They will be victorious over their enemies by the power of God as symbolized in the ensign.

It seems from Isaiah 18 that the ensign will appear first in Ethiopia, be the signal for a great victory which the whole world will recognize, and will then be brought to Mount Zion.

The Ark in Prophecy

Is the Ark itself mentioned in prophecy? If God wanted to preserve the Ark until a certain time, a direct mention of its location or even its existence might defeat His purpose.

In Solomon's prayer of dedication of the temple, when he moved the Ark into its place of rest, he outlined the whole future of Israel, including their dispersion and final return. He closed his prayer with these words. "Now, therefore arise, O Lord God, into thy resting place, thou, and the ark of thy strength." —II Chron. 6:41.

David built a tabernacle for the Ark in Jerusalem, before it entered into its rest in the temple, while it was still the symbol of conquest. Amos says, speaking of the return of the Jews, "In that day will I raise up the tabernacle of David that is fallen, and close up the breaches thereof; and I will raise up his ruins, and I will build it as in the days of old: that they may possess the remnant of Edom, and of all the heathen."—Amos 9:11, 12.

The Ark was kept in the tabernacle of David during the wars of David after which it was transferred to the temple of Solomon. Amos gives the reasons for building again the tabernacle of David as it was in days of old—namely, conquest, prosperity, safety. The tabernacle of David would be quite empty without the Ark. You will note also that the building of the tabernacle of David gives promise of the same blessings as does the lifting up of the ensign.

The seventh verse of this same chapter is rather interesting: "Are ye not as children of the Ethiopians unto me, O children of Israel? saith the Lord. Have not I brought up Israel out of the land of Egypt? and the Philistines from Caphtor, and the Syrians from Kir?" In other words, as I have brought the Syrians out of Kir, and the Philistines from Caphtor, and Israel from Egypt, can not I bring you back even though you are to me as children of the Ethiopians?

Someone has said, "Is it too much to believe that God would guard the Ark and preserve it through all the vicissitudes of Israel's history until its purpose was accomplished and its symbolism fulfilled by reality?" The Ark was a type of Christ. We must look for the fulfillment of the type, therefore, at the first advent of Christ or at the second advent, or both.

The Ark was not in the temple at the time of Christ. It was not in the Holy of Holies when the veil was rent. The Ark was "not in the second temple, but in its stead was a stone called the stone of foundation, three fingers high."—Jamieson, Fausset, Brown.

"A heavy double veil concealed the entrance to the Most Holy Place, which in the second temple was empty, nothing being there but the piece of rock called the foundation stone."—Eldersheim.

At His first advent Christ fulfilled many of the temple types and symbols, but the Ark was not among them. We must look, therefore, to His second advent; and we are not disappointed. Rev. 11:15-19 tells of the preparation in heaven for the Second Coming of Christ. "And the seventh angel sounded; and there were great voices in heaven, saying, The kingdoms of this world are become the kingdoms of our Lord, and of his Christ; and he shall reign for ever and ever." "And the temple of God was opened in heaven, and there was seen in his temple the ark of his testament [covenant]: and there were lightnings, and voices, and thunderings, and an earthquake, and great hail."

This is not the earthly Ark, for the earthly Ark was made after the pattern of a heavenly Ark. It shows, however, that the symbolism of the Ark is to be fulfilled at the Second Coming of Christ, when the terms of God's covenant with Israel will be fulfilled. It is then that Jeremiah says that the Ark of the Covenant will no longer be magnified. Christ, the Antitype, will take the place of the type.

The fact that the Mercy Seat on the Ark was the symbol of blood atonement has led some to believe that it looked forward only to the first coming of Christ. It should be noted that the Ark was a type made up of many symbols. The blood sprinkled on the Mercy Seat on the day of atonement showed the blood of Christ shed for the remission of sin. But the Mercy Seat was also the throne of God, foreshadowing the reign of Christ on earth. Only one of these refers to the first coming of Christ, but they both refer to the second coming of Christ. "Behold, he cometh with clouds; and every eye shall see him, *and they also which pierced him.*"—Rev. 1:7.

"And I will pour upon the house of David, and upon the inhabitants of Jerusalem, the spirit of grace and of supplications: *and they shall look upon me whom they have pierced,* and they shall mourn for him, as one mourneth for his only son, and shall be in bitterness for him, as one that is in bitterness for his firstborn."—Zech. 12:10.

Taken as a whole, the Ark is the earthly manifestation of Christ leading His people into their promised land of rest. The promise (or covenant) was that they would possess the land for ever. The kingdom was to be an everlasting kingdom. The fulfillment is still future.

Ephraim
A name given to the 10 tribes of the north because it was the largest of those tribes.

Epiphaino (appear) Epiphany
Page 28.

Erchomai (come)
Page 28.

Esau
Pages 65, 66, 139.

Esdraelon
The valley of Megiddo (Armageddon).

Eternity
Pages 48, 193.

Ethiopia
Pages 73, 78, 89, 90, 139, 186, 187. Map, page 86.

Ethiopia is probably the most remarkable, if not sensational, of all the countries of prophecy. It is the only nation still in existence today that is mentioned as far back as Genesis 2:13. Job, referring to Wisdom, likened it to the precious Topaz of Ethiopia; Moses selected his bride from Ethiopia, and Asa called upon God to defend him against the Ethiopians who commanded one million men and three hundred chariots (II Chron. 14:19).

Ethiopia has watched the rise and fall of great world empires. She lived while Nebuchadnezzar built the city of Babylon. She witnessed the ascent of Greece. She watched the tramping of the Roman hordes across the face of Europe. She has seen the passing of one civilization after another; civilizations which deemed themselves immortal have died in her presence, but Ethiopia lives on.

Ethiopia's place in history is responsible for her place in prophecy. Although Ethiopia has no written history, it has a very persistent traditional history, which begins in the days of King Solomon. The queen of Sheba was from Ethiopia. According to this history, Jews have reigned in Ethiopia since Solomon. It is literally true that the scepter has never departed from Judah. Haile Selassie's full title is King of Kings, The Lion of Judah, Defender of the Christian Faith, Emperor of the Ancient Kingdom of Ethiopia, The Chosen of God.

Ethiopian Jews are nominally Christian but because there is no written history, Christian doctrine has become badly corrupted. Christianity was taken to Ethiopia by the eunuch (officer) whom Philip met in the chariot. This was a definite act on the part of God. Ethiopian Jews were not represented at Pentecost (Acts 2:8-11) and the gospel had to be sent to them before it could be preached to the Gentiles.

The importance of Ethiopia in prophecy seems to be due to the fact that it possesses what in prophecy is called "the ensign" and which corresponds exactly to the Ark of the Covenant. All authoritative works on Ethiopia mention the Ark. For instance:

The Encyclopedia Britannica says, "It [Aksum] contains the ancient church where according to tradition the Tobot, or Ark of the Covenant, brought from Jerusalem by the son of Solomon and Queen of Sheba, was deposited and is still supposed to rest."

The Nile, by Emil Ludwig, devotes a chapter to this subject and tells a similar story. The Jews of Ethiopia are called Falashas.

The story of the return of the Jews rightly begins in Ethiopia. It is there that the first miracle takes place. When Antichrist sets out to annihilate the Jews, he will not overlook the Falashas; but he does overlook the fact that the Ethiopian Jews have a symbol of God's power

in their possession which will cause a miraculous destruction of the armies of the invaders. The Falashas will then make a present of this symbol of victory, called "the ensign," to Israel and it will be taken to Jerusalem and placed on Mt. Zion (Isa. 18).

After this miraculous event, and after the Jews have returned to Palestine, Ethiopia will become confederate with Egypt (Ezek. 30:4, 5).

Euphrates
Pages 62, 113. Map, pages 61, 70.

European Empire
Page 98.

Ever-expanding Kingdom
Page 193.

Everlasting Kingdom
Page 193.

Everlasting Possession
Page 62.

Exodus from Egypt
Page 17.

Eyes
Page 114.

Ezekiel
Chapters 38, 39. Pages 83, 84, 85, 88, 89, 95, 96.
Dramatized Prophecy—175
430 days (2520 years)—172, 177

Faith
Page 26.

Falashas
Page 90.

Falling Away
Page 184.

Fall of Jerusalem
Page 177.

Fall of Many Nations
Page 191.

False Christs
Page 151, 184.

False Prophet
Pages 118, 126, 189.

Famine
Page 189.

Fig Tree
Page 37.

Fire
Pages 30, 153.

First Reason
Page 65.

First Resurrection
Page 149.

First Step—The Land
Page 59.

Fish in the Net
Page 188.

Flood
Pages 23, 56, 181.

Flood from the Sea
Page 190.

Forever
Page 97.
There is no word in either the Hebrew or the Greek corresponding with our word "forever." In the Bible it is two words. The word "ever" means eternal or perpetually. Sometimes it may be translated "unto the ages of the ages"; and sometimes there is an added explanation, such as "of his kingdom there shall be no end."

Forty Years
Page 142.

Four
The world number: four directions, four seasons, four winds. Four is in evidence when God is dealing with the world. The four world empires of Daniel are sym-

bolic of man's rule over all the earth.
The four Gospels record the life of Christ on earth. The cherubim of Ezekiel are four in number (Ezek. 1). They are a presentation of the heavenly organization for the redemption of the earth. The four living ones of Revelation relay the judgments written under the seals to the four horsemen, who, in turn, transmit them into action on the earth.

Four Horsemen
Pages 45, 189. Chart, page 44.

Four Hundred and Thirty Days (430)
Pages 172, 177. See *Ezekiel*.

Four Hundred and Ninety Years (490)
Page 178.

Four Hundred Thirty Years (430)
Page 172.

Four Wings
Page 109.

Forward Look
Pages 15, 23.

Four World Empires
Page 162.

From Church to Kingdom
Page 43. Chart, page 44.

France
Map, page 110.
Except for the fact that France was in the Roman Empire it has little prophetic significance. It will, of course, be one of the ten horns or nations in the kingdom of the beast. The "little horn," Antichrist, will pull up by the roots three of these horns—that is, he will take by force three nations in his rush to power. Unless France changes materially, such a show of power

would be unnecessary. It is more likely that France would be absorbed, as are all the others but three. If the little horn rises in the northwest as the prophecy indicates, France would be one of the first to be involved.

Fulness of the Gentiles
Page 163. See *Times of the Gentiles.*

Galatians
Page 90.

Gaza
Map, page 70.

Genesis
Page 17.

Gentile Nations
Pages 40, 42.

Germany
Pages 90, 130, 132.

Germany has a unique geopraphic position. It is both inside and outside the Roman Empire. It is also in the northwestern corner of the Roman Empire. The Germans have demonstrated a will to fight and a passion to conquer. It is not essential that Antichrist rise in Germany. Conditions could change; another nation could come to the fore, but that is not foreseeable at the present time. At present Germany is the only country in Europe in a position, physically and geographically, to produce the little horn.

It should be noted that Daniel's symbols stand for both the nation and its head. Daniel said to Nebuchadnezzar: "Thou art this head of gold, and after thee shall arise another kingdom." The head of gold represented both Babylon and Nebuchadnezzar. This is true of the beast out of the sea in Revelation.

It represents both the man and the kingdom.

If the little horn is the head of Germany, then Germany is also the little horn. We know something of the geopraphy in connection with the rise of Antichrist.

First, the country is both inside and outside the Roman Empire. The little horn (Dan. 7:8) is another horn, not one of the ten. The ten horns represent the nations that came out of the Roman Empire. The beast was the fourth or Roman Empire. "The ten horns out of this kingdom are ten kings that shall arise." This was fulfilled when the Roman Empire broke up into nations. (Ten in prophecy is a round number.) Proof of this is found in Dan. 2:41. The ten toes out of the feet of the image correspond to the ten horns out of the head of the beast; and Daniel says this means "the kingdom shall be divided."

The ten horns, therefore, represent the *dividing* of the empire. That has been fulfilled. The horns are here. The only part yet to come is the rise of the little horn. He is not one of the ten, but "another." He is outside the Roman Empire. He comes up "among" (or *between*) them.

The beast represents the empire. The little horn comes out of the head of the beast; therefore, out of the Roman Empire. This is a nation that is at once in and out of the Roman Empire.

Directions are also given. "And out of one of them came forth a little horn, which waxed exceeding great, toward the south, and toward the east, and toward the pleasant land [Palestine]."—Dan. 8:9. This has been erroneously applied to one Antiochus Epiphanes (B.C. 175) who did not fulfill any of this prophecy. Gabriel had no such notion, but said of him: "And through his policy also he shall cause craft to prosper in his hand; and he shall magnify himself in his heart, and by peace shall destroy many; he shall also stand up against the prince of princes; but he shall be broken without hand." Of this verse Scofield says: "Verses 24, 25 go beyond Antiochus and evidently refer to the little horn of Dan. 7." But in verses 24 and 25 Gabriel is explaining the meaning of the little horn of verse 9. It should be noted that the little horn of verse 9 does not necessarily come out of one of the four divisions of Alexander's Empire, but out of one of the four winds of heaven.

If, therefore, the little horn is to establish an empire based on the Roman Empire, and if to do so he waxes great toward the south and east, then he must start in the northwest.

Therefore, Germany is a country to watch, at least until some other country rises with equal possibilities.

Gibraltar
Page 93. Map, page 86.

Gilead
Page 79.

Glory of the Kingdom
Page 45.

Goal
Pages 15, 16, 19.
The end—15, 22
Goal of the church—21, 32, 33
Goal of the nations—95
Goal of all prophecy—20
Goal of redemption—21
Goal of Israel—60

Gog
Pages 85, 88, 89, 96.
Gog and Magog—119, 121, 192

Gold
Head of gold—101

Gold has played a great part in the history of the world; and it will play a larger part in the future of the world. Gold is one of the first things mentioned in Genesis and one of the last things mentioned in Revelation. The Children of Israel carried a tremendous amount of gold out of Egypt, enough to make the fabulous Ark of the Covenant and have enough left over to make a golden calf.

Solomon knew of gold mines somewhere in the eastern world. We are told that "the weight of gold that came to Solomon in one year was 666 talents" (II Chron. 9:13). A talent is estimated to be about $30,000. Gold figures largely in prophecy.

The mention of gold in the Garden of Eden probably has prophetic significance. It came from the land of Havilah and was of especially high grade. The exact location of Havilah is unknown today, but it would have to be somewhere in the Arabian peninsula because a river ran through it which watered the Garden of Eden (Gen. 2:9-12).

Great changes are to take place in the Middle East. Something will cause a great influx of people from the West. Great countries are yet to emerge; great cities are to be built. The new city of Babylon will have buildings decked with gold (Rev. 18:16).

Revelation gives a list of items of commerce flowing from Babylon, and gold heads the list. We should possibly look for new gold discoveries in the Middle East, so great as to change the course of history.

Gomer
Pages 89, 90. Map, page 86.
A grandson of Noah (Gen. 10: 2). "Progenitor of the ancient

Hungary (Romania, Bulgaria)
Page 115. Map, page 86.

Idolatry
Page 143.

Idumea (Edom)
Map, page 61.

Although these names apply to specific places, they are apparently used by the prophets to designate the Arab countries in general (Ezek. 36:5).

Immortals
Pages 40, 42. Chart, page 35.

Impending World Calamity
Page 188.

Indian Ocean
Page 160.

Inheritance
Page 54.

Iniquity
Page 130.

Iran
Map, pages 61, 86.

Iran is Persia. The Persian Empire, of course, was larger in extent than Iran is today; but when all the world empires are revived, they must all be smaller than the ancient empires because their territories overlap. Persia will become a great nation and participate in the tremendous wealth and power that is coming to the Middle East. It will be associated with Antichrist and his kingdom. It is the bear of Revelation 13:2 (Dan. 7:5).

Iraq
Map, pages 61, 86.

Iraq in prophecy is called Babylon, referring not to the city but the nation. The city of Babylon will be the center of a world religion and a world commercial system.

The nation will have a king, called "Nebuchadnezzar" in prophecy. In Daniel he is the king of the north, not because Iraq is north of Palestine (it is in part), but because they would come into Palestine from the north. Iraq was a part of the ancient world represented by the image of Nebuchadnezzar's dream. This image will be standing again when Christ comes. When the stone strikes the image on its toes, the whole image crumbles.

Iron
Page 104.
Legs and feet of iron—102

Iron Curtain
Page 131.

Isaiah
Chapter 19, page 143.

Ishmael
Page 65.

Islands of the Sea
Page 77.

An expression indicating far distant lands and unknown countries.

Israel
Pages 59, 75, 85, 92. Map, pages 61, 70, 71, 86.

Israel's Three Steps to the Kingdom—59

After the Six-day War—70

Jacob's name was changed to Israel (Gen. 32:28). All of the descendants of Jacob are Israelites. After the reign of Solomon, the Kingdom of Israel was divided and the ten tribes on the north were called Israel and the two tribes on the south were called Judah. The northern tribes were also known as Ephraim, because Ephraim was the largest of the ten tribes.

This designation was only for a short time. When all the Jews were scattered among the nations, the tribal identities were lost and they were all known as Jews or Israelites, both names referring to the same people. When the prophets refer to "the whole house of Israel," they are talking about all twelve tribes.

Paul was of the tribe of Benjamin, one of the two southern tribes called Judah, but he called himself an Israelite (Phil. 3:5). He also called himself a Jew (Acts 21:39).

Now that the Jews are returning to their land in fulfillment of prophecy they are one people. The tribal distinctions have all disappeared in fulfillment of Ezekiel 37:15-22.

Now Israel is a nation—but not a kingdom. The kingdom will include all of Palestine, Lebanon, most of Jordan and Syria, and some of the territory that previously belonged to Egypt.

The story begins about 1948 B.C., when God said to Abram, "Get thee out of thy country, and from thy kindred, and from thy father's house, unto the land that I will show thee, and I will make thee a great nation, and I will bless thee, and make thy name great; and thou shalt be a blessing: and I will bless them that bless thee, and curse him that curseth thee: and in thee shall all the families of the earth be blessed."—Gen. 12:1-13.

The next 400 years is divided between Palestine and Egypt. There was no nation, only a few descendants of Abraham, Isaac, and Jacob. But in Egypt they multiplied to become a mighty people, numbering more than a million.

In about the year 1500 B.C. God called Moses to demand that Pharaoh let His people go. In about 1450 B.C. Joshua led the Israelites across the Jordan River into the Promised Land and they became a nation. That was about thirty-four hundred years ago. In that thirty-four hundred years the people called Israel have been in their land only about thirteen hundred years.

They have been confined to other countries about 2,000 years. They have been outside their land more years than they have lived in their land.

The Israelites had a united kingdom after Joshua for only about 450 years. Then the kingdom was divided into two parts. The ten tribes on the north were called Israel or Ephraim; the two tribes of Benjamin and Judah on the south were known as Judah. It is from the word Judah that we get the name Jew, although at the present time the Jews include all of the Israelites of all the tribes.

Israel was taken captive by the Assyrians and scattered over the Assyrian Empire. Later Judah was invaded by the Babylonians and the people were either taken captive or scattered. Some of them were taken to Babylon, others fled into Egypt.

After seventy years of absence from their land they were allowed to return and rebuild Jerusalem and the temple. However, there never was, for any length of time, an independent country, and they never had another king. Palestine, during the years between the Old and New Testaments was dominated by Persia, Greece, and Rome in succession.

In the entire thirty-four hundred years of national existence, there have been less than 500 years of united independence.

But this is not all, for it was only during the reign of Solomon that there was peace in the land of Israel. All the time between Joshua and the end of David's life the people were in more or less war or were suffering invasion from the surrounding tribes. The reign of Solomon was the only time when the Jews had a peaceful, united nation. How is it possible for a nation to exist for thirty-four hundred years, and in all that time to have had less than one hundred years of peaceful independence? Yet in spite of all this the history of the world revolves around this people.

Prophetic events began to take shape with World War I. It was then that the world began to look at Palestine. The underlying cause of the first world war was the desire for Palestine as the gateway to the riches of the East. The Kaiser's dream of a Berlin to Bagdad railroad could not be fulfilled without Palestine. In fact, it was the Kaiser who, among the world rulers, first discovered the wealth of Palestine.

German scientists were the first ones to uncover the wealth of the Dead Sea and to report it to their government. Even in those days it was known in inner circles that the nation that could control Palestine could dictate terms to the whole world. The only lasting result of World War I was the beginning of the return of the Jews to Palestine, for it was during that war that the deal was made with the Jews for the secret of TNT, for which they got a promise of a national home in Palestine.

Between World War I and World War II the importance of Palestine dawned upon all of the nations of the world. In reality World War II was also fought over Palestine. Hitler went farther than the Kaiser did. He knew that the way to insure the lasting possession of that little land was to do away with the people to whom that land belonged by divine decree. Hitler therefore set about to kill all the Jews and to start a world-wide anti-Jewish movement. Satan's purpose, if not Hitler's, was to insure the possession of Palestine. Great Britain followed the example of Hitler, though not quite to the same degree.

Britain did not actually commit Jews to gas chambers. Great Britain was more subtle; she united the Arabs against the Jews and did all she could to foster anti-Jewish sentiment among the Arabs even to supplying them with arms and officers by which the Arabs could do to the Jews what Hitler tried to do. The reason was the same, Great Britain wanted to keep control of Palestine.

Now we have a new nation, Israel. The nation was born and bombed almost the same day. Although it has been recognized by the greatest nations of the world, its future is still very uncertain (except for Bible prophecy).

God said of Jacob and Israel: "Thou art my battle axe and weapons of war: for with thee will I break in pieces the nations, and with thee will I destroy kingdoms; and with thee I break in pieces the horse and his rider; and with thee will I break in pieces the chariot and his rider."—Jer. 51: 20, 21.

The world cannot separate itself from the Jews. Nearly 4,000 years ago God made His first announcement concerning the descendants of Abraham that today we call Jews. That word is still good. "And I will make thee a great nation, and I will bless thee, and make thy name great, and thou shalt be a blessing; and I will bless them that bless thee, and curse him that curseth thee."—Gen. 12:1-3.

Israel Redeemed
    Page 191.

Israelites Sealed
    144,000—46, 189

Italy
    Map, page 86.
    Italy is one of the ten horns of the beast (Dan. 7). It could not

produce Antichrist because, being one of the ten, it could not be "another horn." The little horn is an eleventh. Antichrist will not come out of Italy. He may be born anywhere but, as the head of Italy, he could not fulfill the prophecy. Italy is prophetically significant because of the Roman Catholic Church whose headquarters is there. The fact that these headquarters must be moved to Babylon makes Italy a focal point of prophecy. Rome is now "that great city, which reigneth over the kings of the earth" (Rev. 17:18).

But eventually all false religions, including the Romish, will head up in the new city of Babylon, in the land of Shinar (Zech. 5:5-11). The sudden move may be a rescue by two other religious systems. Any threat to the security of the Pope will have prophetic significance. See *Babylon.*

Jacob's Trouble

Pages 80, 153, 182, 190.

Jeremiah

Chapter 46, page 137.

Jericho

Page 81.

Jerusalem

Pages 100, 171. Map, pages 61, 70, 71.

Jerusalem is a holy city to three religions comprising a large part of the earth. It is disputed territory and the prophecies concerning it entail changes that could come only by a world convulsion. Mt. Moriah, the site of the temple, is now a sacred spot to the Moslems. A Moslem shrine, the Dome of the Rock, is now on the place where the temple stood. It is difficult to imagine changes that could give that to the Jews; the feeling is so intense throughout all the Mohammedan world.

Yet, the Jews are to rebuild the temple. Paul speaks of the coming of the man of sin "who opposeth and exalteth himself above all that is called God, or that is worshipped: so that he as God sitteth in the temple of God, shewing himself that he is God" (II Thess. 2:4).

Jesus said: "When ye therefore shall see the abomination of desolation ... stand in the holy place." —Matt. 24:15. There must be a temple of some kind during the reign of Antichrist and before the coming of Christ.

When Gog (Ezek. 38) invades Palestine, it is an all-Jewish land. The ancient city was built on Mt. Zion which name includes the surrounding hills. The modern city was built on the ruins of the ancient city, but was moved to the north. Zechariah says that half the city will go forth into captivity at the time of the invasion that just precedes the return of Christ (Zech. 14:1-3). Inasmuch as Antichrist will come in from the north, it is the modern city that will suffer. Most of the ancient part will be saved. Mt. Zion is the waiting place of the 144,000 saved Israelites of Revelation (Rev. 14:1).

There is no conflict here with Luke 21:24: "And Jerusalem shall be trodden down of the Gentiles, until the times of the Gentiles be fulfilled." Jesus did not say that the times of the Gentiles began with Nebuchadnezzar. He was talking about the infiltration of Palestine by the forces of Antichrist, even to his occupying the temple, and the subsequent invasion. The Gentiles will be there till their time is fulfilled. That time is about three and a half years.

The prophesied return of the Jews includes all of Palestine and all of Jerusalem.

The Arabs are a mixed race made up of the descendants of Abraham through Ishmael and Esau. Esau took a wife from Ishmael. In prophecy they are called Esau and Edom. Their land is called Mt. Seir and Idumea. This is now Jordan. There are many dire prophecies concerning the destruction of the cities of Jordan. They will be real cities in those days, because the whole Middle East will be full of people and thriving.

The opposition of Jordan to the return of the Jews at the time of their great calamity, when the Lord is there, is the reason for the awful judgments pronounced upon its cities (Ezek. 25:8-14; 35).

The names Edom, Mt. Seir, etc., may be the prophet's way of designating all the Arabs who are now opposing the return of the Jews (Ezek. 35).

Lebanon was a part of God's original grant to Israel, but it was never occupied by the Israelites for any length of time. It will eventually be a part of the Promised Land. This may not happen until the final return after the coming of Christ. Tyre was in Lebanon, and Tyre will be rebuilt, probably by Antichrist, and then destroyed during the wars of Antichrist (Ezek. 26: 28). The final division of the land of Israel into twelve tribes in the Millennium includes Lebanon as well as most of Syria (Ezek. 48).

Palestine is called the Promised Land because it was a land promised to Abram. It was the subject of a covenant, and the boundaries were clearly stated. "In the same day the Lord made a covenant with Abram, saying, Unto thy seed have I given this land, from the river of Egypt unto the great river, the river Euphrates."—Gen. 15:18

There were the north and south boundaries. The Euphrates crosses Syria in its northern part. The river of Egypt would have to be the Nile. There is a brook called the Brook of Egypt, near the ancient boundaries of Egypt; but it is not a river comparable to the Euphrates. The covenant involved a territory which includes all of Lebanon and a great part of Syria.

Now Israel is in the process of recovering the land that was promised. The Israeli have reached the Suez Canal, which is not far from the Nile. This border may be subject to change. They have not extended their possessions very far to the north. The question is, can we expect them to conquer Lebanon now or is that prophecy to be fulfilled at some later time?

God set no time limits on the covenant with Abram. The prophecy could be fulfilled after the return of Christ. God may have been telling Abram the ultimate extent of Israel. The Battle of Armageddon will be much more extensive than we might gather from reading about it in just one place. The fact is there are other prophecies concerning Lebanon, which might be fulfilled before that country can belong to the Jews.

The ancient city of Tyre was in Lebanon not far from the border of Israel. Jesus, we are told, went up to the border of Tyre and Sidon (Mark 7:24).

The question is, when? Will the Jews occupy all this land in connection with the present struggle with the Arabs or will that be postponed to wait for its fulfillment after the reign of Christ in the Millennium?

In Ezekiel's arrangement of the tribes as they will be in the Millennium, he puts Lebanon mostly in the tribe of Manasseh. But his arrangement of tribes does not have to come immediately. It could happen in connection with the final return after the Battle of Armageddon.

Isaiah, Ezekiel and Daniel all mention wars or the results of wars along the coast of Lebanon during which the city of Tyre will be destroyed. The ancient city of Tyre was never destroyed in the way that the prophecies indicate. We therefore must conclude that the prophecies were talking about a future Tyre.

There will be three rival cities in the Middle East during the reign of Antichrist. Two of them will probably be built by Antichrist. These three cities are Jerusalem, Babylon, and Tyre.

Jerusalem is destined to be a world capital. "For out of Zion shall go forth the law, and the word of the Lord from Jerusalem."—Isa. 2:3.

Babylon will be the commercial and religious center of the world.

From Babylon will go out a great radio voice to the whole world (Jer. 51, 55).

Tyre will be the political capital of the world. The prince of Tyre is Antichrist (Ezek. 28:2-11). The King of Tyre is Satan (Ezek. 28: 12-19).

Ezekiel goes into great detail concerning marvelous materials, gathered from all over the world, that will go into the building of this city. It will probably be the world's greatest and most modern city.

Close to the end of Antichrist's reign, when God takes peace from the earth, armies will move across Syria and Lebanon. The king of the south, which almost certainly includes Egypt, will move against the king of Babylon, called Nebuchadrezzar by Ezekiel. In the process, Egypt will be destroyed and so will Tyre.

It is quite apparent that Tyre will not be a part of Israel when all this happens or the war would be against Israel and not against Egypt.

Ezekiel gives three chapters to the future city of Tyre. These chapters have sometimes been applied to the ancient Tyre, and the fact that Tyre no longer exists as a city is cited as proof of the fulfillment of the prophecy.

But the fact is, this prophecy of Ezekiel was never fulfilled exactly as Ezekiel states it. In fact, there is no record in history of any such city as Ezekiel describes. Tyre was still a city in the time of Christ, but not such a city as we find in Ezekiel.

"And say unto Tyrus, O thou that art situate at the entry of the sea, which art a merchant of the people for many isles, thus saith the Lord God; O Tyrus, thou hast said, I am of perfect beauty. Thy borders are in the midst of the seas, thy builders have perfected thy beauty. They have made all thy ship boards of fir trees of Senir: they have taken cedars from Lebanon to make masts for thee.

"Of the oaks of Bashan have they made thine oars; the company of the Ashurites have made thy benches of ivory, brought out of the isles of Chittim. Fine linen with broidered work from Egypt was that which thou spreadest forth to be thy sail; blue and purple from the isles of Elisha was that which covered thee.

"The inhabitants of Zidon and Arvad were thy mariners: thy wise men, O Tyrus, that were in thee, were thy pilots. The ancients of Gebal and the wise men thereof were in thee thy calkers: all the ships of the sea with their mariners were in thee to occupy thy merchandise."—Ezek. 27:3-9.

The Tyre that Ezekiel is talking about could not possibly escape notice in historic records. No city ever existed that came anywhere near fulfilling what Ezekiel described of Tyre, especially its destruction. The destruction of that city is a world calamity. Such a city is yet to come and probably will be Antichrist's crowning glory.

"These were thy merchants in all sorts of things, in blue clothes, and broidered work, and in chests of rich apparel, bound with cords, and made of cedar, among thy merchandise. The ships of Tarshish did sing of thee in thy market: and thou wast replenished, and made very glorious in the midst of the seas.

"Thy rowers have brought thee into great waters: the east wind hath broken thee in the midst of the seas. Thy riches, and thy fairs, thy merchandise, thy mariners, and thy pilots, thy calkers, and the occupiers of thy merchandise, and all thy men of war, that are in thee, and in all thy company which is in the midst of thee, shall fall into the midst of the seas in the day of thy ruin.

"The suburbs shall shake at the sound of the cry of thy pilots. And all that handle the oar, the mariners, and all the pilots of the sea, shall come down from their ships, they shall stand upon the land; and shall cause their voice to be heard against thee, and shall cry bitterly, and shall cast up dust upon their heads, they shall wallow themselves in the ashes:

"And they shall make themselves utterly bald for thee, and gird them with sackcloth, and they shall weep for thee with bitterness of heart and bitter wailing. And in their wailing they shall take up a lamentation for thee, and lament over thee, saying, What city is like Tyrus, like the destroyed in the midst of the sea? When thy wares went forth out of the seas, thou filledst many people; thou didst enrich the kings of the earth with the multitude of thy riches and of thy merchandise.

"In the time when thou shalt be broken by the seas in the depths of the waters thy merchandise and all thy company in the midst of thee shall fall. All the inhabitants of the isles shall be astonished at thee, and their kings shall be sore afraid, they shall be troubled in their countenance. The merchants among the people shall hiss at thee; thou shalt be a terror, and never shalt be any more."—Ezek. 27:24-36.

Almost the same thing is said about Babylon, which is also a great commercial city and which is destroyed at about the same time.

"And the kings of the earth, who have committed fornication and lived deliciously with her, shall bewail her, and lament for her, when they shall seek the smoke of her burning, standing afar off for the fear of her torment, saying, Alas, alas, that great city Babylon, that mighty city! for in one hour is thy judgment come. And the merchants of the earth shall weep and mourn over her; for no man buyeth their merchandise any more."—Rev. 18: 9-11.

Revelation 16:19 also mentions the fact that other cities fall with Babylon.

"And the great city was divided into three parts, and the cities of the nations fell: and great Babylon came in remembrance before God, to give unto her the cup of the wine of the fierceness of his wrath." —Rev. 16:19.

Ezekiel says concerning Tyre, "Thou shalt be built no more." The Revised Version says it will never be rebuilt.

This poses a problem, because Isaiah also describes the fall of Tyre, and says:

"And it shall come to pass in that day, that Tyre shall be forgotten seventy years, according to the days of one king: after the end of seventy years shall Tyre sing as an harlot.

"Take an harp, go about the city, thou harlot that hast been forgotten; make sweet melody, sing many songs, that thou mayest be remembered.

"And it shall come to pass after the end of seventy years, that the Lord will visit Tyre, and she shall turn to her hire, and shall commit fornication with all the kingdoms of the world upon the face of the earth.

"And her merchandise and her hire shall be holiness to the Lord: it shall not be treasured nor laid up; for her merchandise shall be for them that dwell before the Lord, to eat sufficiently, and for durable clothing."—Isa. 23:15-18.

Isaiah says that after seventy years Tyre will return to her former prosperity. When Isaiah mentions the song of the harlot and commiting fornication, he isn't putting any particular evil connotation on these words, but is using them as a metaphor. For a nation to commit fornication as a nation refers to commercial activity.

The fact that "her merchandise and her hire shall be holiness to the Lord" would indicate that this seventy years would run into the Millennium.

So we have a statement by Ezekiel that Tyre will never be rebuilt and a statement by Isaiah that Tyre will come back to life after seventy years.

There were two Tyres: one on the mainland and one on an island, about half a mile off shore, something like Miami and Miami Beach. The original island city was built by the people of Tyre as protection against an invading army. On a number of occasions the island city was saved due to the water barrier.

But Alexander the Great built a causeway from the mainland to the island and destroyed the island city as well as the mainland city.

It has been thought by some that Alexander fulfilled this prophecy, but many of the details are missing in Alexander's campaign.

Tyre has never been the city that Ezekiel describes and never was destroyed in anything like the fulfillment of these prophecies in Ezekiel and Isaiah. Therefore we must conclude that both Ezekiel and Isaiah are talking about a future Tyre, a city built both on the mainland and on the island.

The island city will never be rebuilt. The mainland city will be revived after seventy years. We know that Ezekiel is thinking about the island city, because he says: "And in their wailing they shall take up a lamentation for thee, and lament over thee, saying, What city is like Tyrus, like the destroyed in the midst of the sea?"—Ezek. 27:32.

Many cities will be destroyed at the time of the return of Christ, some by great earthquake, and some by invading or conquering nations. It would seem that Babylon will be destroyed by a bomb. "And a mighty angel took up a stone like a great millstone, and cast it into the sea, saying, Thus with violence shall that great city Babylon be thrown down, and shall be found no more at all."—Rev. 18:21.

Both the mainland and the island city of Tyre will be destroyed by a general whom Ezekiel calls Nebuchadrezzar.

There may be good reason why the island city will not be rebuilt—the island itself may disappear. Revelation says: "And every island fled away and the mountains were not found."—Rev. 16:20.

Inasmuch as this will happen at about the time of the return of Christ, the seventy years that Tyre remains desolate would have to be the first seventy years of the Millennium. Isaiah and Zechariah both looked into the Millennium. Zechariah tells about the religious conditions, Isaiah the political and economical conditions. Economics would present a major problem to anyone except God himself.

The bad handling of laws of economics is bringing this country to almost certain ruin. The leaders of the world have never been able to solve the problems of economics or handle the problems of food and money.

These problems will be greatly increased if there is extremely long life. Life expectancy in the Millennium will be many hundreds of years. Isaiah says that a man a hundred years old will be considered a child (Isa. 65:20).

Today we have the have and the have-not nations, and rich and poor people—a situation which would be unthinkable in a divinely governed world.

Isaiah suggests that the economy will be based on Christian principles rather than on communistic, socialistic or even democratic principles.

Isaiah says concerning the new Tyre after the seventy years: "And her merchandise and her hire shall be holiness to the Lord: it shall not be treasured nor laid up; for her merchandise shall be for them that dwell before the Lord, to eat sufficiently, and for durable clothing." —Isa. 23:18.

Legs and Feet of Iron
Page 102.

Leopard
Page 109.
A symbol of the Grecian Empire.

Lesson of Habakkuk
Page 136.

Libya
Pages 89, 90, 139. Map, page 86. See *Egypt.*
Libya, R.V. "Put" (Jer. 46:9; Ezek. 30:5), was in the Roman Empire and so will eventually be in the kingdom of the beast. It will be included in the federation with Egypt.

Lion
Symbol of the Babylonian Empire —page 109.
Lion of Judah, a title of Christ (Gen. 49:10, Rev. 5:5)
A title held by Haile Selassie, emperor of Ethiopia, who claims to be a descendant of Solomon.

Little Book
Pages 53, 54.

Little Horn
Pages 43, 113, 119, 125, 132. Chart, page 44.
Symbol of Antichrist

Living Ones
Page 45.

Living Saints Caught Up
Page 188. Chart, page 44.

Lot's Wife
Page 27.

Lud, Ludim
Map, page 86.
North Africa

Lydians
Page 186.

Magog
Pages 88, 89, 96.
Magog (Ezek. 38:2; Rev. 20:8) was a grandson of Noah (Gen. 10: 2). In prophecy he is associated with Gog. In both Ezekiel and Revelation the term "Gog and Magog" or "Gog and the land of Magog" applies to a time when Satan is manifest in the flesh. Gog is Satan, Magog is his earthly counterpart. This situation is apparent both at the time of the return of Christ (the so-called Battle of Armageddon) and after the Millennium when Satan is again let loose and operates on the earth.
The land of Magog is the name given in Ezekiel to the kingdom of the beast. It is the land over which Gog reigns in the person of Antichrist. The countries are named or indicated. Those countries which were known in Ezekiel's day are named—Persia, Ethiopia, Libya; the others are called by the names of their founders, the grandsons of Noah.

Man of Sin
Pages 119, 126.

Mark of the Beast
Page 189.

Marriage Supper
Page 191.

Massacre of the Jews
Page 141.

Messiah
Page 180.

Meaning of the Last Days
Page 37.

Media
Pages 102, 109. Map, page 61.
Medes, page 160

Megiddo
Page 83.
Armageddon

Merchants of Tarshish
Page 93.

Meshech
Pages 89, 90. Map, page 86.
Meschech and Tubal are names of men, grandsons of Noah (Gen. 10: 1-3). They settled somewhere between the Black and Caspian Seas in territory that now belongs to Russia. In the past it has been a separate country and in the future it will be again. It will be a part of the kingdom of the beast. If it is Antichrist that beats back Russia, he could form this state. Connecting these names with present-day Russian cities is not based on any ethnological nor etymological considerations but only on the accidental similarity of sounds.

Messengers
Pages 38, 129.

Messiah Cut Off
Page 180.

Michael
Page 52.

Shinar
Page 77.

Shout, Voice, Trumpet
Page 188.

Signs of Christ's Coming
Pages 191, 124.

Silver
Arms of silver—page 102.

Sinai
Map, pages 61, 70.

Six
The number of evil. Satan's number (Dan. 3:1; Rev. 13:18).

Sodom and Gomorrah
Page 147.

Some Cast Out, Some Left Out
Page 188.

Some Taken, Some Left
Page 188.

Spain
Page 91. Map, page 86.

Specific Times
Pages 172-182.

Spirit
Page 76.

Spoil
Page 93.
Spoiling—130

Stone
Pages 107, 120.

Stone, Nathan J.
(Concerning Rosh)—page 85.

Story
Page 88.

Strangers
Pages 75, 78.

Strife
Page 130.

Structure of Prophecy
Page 19.

Sudan
Page 140. Map, page 86.

Suez
Map, pages 61, 70, 71, 86, 110.

Sword
Pages 92, 94. See *Weapons*.

Symbols
Page 108.
Symbolism of the ark fulfilled—191

A symbol is an arbitrary use of one thing to portray another. A symbol may be an imaginary object. Many symbols may be used of one thing to picture different phases: a seed, a stone, buried treasure, a pearl, a fish, and a manchild may all be symbols of the same thing.

A symbol cannot be understood unless it is explained in some way. Usually a symbol is explained the first time it is used, but not afterwards. Symbols, unlike types, may be understood before they are fulfilled. The Bible is consistent in its use of symbols.

In symbolical language where action is added, the action is always literal.

Some literal language may seem like symbols because heavenly things are in view. When the prophet was given a vision of something in heaven, he used the nearest possible earthly word to describe it. It should be treated as literal but heavenly.

Many things in heaven are entirely beyond our experience. They are things that eye hath not seen nor ear heard. Their understanding is only through the spirit, for there are no human words to express these things. For instance, there are no exact words to express what the Prophet Ezekiel saw when he was given a vision of the cherubim. John saw scenes in heaven that there are no human words to describe. Symbols would be useless in this case. There is only one way heavenly things can be made known to us and that is through the nearest corresponding earthly word. Sometimes this may not be very near.

The cherubim are not symbols of something on earth. They are a heavenly group or organization having a part in the redemption of the earth. John saw the same things (Revelation) but used different earthly words to describe them and their work.

Surely, nothing can be learned by treating these wonderful scenes in heaven as though they were symbols of things on earth. The transparent gold of the Holy City is not a symbol of something on earth. John saw whatever in this heavenly city corresponds in value and beauty to gold.

"Ten thousand times ten thousand" (Dan. 7:10; Rev. 5:11; Matt. 25:1; Rev. 2:10).

Twelve

The number of the redeemed. In the Old Testament, they were represented by the twelve tribes; in the New Testament, by the twelve apostles. The Holy City has twelve gates and twelve foundation stones named for the saints of the old and new covenants.

Two Witnesses

The Two Witnesses (Rev. 11:34) are the prime movers in conditioning the Jews to receive Christ when He comes again. They operate from Jerusalem for 3 1/2 years just before the return of Christ. Their main function seems to be to cause the Jews to receive Christ, not just as King, but as the one they crucified, fulfilling the words of Zechariah, "They shall look upon me whom they have pierced."—Zech. 12:10.

The Two Witnesses re-enact the death, resurrection, and ascension of Christ. The length of their ministry is the same as that of Christ's. On the other hand, they will repeat the methods and miracles of Moses and Elijah, even to causing that it rain not on the earth for 3 1/2 years (James 5:17). They will withstand Antichrist and prevent him from getting complete control of Jerusalem.

Moses demonstrated the power of God by sending plagues on Egypt. The works of these Two Witnesses will continually remind the Jews of Moses and Elijah, yet their experiences will run parallel to those of Jesus in many ways. Here we have, on one hand, all the power that the Jews would expect in their Messiah combined with the testimony and atoning work of Jesus.

After 3 1/2 years, Antichrist will be allowed to kill the Two Witnesses and this will be the signal for the gathering of the armies of the world against Christ, which is called the Battle of Armageddon.

The bodies of the Two Witnesses will not be buried. Antichrist will not make the same "mistake" that Pilate made in allowing the bodies to be buried in such a way that they might be stolen or otherwise disappear. This time the bodies will be left in the street for everyone to see. No one can say that their bodies were stolen by friends to make possible a resurrection story.

At the report of the death of the Two Witnesses a strange thing happens. People all over the world begin to make merry and send presents, one to another. This is a remarkable prophecy. There naturally will be no celebration of Christmas during the reign of Antichrist. The Christmas habit, however, is of long standing and deep seated. At the first provocation it breaks out afresh and they make merry and send presents. This prophecy could not have been fulfilled in John's day. In three and one half days the news of the death of the Two Witnesses travels around the world, a holiday is declared and presents are purchased and sent. This requires fast communication and travel.

Aside from the armies of Antichrist which are trying to take possession of Palestine, Jerusalem is a Jewish city at this time. If people of all nations are going to see those dead bodies in the streets of Jerusalem, they must do it by some kind of television.

The resurrection and ascension of the Two Witnesses will make a profound impression upon the Jews. No longer can they deny the death, resurrection, and ascension of Jesus. So, the Two Witnesses will accomplish their main purpose by their death, the same as Jesus did.

Revelation identifies the Two Witnesses as "the two olive trees and the two candle sticks, standing before the God of the earth" (Rev. 11: 4). This is a reference to Zech. 4: 11-14.

"Then answered I, and said unto him, What are these two olive trees upon the right side of the candlestick and upon the left side thereof? And I answered again, and said unto him, What be these two olive branches which through the two golden pipes empty the golden oil out of themselves? And he answered me and said, Knowest thou not what these be? And I said, No, my Lord. Then said he, These are the two anointed ones, that stand by the Lord of the whole earth."

The candlesticks, in Revelation, stand for churches. Zechariah 4 is a symbolic picture of the church. The anointed ones stand for the two parts of the church: those who, like Moses, die and are raised from the dead, and those who, like Elijah, will be caught up.

Type
See *Symbol.*
A type differs from a symbol in the way it is to be interpreted. A type must be in some respects like the fulfillment, or antitype. In those respects only is it a type. For that reason a type can be understood only after the antitype has come or is in view. A type is usually a person or thing that has actually existed and that has a single counterpart in the future.

Illustration: Jonah was a type of Christ in those respects wherein he was like Christ.

Tyre, Tyrus
Page 186. Map, pages 61, 70. See *Lebanon.*

United Nations
Page 148.

United States
Pages 93, 133.

United States of Europe
Page 105.

Unsaved Nations
Page 47.

Vials
Page 46.

Vile Person
Page 119.

Violence
Page 130.

Wars and Rumours of Wars
Page 184.

Wars Cease
Page 192.

Water
In the Sahara—page 141.

Weapons
Wooden—pages 88, 96.

Wheat and Tares
Page 188.